SO-ALJ-268

WITHDRAWN

RELIGION AND THE MUSE

Religion
and the
Muse

The Vexed Relation between
Religion and Western Literature

Ernest Rubinstein

STATE UNIVERSITY OF NEW YORK PRESS

COLORADO COLLEGE LIBRARY
COLORADO SPRINGS, COLORADO

Published by
State University of New York Press, Albany

© 2007 State University of New York

All rights reserved

Printed in the United States of America

No part of this book may be used or reproduced
in any manner whatsoever without written permission.
No part of this book may be stored in a retrieval system
or transmitted in any form or by any means including
electronic, electrostatic, magnetic tape, mechanical,
photocopying, recording, or otherwise without the prior
permission in writing of the publisher.

For information, contact State University of New York Press, Albany, NY
www.sunypress.edu

Production by Michael Haggett
Marketing by Michael Campochiaro

Library of Congress Cataloging in Publication Data

Rubinstein, Ernest.
  Religion and the muse : the vexed relation between religion and
Western literature / Ernest Rubinstein.
     p. cm.
  Includes bibliographical references and index.
  ISBN-13: 978-0-7914-7149-4 (hardcover : alk. paper) 1. Religion and
literature. I. Title.

PN49.R76 2007
809'.93382—dc22

2006027381

10 9 8 7 6 5 4 3 2 1

PN
49
.R76
2007

In memory of my mother,
Jeanne Rubinstein (1922–2001),
who favored the muse

Religion und Kunst stehen nebeneinander wie zwei befreundete Seelen, deren innere Verwandtschaft, ob sie gleich ahnden, ihnen doch noch unbekannt ist. Freudliche Worte und Ergiessungen des Herzens schweben ihnen immer auf den Lippen und kehren immer wieder zurück, weil sie rechte Art und den letzten Grund ihres Sinnens und Sehnens noch nicht finden können. Sie harren einer näheren Offenbarung, und unter gleichem Druck leidend und seufzend sehen sie einander dulden, mit inniger Zuneigung und tiefem Gefühl vielleicht, aber doch ohne Liebe. Soll nur dieser gemeinschaftliche Druck den glücklichen Moment ihrer Vereinigung herbeiführen?

—Friedrich Schleiermacher, *Über die Religion:*
Reden an die Gebildeten unter ihren Verächtern
(Göttingen: Vandenhoeck & Ruprecht, 1967).
Originally published in Berlin, 1799.

[Religion and Art stand next to each other like two friendly souls, whose inner relationship, whether they immediately suspect it or not, is still unknown to them. Friendly words and outpourings of heart are always hovering on their lips, but always return back to them, because they cannot yet find the proper way to express their inclinations or longings, or the ultimate reason of them. They await a further revelation, and suffering and sighing under the same oppression, they see each other patiently enduring, with inner affection and perhaps deep feeling, but still without love. Might this shared oppression produce the happy moment of their union?]

Contents

Preface

At least two practices inform the history of meditative reading, one of them sacred and the other secular. The sacred practice, cultivated by the schools of monasticism, is *lectio divina*. The medieval monks took to heart the teachings of the church fathers by copying their words into anthologies that went by the botanically evocative name *florilegia*. There is no more effective or affective tribute to this practice than Jean Leclercq's in his now-classic book *The Love of Learning and the Desire for God*,[1] which, itself, invites devotional reading. The complementary secular practice, with roots in classical and Renaissance humanism, is the commonplace book, an anthology of quoted passages from works that especially moved the author or keeper, who stored them up for future use. In the very act of being copied, these passages, too, kept close to the heart of their anthologist.

Survivals of both these practices help determine the selection of literary works that propel this book, especially in its last, thematic part, whose chapter titles might serve as subject headings for a commonplace book. Some of the novels excerpted and critiqued here have been with me since my teenage years. As a high school student, I could not have suspected when I first opened the pages of *The Scarlet Letter* how many times after that I would return to it for its unexpected consolations. The romance of that novel, which its often forgotten subtitle claims for it, tells a story of illicit love against the backdrop of a translucent skein that simultaneously conceals and reveals an other-world. Romance so defined interweaves two tales of love, one between an ill-fated human pair and the other between this world and an other. This kind of romance implicitly scripts a part for the reader, not simply by the identification it invites with one of the human lovers but by the welcome it extends to enter the embrace of the other-world, whose portals it limns.

The two-tracked romance of this type has many instances among novels, stories, and poems. If any one quality unites all of the works of literary art presented here it is that they all participate, to greater or lesser extents, in this kind of romance. And it may well be that every other piece of fiction that has moved me since I read *The Scarlet Letter* has done so through the lens of that one work. In time, other imagined characters joined Dimmesdale in a personal anthology of what I came to call "fictional mystics," the characters cited and discussed in the introduction to this book. By my early adulthood, I had assembled my own *florilegium* of readings from the six novels that hold those characters, which, for a time, I consulted in a devotional way.

Later, while living in Chicago, and upon the advice of my good friend, Jan Richardson, I enrolled in a great books seminar offered by the University of Chicago, called the "Basic Program." It was there, as part of an ongoing community of readers, that I first seriously attended to the works of Homer, Dante, and Shakespeare, who supply so much of the literary representation in this book.

As to the religious voices present here, these have been speaking to me since late childhood, alternatively and conjointly in the sacred and devotional texts of Christianity and Judaism. This book attempts a dialogue between two sets of voices, from literature and religion, in conjunction with a third, which both spans the distance between them and links them to philosophy, namely, Plato's, whose myth of the cave carries as much, if not more, meaning for me as the mythic foundations of either Judaism or Christianity. All of this is to say that the readings that inform this book are largely selected on the basis of autobiography, and so, in the final analysis, arbitrarily. But that so many other novels, plays, stories, and poems could as easily have served the themes of this book hopefully testifies more to the ubiquity of religious ideas in literature than to the limitations of my own life story.

This study follows a three-part structure of comparison between religion and literature—the first historical, the second theoretic, and the third thematic. The character of the comparison changes across these three successive views. History sets the stage for a relation of mutual rejection between religion and literature, each of the other; theory, for one of harmonious pairings between them; and the assembled themes, for one of reciprocal assimilation and differentiation. This configuration of relations roughly corresponds to patterns of intellectual life today. Academic historical or literary treatments of religious themes in literature are likely to be written from agnostic perspectives that either mute or problematize the religious voice itself, while theory, in its literary, critical form, has taken what some have called a "religious turn."[2] If the relationship between religion and literature, broadly conceived, is therefore ambivalent, then the relation itself most naturally allies with literature, which channels that quality more easily than religion does. Perhaps the lesson is that literature inhabits the space between religion and literature more comfortably than religion can. After centuries of acting the part of patron to the arts, it is difficult for religion to speak unpatronizingly of literature. Pope John Paul II tried to do so in his superficially affirming *Letter to Artists* (1999). But this document, despite its evident insights and good intentions, retracts with one authoritative hand the play of freedom it appears to grant with the other.[3] Literature is more attuned than religion to the duplicities of reality. Is reality a product of design, whose meaning is finally as simple and whole as its presumed creator? Or is it inherently double, a simultaneity of opposites that pull at once in mutually incompatible directions, on the model of an optical illusion, devoid of any criteria for determining which of its faces carries the deeper truth? Whether our spirituality finally aligns with religion or literature may depend on how a mediating third between them, namely, philosophy, resolves this question for us.

Acknowledgments

This book is based on lecture notes I prepared for a class I taught at the New School University in New York City in the fall of 2001 entitled "Religion and the Muse: The Vexed Relation between Religion and Western Literature." Intellectual energy and support from many quarters helped the notes for the class evolve into this book. I would like to mention especially the following individuals: Almaz Zelleke and Donna Axel, who admitted the class into the New School curriculum; the six class participants, who together brought life to the ideas in our readings: Natalie Devoe, Rica Fujihira, Richard Gudonsky, Isabelle Holland (may her memory be for blessing), Lindsey Lafferty, and last, and most especially, Laura Lombard, with whom I have since enjoyed so many memorable conversations of ideas; the Rev. Roger Ferlo, who taught a stimulating class on *Paradise Lost* at the Church of St. Luke in the Fields, from which I drew in writing the sections in the book on Milton; Barth scholar Dr. Suzanne Selinger, who kindly read and critiqued the chapter on ethics; State University of New York Press Acquisitions Editor Nancy Ellegate, for accepting the manuscript for publication and Production Editor Michael Haggett for seeing it through production; the two anonymous readers who commented on it so helpfully; and my life partner, Paul Glassman, whose realizations of beauty in matters of design are an ongoing revelation for me. All errors in the book are, of course, my own.

Lines from W. B. Yeats's *To a Rose upon the Rood of Time* and *Ego Dominus Tuus* are reprinted with the permission of Scribner, an imprint of Simon & Schuster Adult Publishing Group, from *The Collected Works of W. B. Yeats, Volume 1: The Poems Revised*, edited by Richard J.

Finneran (New York: Scribner, 1997). Permission from A. P. Watt for markets outside of the United States, is on behalf of Michael B. Yeats.

Lines from W. B. Yeats's *Vacillation* are reprinted with the permission of Scribner, an imprint of Simon & Schuster Adult Publishing Group, from *The Collected Works of W. B. Yeats, Volume 1: The Poems Revised*, edited by Richard J. Finneran. Copyright © 1933 by Macmillan; copyright renewed © 1961 by Bertha Georgie Yeats. Permission from A. P. Watt for markets outside of the United States, is on behalf of Michael B. Yeats.

Lines from W. B. Yeats's *Sailing to Byzantium* are reprinted with the permission of Scribner, an imprint of Simon & Schuster Adult Publishing Group, from *The Collected Works of W. B. Yeats, Volume 1: The Poems Revised*, edited by Richard J. Finneran. Copyright © 1928 by Macmillan; copyright renewed © 1956 by Bertha Georgie Yeats. Permission from A. P. Watt for markets outside of the United States, is on behalf of Michael B. Yeats.

Lines from W. B. Yeats's *The Circus Animals' Desertion* are reprinted with the permission of Scribner, an imprint of Simon & Schuster Adult Publishing Group, from *The Collected Works of W. B. Yeats, Volume 1: The Poems Revised*, edited by Richard J. Finneran. Copyright © 1940 by Georgie Yeats; copyright renewed © 1968 by Bertha Georgie Yeats, Michael Butler Yeats, and Anne Yeats. Permission from A. P. Watt for markets outside of the United States, is on behalf of Michael B. Yeats.

Lines from W. B. Yeats's *A Vision* are reprinted with the permission of Scribner, an imprint of Simon & Schuster Adult Publishing Group, from *A Vision* by W. B. Yeats. Copyright © 1965 by Bertha Georgie Yeats. Permission from A. P. Watt for markets outside of the United States, is on behalf of Michael B. Yeats.

Lines from Homer's *Iliad* are reprinted with the permission of University of Chicago Press from *The Iliad of Homer*, translated and with an introduction by Richmond Lattimore; copyright 1951 by University of Chicago Press.

Chapter 1

Introduction

The ancient Greek muses were the divine daughters of Zeus and
Mnemosyne, goddess of memory. As daughters of the master god, they
were themselves masters of the arts and sciences. But Mnemosyne's
gifts surface more ambiguously in the muses' nature. Like their half
brother Apollo, who as consummate healer had also the power to harm,
the muses, as aids to memory, were also agents of forgetfulness. Part of
the point of the epic recitations, themselves feats of memory, that the
muses inspired in ancient Greek poets was to so vivify a mythic past
that listeners forgot the troubles of the present.[1]

At just this juncture Judaism and Christianity raise their voices in
protest against the muses. These religions understand themselves to
reveal truths that sharpen attention to the present. The memory of the
past does not so much eclipse the present as infuse it with meaning. If
the muses were artists of forgetfulness, then from either a Jewish or
Christian standpoint the products they inspired—epic and lyric poetry,
comic and tragic drama—are merely tools of escape from the serious
business of living in history-making time. The point of remembering
history, from a Judeo-Christian standpoint, is to participate in the further making of it, not withdraw from it. And so the mere invocation of
the muse already challenges monotheism's historic life in time and
incites the religious critique of literature sometimes heard, that stories,
poems, and plays are simply frivolous diversions from the serious business of life.

Judaism and Christianity are not casual or arbitrary representatives of the religious voice in the quarrel beginning to unfold before us between Western religion and literature. Christianity has been the dominant religion of the West for 2,000 years. And as Judaism is its ground, the two religions are natural partners in the critiques they issue of the arts. That they are monotheisms binds them in a further united front against Western literature, for if the goddesses of memory become agents of forgetfulness then these are figures that drive simultaneously in two opposed directions, a self-divided movement they share with other gods that supplies the root meaning of ambiguity (from the Latin: amb + agere). The paragon patrons of the arts are radically ambiguous, but as the muses also personified the arts, they infect the arts with the same radical ambiguity. Monotheism again protests, this time from the roots of its being. For by the mono- of monotheism in which Judaism and Christianity together participate, neither religion can rest easily with ambiguity. Where the ideals of literature incorporate and even celebrate ambiguity, the monotheistic ideal is univocity: speaking in one voice, at least on the central issues of faith and practice.

Of course, the broadest category Judaism and Christianity together share is religion. And here too a division from literature springs up from the root, for on at least one etymological reading of the word, "religion" descends from re-legere: to reread. This is a fitting etymology for the literary religions of Judaism and Christianity, which do indeed incessantly reread their own sacred texts in both public and private settings. By contrast, one of the marks of literature, insofar as it participates in the larger category of the arts, is that each new manifestation of it is understood as new and original. Literature might be defined as the collective body of linguistic products of the creative imagination.[2] The imagination would not be imaginative if it simply repeated and reread the old, whereas monotheistic religion positively turns on ritual repetitions of the old that come to define tradition. So once again, monotheistic religion and ambiguous literature point in opposite directions.

The dispute between religion and literature had an early theorist, outside of Judaism and Christianity altogether, in Plato, who wrote about "the ancient quarrel between philosophy and poetry."[3] Plato casts literature's opponent as philosophy, but philosophy in his hands is not so very different from religion in ours. Plato's philosophers are mythmakers. They critique the stories of the gods inherited from the Greek

poets and substitute new stories of their own. Philosophers also legis-
late as much as Moses did. In his late dialogue *The Laws,* Plato contrasts the philosophical legislator, who "must give not two rules about
the same thing, but one only," to the poet, who "is often compelled to
represent men of opposite dispositions, and thus to contradict himself."[4] Plato's evident preference for the single-mindedness of the
philosopher over the double-mindedness of the poet allies him with
Judaism and Christianity in their dispute with literature over the relative merits of univocity and ambiguity. Platonic religion is not revela-
tional in the way the monotheisms are. The highest object of desire, for
Plato, is an idea that human reason ascends to contemplate, as opposed
to the god of Judaism and Christianity, who descends to encounters
with earthly human beings. And Platonism, unlike monotheism, does
not typically found communities of worship. Platonic religion is more a
sensibility than a communal structure, but that has not lessened its
impact on Western culture, nor does it disqualify it from playing a religious third to Judaism and Christianity, which it often has inflected
toward its own characteristic ideals. What further allies it with the
monotheisms in their quarrel with literature is the nature of Plato's own
opponent in the Greek religious world of the fifth century BCE. Plato
did not openly object to the civic religion of the times, which turned on
temple sacrifice to the patron deities of the Greek city-states, nor to the
mystery cults that initiated followers into intimate relations with the
gods. On the contrary, *The Laws* provides for polytheistic temple worship, and Plato's own mysticism of ideas has been likened to the ecstatic
experience sought by the Eleusian and Orphic adepts.[5] The strand
within the multiple levels of ancient Greek religion that Plato contested was the distinctly literary one: the Homeric strand of epic stories
of gods and heroes, and its descendants in the tragic dramas of Aeschylus, Sophocles, and Euripides. Plato so distrusted the literary expression of religion that in one of his own dramatic gestures, in the middle
dialogue, *The Republic,* he famously and notoriously banished poets
from his ideal state. Plato, having defined a religious sensibility of his
own, distinct from the polytheistic mythology of his inheritance,
focused his critique of that mythology not on its cultic expressions but
precisely on its poetic renderings, so much so that the quarrel between
Plato and his inheritance is not so much between one type of religion
and another as between one type of religion and literature.

But then we have a threefold front of religion, comprising Judaism, Christianity, and Plato. These are distinct currents in Western religious history that nonetheless overlap and borrow from each other. Conceived in contrast with Western literary history, their loosely united front is against a body of imaginative works that extends from Homer to the modern age. In the chapters that follow, Jewish, Christian, and Platonic texts voice a complex religious sensibility in contrast to a literary one, represented by selections from the Western literary canon. Our themes of comparison and contrast divide into three natural groups: first, a divisive grouping of mutual critiques that the religious and literary voices have issued of each other; second, a more harmonious grouping of analogous relations between the two suggested by three features of an artwork: its creation, beauty, and appreciation; and third, a grouping, alternatively divisive and harmonious, of religious and literary voices speaking to an interlocking series of perennial themes: love, death, evil, suffering, forgiveness, and saintliness.

The ancient and modern worlds supply most of our voices, because it is just in those eras that religion and literature speak so distinctively from each other. In the Christendom of medieval Western Europe, religion breathed through so much of culture that literature, with some notable exceptions, did not sound out distinctively enough to make a contrast. Indeed, so intertwined were the medieval voices of religion and literature that it took a new genre of literature to mark the break with a past so dominated by religion. And that genre, as though seeking to carry through history the novelty of its break with the past, we call the "novel."

If the Hungarian literary critic, George Lukacs, was right about the novel, that it is "the epic of a world that has been abandoned by God,"[6] then novels mark the site of a particularly stark departure of literature from religion. Implicit in Lukacs's famous claim is that part of what defined the epic, in its ancient and medieval form, was precisely the presence of God or gods. The novel proclaims its novelty just by absenting that presence. Of course, by the time of our own reading lives, novels are no longer novel, but they were some 400 years ago, when, by a consensus of reckoning, the first one, *Don Quixote*, appeared in the west.[7]

Certainly on the surface *Don Quixote* fashions not so much a world without God as a world without chivalry, the arts of medieval romance that focus this novel by their simultaneous absence from the real world of the story and centering presence in the fantasies of the don. This novel self-consciously locates itself in a postchivalrous age—Cervantes' and Don Quixote's own time. Cervantes doubly distances the world of Don Quixote's fancy, for that world belongs not so much to the historical past that precedes the novel's time as to the fantastic literature of that earlier time, which itself never portrayed the real world, even of the Middle Ages. The literature of fantasy is not only the foil of the priest, who burns the don's books on chivalry, but of Cervantes too. It is against the backdrop of the medieval, secular literature of fantasy, which according to later typologies of literature would be called the "romance," that Cervantes fashioned what those same typologies would call the "novel." The novel, in the form of *Don Quixote*, rejects the romance with so much verve that we hardly notice how much, in the process, religion is simply eclipsed. It fades not so much from being defeated, or having its books burned, as from being denied the vocabulary in which it formerly expressed itself. One of the chief representatives of grounded this-worldliness in Cervantes' novel is a priest. Between the otherworld of chivalry and the no-nonsensical this-worldliness of the priest, religion's putative representative in the novel, actual religion loses any means of self-expression at all. It can identify neither with the delusive otherworldliness of the don nor the untranscendental pragmatism of the priest. But Cervantes gives religion no other alternatives, and so it is simply silenced. This silence of religion in literature Cervantes bequeathed to succeeding novelists.

But religion is irrepressible. For a reading of Cervantes' novel developed according to which Don Quixote himself mediates the religious voice.[8] This reading teaches that he is the comic result of transporting a definitively antique figure, namely Christ, into the modern age. And this indirect reentry of religion into a literary work from which it had seemed to be banished becomes a parallel legacy of Cervantes, or at least of his interpreters. Later novelists may have fashioned worlds without God, but their works are not always without religious feeling, sensibility, or interpretability.

Six novels that lend themselves to religious interpretation concretize the abstractions in which we have up until now been hovering. They are *The Scarlet Letter* (1850) by Nathaniel Hawthorne; *Sons and Lovers* (1913) by D. H. Lawrence; *The Bulwark* (1946) by Theodore Dreiser; *Eustace and Hilda* (1944–1947) by L. P. Hartley; *Anna Karenina* (1877) by Leo Tolstoy, and *The Idiot* (1868) by Fyodor Dostoevksy.

Bound by a single century (1850–1950), these novels speak to us from a variety of other times. The otherness of the periods that gave rise to them may serve our goal of awakening, for purposes of study, the otherness of feeling that at least partially constitutes religious experience. Only two of the novels—*The Scarlet Letter* and *The Bulwark*—foreground the religious backdrop of their settings. But this only shows how little the literary mediation of religious sensibility requires the explicit display of either doctrines or practices from institutional religion. As one critic observes about moments of religious epiphany in novels: "Our understanding of religious belief must be revised; for the forms of belief, desire and dread we so often encounter in such moments of epiphany are at the furthest remove from any set of dogmatic propositions."[9]

All of our selected novelists were raised in Christian traditions: Hawthorne and Lawrence in Congregationalism; L. P. Hartley in Methodism, though he later became a nominal Anglican; Dreiser in Catholicism; Tolstoy and Dostoevsky in the Russian Orthodox Church. As mature artists, all of these writers, except Dostoevsky, referred to aspects of institutional religion in tones that ranged from indifference to hostility. Dreiser and Lawrence wrote novels that were placed on the Catholic Church's Index of Prohibited Books. But that is not to say that these writers lacked a religious sensibility of their own. Ever since the so intimately interrelated periods of Enlightenment and Romanticism, two channels of religious feeling emerged to compete with the doctrine and liturgy of the institutional church: (Enlightenment) ethics and (Romantic) nature. And in very broad strokes, Hawthorne, Hartley, and Tolstoy take their place among the religious ethicists and Lawrence and Dreiser among the religious naturalists. Let us consider what each of these writers has to teach us about the relation between religion and literature.

HAWTHORNE AND THE
LITERARY IDEAL OF AMBIGUITY

It is not that religious texts are not also ambiguous, but the weightiest texts of Jewish and Christian history, the ones that determine religious life—the creeds and confessions for Christians, halacha for Jews—do strive for univocal clarity. If later interpreters find ambiguous meanings in these texts, then it is largely for the purpose of resolving them. Creeds and laws proclaim by their very form their aspiration to univocity. Literature, in contrast, which lacks the same life-determining mission, is free to weave multiple meanings into its narratives and even celebrate their cross-purposes. If we are seeking a literary illustration of sustained ambiguity that chastens the Christian hope to speak univocally, then we can probably do no better than Hawthorne, whom one critic called a master of "magnificent hedging."[10] Hawthorne's own spiritual biography is ambiguous. The New England congregationalism of Hawthorne's day was divided between Calvinist and Unitarian theology. Adding to the conflicting crosscurrents was transcendentalism, a literary pantheism inspired by German philosophical idealism that, like Emerson, its most famous proponent, broke with the Church entirely. Hawthorne did not explicitly ally with any of these trends. As a backdrop to his literary probings of the darker recesses of the human soul, Calvinism served his artistic purposes, but it was too weighted with unnecessary doctrinal baggage and a heritage of oppression that Hawthorne himself felt acutely (as he confesses in the preamble to *The Scarlet Letter*, with regard to his witch-burning Puritan ancestors) to figure believably in his own religious life. On the other hand, transcendentalism and Unitarianism too readily suppressed anything that compromised their sunny moral psychology. Hawthorne attended no church as an adult. He seemed to hover iconoclastically between the instituted faith options of his time.

Hawthorne's religious ambiguities have social and historical roots beyond his own personal life. He descended from seventeenth-century Puritan theocrats, but he was born in 1804, the first year of the second term in the presidency of Thomas Jefferson, a figure so un-Puritan that he rewrote the New Testament to purge it of miracle and harmonize it with enlightened moral reason. Hawthorne set *The Scarlet Letter* in colonial Puritan Boston, but the narrative voice of the story betrays sympathies with the moral reason that the Founding Fathers only a generation or two before him idealized. It is just from the standpoint of reasonableness that the Puritans in Hawthorne's novel can appear as cruel and gullible as they do. But at least one Puritan idea escapes censure by the enlightenment sensibility of the narrator, and so projects itself into the tone of the novel that the narrative voice reads ambiguously, poised indecisively between seventeenth- and nineteenth-century

worldviews—that inner, moral states of soul, in obedience to a supernatural moral law, inevitably manifest externally.

It was Max Weber, in his now-classic *Protestant Ethic and the Spirit
of Capitalism*,[11] who first popularized the idea that Calvinism provided
a motivating theology for capitalism. His thesis was that Calvinist theories of predestination raised an anxiety over future salvation that
necessitated a further, compensatory teaching, that a sign in this life of
salvation in the next was a gainfully productive activity in Christian
society. This in turn encouraged Christians to succeed in their work in
just the ways that sustained a capitalist economy. Economic success was
the this-worldly assurance of future salvation. Scholars of Calvinism do
not find in Calvin himself any such doctrines of salvation's assurance.
Calvin's own aim in preaching predestination was to restore the tran-
scendent majesty of God after centuries of Catholic teaching about, for
example, the mediation of the saints, had, in his judgment, compromised it. Nonetheless, Calvin did subscribe more fully than his sixteenth-century Reforming colleagues to a theory of vocation, or calling,
that linked the inner predispositions of each human being to some
form of gainful and productive work in Christian society. Calvin's successors, including the Puritans, did develop theories of salvation's assurance that invite Weber's interpretation. The notion that inner states of
soul, especially the bad ones, bleed through to the surface of the body—
an outward moving inwardness—was the quasi-Calvinist idea[12] that
flourished so artistically at Hawthorne's hand.

This idea furnished the form of Hawthorne's novel, but Hawthorne parted from the Puritans over the specific contents of the idea,
that is, over the actual inner evils that were powerful enough to bleed
through to the surface of the body. The narrator shows little sympathy
for the Puritans' collective, unquestioning outrage over Hester's adultery. He suggests that in satisfying the one biblical mandate, to punish
adultery, the Puritan townsfolk violate another, against following a
multitude to do evil (Exodus 23:2), as they do when they act in mass to
ostracize Hester. Hawthorne recalibrated the Puritan scale of sinfulness
so that in the deadly spot where the biblical sin of adultery once
weighed so heavily, malicious cruelty now showed.[13]

Time and again in the novel, Hawthorne plays a moral-supernatu-
ralist form of explaining outward appearance against its enlightened,
naturalistic counterpart. Perhaps the most famous instance is Dimmes-

dale's death scene, where a scarlet letter appears to horrified spectators as though branded on his chest. The narrator commends to the reader both naturalistic and supernaturalistic intepretations of that manifestation, without deciding between them. Dimmesdale is framed by such ambiguous allusions, for another, less often noticed one occurs at his moment of introduction. After giving a brief physical description of the minister, the narrator comments, "Notwithstanding his high native gifts and scholarlike attainments, there was an air about this young minister . . . as of a being who felt himself quite astray and at a loss in the pathway of human existence."[14] The passage is not so much ambiguous as deceptively innocent (like Dimmesdale himself). It seems merely to register about Dimmesdale what many believe to be true of scholars generally, that because their heads are lost in the clouds, their feet are lost on the world's human paths. This would be a reasonable interpretation of the minister's demeanor of estrangement, but that could be the meaning of the sentence only if the subordinate clause that opens it began with "Because of." The "Notwithstanding" suggests that the minister's appearance of being lost is at odds with his scholarly attainments. The dissonance concealed in the "Notwithstanding" opens up beneath it onto that dark Puritan belief in the outward moving inwardness. Arthur's appearance of being lost cannot owe to his scholarly attainments, for these, as his assurance of salvation, would work to integrate him further into Puritan society, not alienate him from it. If Arthur appears lost, then something decidedly wayward inside of him is causing that outward impression. In Arthur's debut, as at his death, he hovers ambiguously between opposed interpretations of the appearance he makes.

This is the ambiguity that justifies the often-forgotten subtitle of *The Scarlet Letter: A Romance*. It is not the muted love interest between Arthur and Hester that makes the book a romance, but its supernaturalism, which harks back to that very same tendency that Cervantes parodied in *Don Quixote*. Already in Hawthorne's day it was understood that novels simulated reality; in contrast, romance was the genre of fantasy. Hawthorne inherited enough of Cervantes' skepticism toward romantic fantasy that he could only portray it as one of two intertwined threads, the other of which—the enlightenment one—worked against it. The simultaneous driving in opposite directions makes his novel a literal model of ambiguity.

D. H. LAWRENCE AND THE
LITERARY CRITIQUE OF RELIGION

What ambiguity implies when it is raised to the level of an ideal is that truth is less a static fact, waiting to be captured in doctrine, than a movement that vibrates elusively between the poles of opposites. Creeds and laws inevitably freeze the movement and so just as inevitably distort the truth. In this way, *The Scarlet Letter* indirectly critiques both the Puritans and the Enlightenment for presuming to formulate truth as doctrine. But far more direct rebukes of religious doctrine occur in other writers, perhaps in no other twentieth-century writer as forcefully as in D. H. Lawrence. Lawrence shares with Hawthorne the same religious roots in Congregationalism, and analyses of Lawrence analogous to those of Hawthorne, that trace themes and emphases of his novels back to Puritanism, have been written.[15] But Lawrence was more direct about rejecting Christianity, as when he wrote, "By the time I was sixteen I had criticized and got over the Christian dogma."[16] Whatever specific dogmas Lawrence had gotten over at sixteen, the Christianity he was rejecting in his late twenties, when *Sons and Lovers* was published, is clear from the letter he has the hero of that novel, Paul Morel, send his girlfriend, Miriam Lievers, by way of breaking off their intense romantic friendship:

> See, you are a nun. I have given you what I would give a holy nun—as a mystic monk to a mystic nun. In all our relations no body ever enters. I do not talk to you through the senses—rather through the spirit. Ours is not an everyday affection. As yet we are mortal, to live side by side with one another would be dreadful, for with you I cannot long be trivial, and to be always beyond this mortal state would be to lose it. If people marry, they must live together as affectionate humans who may be commonplace with each other without feeling awkward—not as two souls. So I feel it.[17]

Lawrence identified Christianity with disembodied love. Miriam Lievers, who represents that love in the novel, "knew that one should be religious in everything. . . . All the life of Miriam's body was in her eyes, which were usually dark, as a dark church. . . . Her body was not flexible and living."[18] The point of Paul's letter is that this kind of love cannot support human relations. Disembodied, Christian love coerces, forces, its objects by alternately passive and aggressive means to receive it and in coercing them enervates them. Paul's rejection of Miriam parallels Lawrence's rejection of his understanding of Christian love.

There is little resonance in this letter on love of that other, Pauline letter on love, to the Corinthians, part of the New Testament canon, but the coincidence of name and theme does invite comparison, if only to test how accurately Miriam's love, as Lawrence portrays it, conforms to early Christian ideals. And of course as many critics note, the Christianity Lawrence targeted is neither biblically nor historically normative. Far from freeing the soul from the body, or exalting it to a station above the body from which it can radiate disembodied love, St. Paul weds the soul to the body so intimately, as indeed his Jewish roots would have him do, that he can only conceive final salvation in bodily terms. There is a love that is visionary, mediated by the eyes as Miriam's is, and that emanates ideally from a disembodied soul, only it is not Christian but Platonic. Paul Morel, speaking for Lawrence, has simply mislabeled the love he condemns. So Lawrence turns out to be a serious rejector of religion after all, only not of Christian religion but Platonic religion.

Lawrence's rejection of Platonism was so virulent that it could not remain bound by the limits of negation. It needed a channel of affirmation, which it found in the direction of sexual love. Lawrence's affirmation of sexual love carried all of the extremity of his rejection of Platonism. And it was really the extremity of that affirmation—sacralizing what Platonism demonized—that offended Christians. Christianity becomes the unwitting target of Lawrence's critique after all, for resting content merely to bless, but not sacralize, sexual love. And so it is through Christianity that Lawrence's rejection of Platonism is reflected back to him, by the celebrated obscenity trial against *Lady Chatterly's Lover*, and the addition of that book to what was once the Catholic Church's Index of Prohibited Books. In this way, Lawrence illustrates not only literature's critique of religion but religion's critique of literature.

THEODORE DREISER AND THE IDEAL OF BEAUTY

There is a still deeper level to the dispute between Lawrence and Platonic religion. It is not merely the anti-Platonist in Lawrence that rejects all aspirations to transcend the body, it is also the artist in him, for it was not so much sex as creativity that was sacred to him. Nineteenth-century romanticism had already taught that the artist unconsciously mediates, more passively than actively, imaginative energies that flow naturally through him (provided nothing blocks them). Sex is Lawrence's chief trope for the unimpeded natural energy by which creative artworks arise. This does not reduce the offense that Lawrence is to Christianity, for in Christianity human creativity has no more claim to being sacred than does sex or nature. But it does position Lawrence to represent writers (and artists generally) in their claim upon a quality that the church had taught, for centuries, was exclusively God's own, namely, creativity and to represent them in a way that offers promise of rapprochement with Christianity. For part of what makes the natural creative energies animating the artist natural is that they come from beyond his will. And if the originating will is divine, then God and humanity are apportioned complementary, not conflicting, roles in the genesis of artworks. This harmonization extends beyond monotheism to Platonic religion, the original source of the breach between Lawrence and Christianity, since Plato taught that poets composed in an ecstasy of divine possession.

When we move beyond the critiques that religion and literature have separately issued of each other, which make a battleground of the space between them, to artworks themselves—to the creation, beauty, and appreciation of them—then it is striking how easily analogies to the divine—its creative activity, sublimity, and manifestability in human experience—suggest themselves. Lawrence has introduced the first analogy, between divine and human creativity. And now Theodore Dreiser serves to introduce the second, between divine and artistic beauty.

From the standpoint of the novel's dialogue with religion, Dreiser and Lawrence have so much in common that it is surprising that so few comparisons between them have been made. Both of them rejected the Christianity of their youth, suffered having books censored by the Catholic Church, and looked to nature for spiritual sustenance. Dreiser differs from Lawrence religiously by coming late in life to affirm one branch of Christianity, Quakerism. But what he affirms in Christianity mirrors what Lawrence rejects in it, namely, a projection onto it of a religious sensibility from outside it. If Lawrence's rejection of Christianity is more truthfully of Platonism, then Dreiser's affirmation of Quaker Christianity is more truthfully of pantheism.

Dreiser was raised a Catholic. Like Lawrence, he rejected institutional Christianity early on, on experiential grounds, because of the terrible poverty he observed around him, and on intellectual grounds, under the influence of such social Darwinist thinkers as Herbert Spencer. Dreiser is typically identified as a naturalist, or social realist, who narrated the tragic subjection of his characters to social forces beyond their control. But his naturalism late in life took a romantic turn, due at least partly to his sympathetic reading and editing of Henry David Thoreau. He came to believe that a Creative Force underlay the natural world, and that it revealed itself to us in the beauty and design we discerned in our environment. Another late-life discovery for Dreiser was Quakerism. This liturgically spare, governmentally flat, mystically charged expression of Christianity came as close in his eyes as religion could to pure institutionlessness without losing an organizational presence in the world. In his late novel, *The Bulwark*, these two quite different religious streams, of neotranscendentalism and Quakerism, combine to shape a theme of which the first supplies the inner content and the second the outward form. "Dreiser used Quakerism in the novel as a vehicle for expressing his own emergent exultation in the Creative Force."[19] Traditional Quaker readers were not deceived. For all of its radicalism, Quakerism is still Christian in its roots, not pantheist. As one Quaker critic commented about this book, "Friends will read it with strong to violent disapproval."[20]

One of Dreiser's inheritances from his economically impoverished childhood was a fascination with beauty. The beauty that wealth enabled represented an attractive alternative to poverty, but beauty also showed in the midst of poverty (as in the rural, Indiana landscapes of his boyhood), offering there momentary consolations. Beauty is the fascination that draws some of Dreiser's characters to their doom, but it also works, conversely, to elevate, in the character of Etta Barnes from *The Bulwark*, one of Dreiser's most attractive heroines.

> From her very youngest days, Etta was a dreamer, stricken with those strange visions of beauty which sometimes hold us all spellbound, enthralled, but without understanding. In no way in which her father, her sisters, and her brothers were wise, was she wise. There is a wisdom that is related to beauty only, that concerns itself with cloud forms and the wild vines' tendrils, whose substance is not substance, but dreams only, and whose

dreams are entangled with the hopes and yearnings of all men. Etta was such a one.[21]

Dreiser does not interrupt the poetry of this passage to elucidate the wisdom that is related to beauty only, but we may surmise that it turns on attunement to the Creative Force of nature. That Dreiser bestows this wisdom on Etta, a Quaker, makes of her a point of synthesis between the novel's conflicting undertone of pantheism and overtone of Quakerism. It is all the more to our purpose if we can trace the pantheism, as some critics do, back to so eminent a literary figure as Thoreau, for then Etta personifies the tension between literary and Christian voices over the value of beauty. It is already an irony that a Quaker, schooled to discipline natural human responsiveness to aesthetic allure, should show the wisdom of beauty. We might expect that wisdom to carry Etta out of Quakerism entirely and for awhile it does, in the form it takes of an attractive Greenwich Village artist, with whom she has an affair. At the end of the novel, Etta returns to her Quaker roots, but only at the end, so Dreiser is spared having to show how the alternative wisdoms of beauty, and of the Inner Light, can coalesce enduringly in one person. But at least he has raised the question for us, his readers, of whether they can.

L. P. HARTLEY AND THE AESTHETIC DIMENSION OF RELIGIOUS EXPERIENCE

The English novelist, L. P. Hartley (1895–1972), is probably the least well known of our six novelists. His best-known book, *The Go-Between* (1953), became a successful film (1970). Hartley is the sort of novelist a librarian would commend to the hapless lover of Hawthorne who, having read all of his novels and stories, is bereft of any more to read. Hartley himself admired Hawthorne and wrote about him. Like Hawthorne, Hartley rejected the religion of his childhood, in his case, Methodism, and though he later converted to the Church of England, he was as muted in his Anglicanism as Hawthorne was in his Congregationalism, except in one area of appreciation that he further shared with Hawthorne: a love of gothic cathedrals.

Hartley grew up near the English cathedral city of Peterborough. One biographer speculates that it was just the aesthetic lure of the cathedral that drew Hartley into the Church of England.[22] In the work considered his masterpiece, *Eustace and Hilda*, a local cathedral sets the context for an unusual religio-aesthetic experience in the life of the young hero, Eustace. As a young child, he is on an outing with his family when he looks up at the cathedral window:

> Here they were, under the shadow of the church ... [whose west window the guidebook called] "an earthly echo of a symphony made in heaven." The word, "heaven," . . . released Eustace's visual eye from dwelling on the material structure of the medieval mason's masterpiece. The design, with all its intricacy, faded from his sight, to be replaced in his mind's eye by the window's abstract qualities, its beauty, its vigor, its originality, its pre-eminence, its perfection. With these . . . he began to feel as one. He . . . floated upwards. Out shot his left arm, caught by some force that twisted this way and that; he could feel his fingers, treble-jointed and unnaturally long, scraping against the masonry of the arch as they groped for the positions assigned to them. . . . Even his hair ... rose from his head and swaying like seaweed, strove to reach up to the keystone. Splayed, spread, crucified . . . into a semblance of the writhing stonework, he seemed to be experiencing the ecstasy . . . of petrifaction. Meanwhile . . . pictures of saints and angels, red, blue and yellow pressed against and into him, bruising him, cutting him, spilling their colors over him. The pain was exquisite, but there was rapture in it, too. Another twitch, a final wriggle, and he felt no more; he was immobilised, turned to stone. High and lifted up, he looked down from the church wall, perfect, preeminent, beyond criticism.[23]

This is as much a portrait of religion in aesthetic experience as of aesthetics in religious experience. Like Etta in *The Bulwark*, Eustace is a point of convergence for both religious and aesthetic sensibilities. It is a highly impressionable child who imagines himself transposed into the figures of a stained glass window. As Eustace matures, this impressionability takes on self-sacrificial hues that ally him with certain kinds of religious figures. At the same time, he develops artistic talents as a writer and becomes a novelist. But Hartley is astute enough to shade the self-sacrificial behavior with suggestions of self-destructive self-indulgence.

The first book of the trilogy constituting *Eustace and Hilda* is entitled *The Shrimp and the Anemone*. It tells the story of Eustace's childhood relation with his older sister, Hilda. In the episode for which the first book is named, the two children witness by the seashore one of nature's cruelties, a beautiful anemone in the process of devouring a shrimp. In sympathy for the shrimp, Eustace tries to extract it from the anemone's clutch but in the process beheads the shrimp and disembowels the anemone, so that both die. Critics see the episode, which comes at the very beginning of the novel, as a metaphor for the relation between Eustace and his older sister. The relation is precipitously if not actually incestuous. Eustace is the shrimp who sacrifices himself to the guidance and wishes of his sister, the beautiful but devouring anemone. But the sacrifice is ultimately not willing or whole. By the end of the novel, Eustace rebels against it and in the process accidentally nearly kills his sister and actually dies himself, in imitative repetition of the shrimp and anemone scene from the start. That this troubled and troubling fate falls to the character who, at an early age, is already weaving together elements of religious and aesthetic experience raises the question of how successfully the two can be combined. The imaginative self-sacrifice implicit in Eustace's projection of himself into the stained glass is quite different from the actual sacrifice he tries to make of himself in relation to his sister. Self-sacrifice shows differently in the aesthetic experience of art and the religious experience of life, or, at least, the novel raises the question of whether it does. Perhaps Hartley is suggesting that to work without self-destruction, self-sacrificial behavior must be religiously and not aesthetically motivated, and Eustace, tragically, has failed to distinguish the two. But Hawthorne, in one of his magnificent hedgings, may already have warned against the temptation to mix artistic with religious experience when he showed the relation between the minister, Dimmesdale, and the textile artist, Hester Prynne, come to such a sorry end.[24]

LEO TOLSTOY AND THE RELATION OF RELIGION AND ART TO ETHICS

Perhaps there is no more dramatic example of separation between religion and literature than early nineteenth-century Russia where, it is said, the preeminent writer of the day, Alexander Pushkin, and the preeminent saint, Serafim of Sarov, did not know of each other's exis-

tence.[25] That separation surprises, if only because the Russian Orthodox Church seems to provide a more hospitable climate for the arts
than, say, early American Puritanism. "The Orthodox liturgy has a
beauty that does not escape the most secular visitors."[26] At the same
time, the Orthodox Church, which preserves more of the substance and
mood of its ancient roots than perhaps any other form of Christianity,
is not known for bold intellectualizing. Its doctrinal life effectively
closed in 737, the year of the last ecumenical church council that is
authoritative for it. And so when the European Enlightenment moved
East, under the encouragements of Tsar Peter the Great, the church
had no resources to contain it, and a new intellectual class arose outside
itself. It was to this class that writers such as Pushkin, Turgenev, and
Tolstoy belonged.

Tolstoy is the only one of our six authors to undergo a dramatic
religious conversion, which itself received literary expression in his
book *Confession*. The conversion experience marks a turn in his literary
output. His two great novels, *War and Peace* and *Anna Karenina*, precede the conversion. Afterwards, much, although not all, of his work
took the form of religious tracts. Critics largely agree that, with some
notable exceptions, such as "The Death of Ivan Ilych," the novels and
stories that followed the conversion are less memorable than those that
preceded. And this could open up another vantage point on religion's
critique of literature, or literature's of religion, that stories that channel
religious doctrine invariably sacrifice their aesthetic potential. But the
form of religion into which Tolstoy converted points us down another
track. He did not become normatively Russian Orthodox. Rather, in
the spirit of the Enlightenment, he emphasized the ethics of Christianity, to the explicit detriment of its theology. "The will of God is most
clearly expressed in the teaching of the man Jesus, whom to consider as
God and pray to, I consider the greatest blasphemy."[27] Moral principles
such as nonviolence and pacifism constituted Tolstoy's personal religion. That fact challenges Christianity (and Judaism) with the possibility of being supplanted by ethics. Typically, it is much more
philosophers of the Kantian type who raise that challenge. But literature, in Tolstoy's hands, does too.

The ultimate effect of Tolstoy's challenge to religion draws it and
literature together, for they face in ethics a shared threat to their respective autonomies. If Tolstoy's aesthetic gifts were chastened by a
religious conversion that proves on inspection to be more moral than

religious, then it is really ethics that reins in his literary talents. The theory of literature Tolstoy expounds in his postconversionary essay *What Is Art?* most explicitly subordinates aesthetic drives to moral ends. No literature is good that is not also morally improving. By this standard, it is not clear whether *Anna Karenina* is good literature. Certainly what stands out for most readers about this novel is the vividness, not the ethics, of the characters. Critic Wayne Booth speaks for many Tolstoy lovers when he writes, "When reading *Anna Karenina* in my late teens, I found myself detesting everyone I met outside the book; . . . nobody in my world was half as interesting as the much more vividly imagined people in Tolstoy's. At such times, relatives and friends found me unbearably, contemptuously rude and distant."[28] In this case, the novel has had a positively immoral effect on its reader.

Indirectly, Tolstoy himself points to a tension between the vividness of life he sought to communicate in this novel and at least one version of moral idealism. There is a minor character in *Anna Karenina* called, simply, Varenka. Orphaned as an infant and raised by an aristocrat whom she serves, Varenka first appears in the novel at a spa, where one of the main characters, Kitty Shcherbatsky, has retired with her mother to recover from an unhappy love interest. The lovelorn Kitty is fascinated by Varenka's seeming indifference to romance and her single-minded devotion to serving others. Her ministrations to the ailing guests at the spa unfailingly have a good effect. In addition, she is musically talented but without pride in her gifts. Kitty "was entranced by her art, her voice, her face, but most of all by her manner, by that fact that Varenka . . . was completely indifferent to praises."[29] And Kitty wonders, "What has she got that gives her this power to disregard everything and to be so serenely independent?"[30]

Tolstoy wrote *Anna Karenina* between 1873 and 1877, on the cusp of his conversion. He began writing his *Confession* only two years later, in 1879. In *Anna Karenina*, Tolstoy never explicitly answers Kitty's question about Varenka. If he had been asked it several years later, he might have answered that what Varenka had that so enobled her was unselfishness. Especially in light of his postconversionary story, "The Kruetzer Sonata," which reads as a moral judgment on sex, Varenka's seeming sexlessness is an outward sign of moral elevation. Varenka surely appealed to the postconversionary Tolstoy, but there are signs she did not appeal to Tolstoy at the time he created her. Here is how Varenka appears through Tolstoy's own narrative voice:

She seemed to be a person who had never been youthful. She might be 19 or she might be 30. She was . . . good-looking rather than plain. . . . But then she was not the type of person who was attractive to men. She was like a beautiful flower which, though its petals had not yet begun to drop, was already faded and without fragrance. Besides, she could not be attractive to men because she lacked what Kitty had too much of—the suppressed fire of life and consciousness of her own attractiveness.[31]

According to distinguished historian and critic Isaiah Berlin, the religio-moral beliefs of the preconversionary Tolstoy were closest to Rousseau's.[32] His conversion had less to do with Christianity than with the two non-Christian options for religious veneration that opened up after the Enlightenment: nature and ethics. Tolstoy converted from nature to ethics. It was just his preconversionary faith in the natural and spontaneous that enabled him to write such vivid stories.[33] The problem with Varenka is that she is not vivid. This judgment falls on her most harshly, not by what Tolstoy says of her but by the minor role he assigns her. Even her name is attenuated. The aristocrat who raises her never formally adopts her, so she cannot go by her patron's name. Neither can she go by her biological parents' name, since that is never disclosed. As though to seal his judgment on her, Tolstoy later invests her with a love interest—she is not above romance, after all, as Kitty mistakenly imagines—that he foils.

Varenka, at least upon first appearance, models a quality that has captivated and inspired a wide range of moral idealists, from the stoic and the Kantian to the mystical and saintly, namely, disinterest. That a picture of this moral ideal occurs so unvividly in one of his most vivid novels poses the further question: How aesthetically memorable can uniformly moral characters be?

DOSTOEVSKY AND THE LITERARY PROBLEM OF SAINTLINESS

That question, transposed back into religious terms, proved more troubling to Dostoevsky than to Tolstoy, for Dostoevsky wanted to portray a saint. Can that be done in modern literature? A surprising consensus of critical opinion is that it cannot. Of the six themes addressed in the third part of this book—love, death, evil, suffering, forgiveness, saintliness—the last raises a border between religion and literature that may prove unpassable.

Dostoevsky, like Tolstoy, was raised in the Russian Orthodox Church. As a youth, he, again like Tolstoy, rejected it, but unlike Tolstoy, he returned to it in later years. Christianity in general, Russian Orthodoxy in particular, and the heritage of the novel are all originating points for Dostoevsky's much-quoted aspiration "to portray a positively beautiful man."[34] For the character who bears the brunt of realizing that aspiration, Prince Myshkin of *The Idiot*, has roots in the figure of the New Testament Christ, in the Russian Orthodox institution of the "holy fool," and in that literary character who helped launch the novel on its course, Don Quixote. Myshkin, like Eustace Cherrington and Etta Barnes, mingles dual heritages from religion and literature.

The worry over saints in literature is that their sanctity deprives them of aesthetic interest. The assumption is that sanctity, like God as traditionally conceived, is simple, and so without the complexity that underlies the capacity of a character to sustain interest. But it is by no means obvious that sanctity is simple. The holiness of God as the Bible portrays it carries as much potential destructiveness as blessing. Religious experience, according to the now-classic analysis by Rudolf Otto, divides between feelings of terror and love. If the simplicity of God turns out to be, as some church traditions teach, a *coincidentia oppositorum*, then there is ample room for literary characters who imitate that simplicity to arouse and sustain interest.

Certainly Dostoevsky was fascinated by juxtaposed, if not coinciding, opposites. At several points throughout *The Idiot*, Myshkin is paired with his sinister opposite, Rogozhin. Originally in Dostoevsky's mind, Myshkin was himself to embody moral opposites, but as the novel evolved, the darker side of his nature manifested as the separate character, Rogozhin.[35] But Myshkin was not entirely relieved of darkness; it descended on him physically in the form of a darkening disease, epilepsy. Epilepsy itself has, in the annals of medical history, a religious side. It once was known as "the sacred disease" because the convulsions associated with it seemed religiously inspired. That is how Dostoevsky presents Myshkin's own epilepsy in this well-known passage from *The Idiot*:

He remembered among other things that he always had one
minute just before the epileptic fit . . . when suddenly in the
midst of sadness, spiritual darkness and oppression, there
seemed a flash of light in his brain, and with extraordinary
impetus all his vital forces suddenly began working at their
highest tension. The sense of life, the consciousness of self were
multiplied ten times at these moments which passed like a flash
of lightening. His mind and his heart were flooded with
extraordinary light; all his uneasiness, all his doubts, all his anx-
ieties were relieved at once; they were all merged into a lofty
calm, full of serene harmonious joy and hope. But these
moments . . . were only the prelude of that final second . . .
with which the fit began . . . [which plunged him into] stupefaction, spiritual darkness, idiocy.[36]

So intimate a pairing of harmonious joy with spiritual darkness is surely
ripe with dramatic potentials, which Dostoevsky exploits in the
epilepsy scenes of the novel. The question is whether Myshkin's sanctity of character shows through the drama or is eclipsed by it. Myshkin
himself reasons that the split second of harmonious joy weighs so much
more in good than the resultant darkness does in evil that the tension
between them resolves in favor of the good. The trouble is that joy and
idiocy are not the only opposites between which Myshkin's sanctity
hovers. Much of the plot is driven by the division of his affections
between the beautiful but tragic Nastasya, whom he loves compassion-
ately, and the beautiful but normal Aglaia, whom he loves romantically.
And far from resolving that affectional rift, he himself is torn in two by
it and regresses in the end to a permanent state of "stupefaction, spiritual darkness and idiocy." That regression can be read two ways—as the
failure of his sanctity or the failure of a desanctified world to tolerate
sanctity. If the first, then Dostoevsky has sacrificed Myshkin's sanctity
to the dramatic requirements of literature; if the second, then the opposite danger looms, since the authorial voice then takes on a posture of
sanctity that in a fictional world abandoned by God becomes inauthen-
tic, becomes sanctimony. Dostoevsky is too religious a writer for the
first course and too honest a writer for the second. And so, like
Myshkin, he hovers between the opposites. But in so doing, he raises
our last question: Can saints appear in modern literature?

Part 1

Mutual Critiques

Chapter 2

A Religious Critique of Literature
The Platonic Line

One of the most touching portraits of a childhood deliberately deprived, on religious grounds, of imaginative literature is Edmund Gosse's, in his memoir of his own youth, *Father and Son*. A Victorian writer and critic whose fame today is much eclipsed by his better-known contemporaries, Oscar Wilde and George Bernard Shaw, Gosse was widely read in his own time (1849–1928), especially for his biography of John Donne. Edmund was the son of Philip and Emily Gosse, who belonged to a small sect of Christians known today as the Plymouth Brethren. The Brethren were founded by the Anglican priest, John Nelson Darby (1800–1882), who sought to foster in small worship and study groups a more profoundly biblical Christianity than he thought available in the established Church of England. His movement was so anti-establishment that it resisted taking any name, thus others dubbed it, after the meeting place of its most prominent worship circle, in Plymouth, England, the Plymouth Brethren. The spiritual descendants of Darby today remember him best for his theory of biblical dispensation: the Bible is divisible into portions in each of which God reveals a stage of his ultimate plan for world salvation. The issue of salvation, and its apportionment over distinct dispensations, was so intensely foregrounded that it fostered an asceticism with regard to other human endeavors. As the Jewish theologian, Martin Buber, observed of asceticisms in general, they spring from a "despair of being able to subjugate . . . the fullness of life to the religious."[1] And the nineteenth century, which gave us, among other things, Charles Darwin and the Industrial Revolution, offered up a range of challenges that at least superficially resisted subjection to the religious. One of the casualties of that subjugation in the Gosse household was imaginative literature.

In some ways, that is surprising. Edmund's father, Philip, was a zoologist. A hidden debt that every lover of live fish, on display, owes to him is the very word "acquarium," which he coined.[2] Philip's commitments to scientific method and classification might be thought to explode the confines of any religious asceticism, especially since he both knew and accepted the findings of Charles Darwin. But the ingenious Philip did indeed succeed in subjugating Darwin to the religious through a theory he advanced in a book called *Omphalos*, Greek for "navel." According to Philip, God created the world as the Bible describes, but with the addition of fossils, implanted in the earth, so as to highlight, for the humans who discovered them, that God orders the world according to just such natural law as Darwin unveiled. Questioning the meaning of fossils was, for Philip, like asking of Adam and Eve whether they had navels: given the biblical account of their origin, neither would have a navel, but nonetheless God supplied them with one in order that they conform to the divinely ordained laws of human propagation. Philip's interests were broad enough to require further exercise of his ingenuity in additional subordinations of the nonreligious to the religious. Novels, which might invite inordinate interest in romantic love, were nonetheless admissible, according to Edmund's account of his father's opinions, if, as in the case of Dickens's works, they "exposed the passion of love in a ridiculous light."[3] Pagan poets who might tempt to false religion were nonetheless readable, if, like Virgil, they can be "enjoyed with least to explain away and least to excuse."[4]

But in the end it was not Philip but the imaginatively gifted Emily who had the most ascetic and inhibiting effect on Edmund's childhood reading. The portrait that Edmund paints of his birth mother, who died young, is sympathetic. Her severity toward literature was more toward her own storytelling proclivities; the restrictions she placed on her child read like an irrepressible excrescence of ones she imposed more rigorously and painfully on herself. Here is her self-condemnation, as Edmund presents it, in her own words (the bracketed insertions are Edmund's):

When I was a very little child, I used to amuse myself and my brothers with inventing stories, such as I read. Having, as I suppose, naturally a restless mind and busy imagination, this soon became the chief pleasure of my life. Unfortunately, my brothers were always fond of encouraging this propensity, and I found in Taylor, my maid, a still greater tempter. I had not known there was any harm in it, until Miss Shore [a Calvinist governess], finding it out, lectured me severely, and told me it was wicked. From that time forth I considered that to invent a story of any kind was a sin. But the desire to do so was too deeply rooted in my affection to be resisted in my own strength . . . and unfortunately I knew neither my corruption nor my weakness, nor did I know where to gain strength. The longing to invent stories grew with violence; everything I heard or read became food for my distemper. The simplicity of truth was not sufficient for me; I must needs embroider imagination upon it, and the folly, vanity and wickedness which disgraced my heart are more than I am able to express. Even now [at age twenty-nine], though watched, prayed and striven against, this is still the sin that most easily besets me. It has hindered my prayers and prevented my improvement, and therefore has humbled me very much.[5]

Had religious psychologist William James known of this account, he might well have included it in his chapter "The Sick Soul," which would have been more aptly named "The Self-Divided Soul," in his *Varieties of Religious Experience,* where other, sometimes equally moving self-judgments of sinfulness are gathered. The poignancy of the passage owes much to the fact that it is indeed a *self*-judgment. It is just because the governess, Miss Shore, who first passes this judgment about story-telling, does so on another, not herself, that the impression she leaves on the reader is not so benign. Emily herself might have been remembered much less fondly by Edmund had she not died young and ceded her place to a stepmother more forebearing towards the imagination.

The gist of Emily's judgment on storytelling is that precisely in its attractive inventiveness it is false, and that the falseness of the story morally corrupts all who enjoy it, both creator and audience. The underlying assumptions, that falseness and wickedness are correlative, and that literary inventiveness yields only falseness, are by no means obviously true. What are the origins of these assumptions? Edmund, in his bracketed commentary on the passage, provides a link to a religious origin for this attitude toward imaginative literature. The condemnatory Miss Shore was a *Calvinist* governess. If Calvinism carried these attitudes to Miss Shore, then the ultimate origin of them is presumably the man for whom that theological and ecclesiastical tendency is named, sixteenth-century Reformer John Calvin. But such a presumption would be rash. It is a commonplace among scholars of the Reformation that Calvin's own attitudes do not always match those of his followers, or of others who spoke in his name. In fact, Calvin had a refined appreciation of literary style. There is a sense in which all of the sixteenth-century Reformers were converts out of Catholicism and into the, in their judgment, more authentic Christianity they themselves were fashioning. Before he initiated the Christian movement that took his name, Calvin was a humanist. As a student in Orleans, France, Calvin focused on law, but "his real passion as a student was . . . for the languages, literatures and cultures of antiquity."[6] And though the philosopher, Seneca, was his favorite among the ancient writers, he also cited with approval Homer and Ovid,[7] who were nothing if not storytellers. Of course, the true measure of Calvin's openness toward stories would have been in his attitudes toward the literary genre just about to emerge in his own times, namely, the novel. Cervantes and Calvin were near contemporaries. It requires a creative imagination even to picture them in conversation. But they had more in common than first appears. When Cervantes parodies medieval romances, the note he sounds rings in harmony with Calvin's when he in turn condemns the fanciful allegories of medieval Bible interpretation and commends to exegetes a sober linguistic and historical method. That potential affinity between the two suggests that Calvin might have appreciated a kind of truth in novels, which would have mitigated, without entirely eradicating, the severity of tone we find in Emily Gosse's judgment on storytelling.

It is possible to construct what Calvin's response to Cervantes might have been. In Calvin's now-classic theological treatise *The Institutes of Christian Religion*, he has this to say about the literary greats of Greece and Rome:

> Read Demosthenes or Cicero; read Plato, Aristotle and others
> of that tribe. They will, I admit, allure you, delight you, move

you, enrapture you in wonderful measure. But betake yourself from them to . . . sacred reading [i.e., the Bible]. Then, in spite of yourself, so deeply will it affect you, so penetrate your heart, so fix itself in your very marrow, that, compared with its deep impression, such vigor as the orators and philosophers have will nearly vanish.[8]

Though Cervantes was neither orator nor philosopher, delight and rapture have always been part of his readers' response to him, so much so that had Calvin been able to foretell the future, he might have added Cervantes' modern name to that list of ancient orators and philosophers who so tempt our attention but whose literary achievements pale in comparison to Scripture's. Calvin's argument is that the Bible surpasses literature at its own art of moving us "in wonderful measure." As Calvin develops the argument, it is not simply that the Bible shows greater stylistic grace than a mere human writer can achieve, it is that Scripture's content impresses so much more deeply than literature's form, however accomplished, that it silences all claims for style or form to transformingly move an audience.

This is the argument of one so confident of Scripture's powers that literature no longer even competes with it. The argument carries all the more weight coming from a humanist, or from one academically trained in humanistic disciplines. Part of the reform that Luther, Calvin, and their colleagues initiated was to shift the Bible center stage. And one measure of their confidence in it was their belief that the Christian faithful needed much less besides it than the Catholic Church deemed necessary to ground their spiritual lives. In a household that was truly Calvinist, literature would not be censored. It would be casually tolerated in the serene assurance that next to the Bible (which would be ever on hand), its charms would quickly pale. The figure who, having intervened between Calvin himself and such Calvinists as Emily Gosse, inadvertently worked to accelerate the decline of that assured confidence in the Bible is Darwin, who loomed so large in the Gosses' intellectual life. Calvin, who did not have to contend with Darwin, much less Spinoza or the founder of the German higher criticism of the Bible, Julius Wellhausen, could afford to condescend to literature. Emily Gosse could not. And so if we seek a precursor in Christian history for the troubled intensity of her censoriousness toward literature, Calvin will not do. We must revert to a time before the Bible was so unassailably sure of itself, to a period when contenders for supreme place in readers' and listeners' hearts were as challenging to Scripture as Darwin would become: the period of the early church.

As late as the fifth century, the pagan myths behind the stories Virgil told still showed through the *Aeneid* so compellingly that St. Augustine (354–430), himself a master storyteller, had to discipline his delight in them lest they lure him from the Gospels.[9] Augustine marks a turning point from Hellenistic antiquity to the Middle Ages. In his time, pagan art had not yet frozen into the distanced, objectified past, nor had the serene scholasticism of the high Middle Ages yet been born. Augustine wrote at the end of the period of ancient Christian apologetics, whose theological intensities and moral recriminations come closer in tone to Emily Gosse's mood of judgment. Pagan literature does for Augustine what Darwin did for the Gosses—it supplies the challenge against which an intense censoriousness toward literature can voice itself.

Augustine confides in his *Confessions* how much pleasure he had in the Latin (if not the Greek) classics, especially the *Aeneid*. When early on in the book he recalls with shame his boyish success in declaiming, at school, a scene from the *Aeneid* he inventively enlivened, he sounds very much like Emily Gosse's precursor.[10] He and Emily could wring their hands in unison over the "spectral image . . . and vain show" of the "baubles of literature."[11] But Augustine resisted the lure of literature with even greater urgency than Emily did, for he wrote not merely at the end of an intellectual history, as it could be argued Emily did, but at the end of a state's history, namely, Rome's. When the Goths captured the city of Rome in 410, it was the beginning of the end of the western Roman empire. It was only a century earlier that under Constantine's favor Christianity had begun to flourish. Some observers linked the rise of Christianity to the fall of Rome. Roman religion was a civic affair. The gods protected the cities that worshiped them. As the empire turned from Roman gods to Christian God, it sacrificed the divine protection it previously enjoyed. Christian teachings of love and forgiveness further undermined the martial spirit of self-defense. Augustine wrote *The City of God* to counter these claims. It was not Christianity that undermined the empire from within but the lingering lures of pagan culture, most especially its theatrical literature. Augustine refines

Emily Gosse's assumptions. Emily's storyteller translated back into Augustine's time is the tragic poet who "composed fictions with no regard for truth."[12] Augustine condemns such poets, as Emily no doubt would, but his qualification of their fictions, that they are told with no regard for truth, opens up the possibility of fictions that do transmit some truth. Augustine agrees with Emily that truthless fiction morally corrupts, but the reason he gives for that differs from any Emily might have conceived to explain the ruinous impact of the stories she told. The problem with ancient tragic poets was that they "set the worst possible examples before wretched men, . . . gratuitously fanning the flame of human lust."[13] It is not so much falsity per se that corrupts as the particular form falseness takes when it wants to entertain: it portrays the least attractive side of human nature as though to model it. If Rome fell, it was in part because the Romans' inner nature had been corrupted by watching too many theatrical depictions of corrupt human beings.

If Augustine were writing in the modern age, he might have exempted poets from the criticism he heaped on playwrights and actors, as indeed Calvin did.[14] But for antiquity, poets, playwrights, and actors formed a continuum. Playwrights were poets. Epic poetry asked for dramatic recitation, Augustine declaiming Virgil was a playwright and an actor. If there was evil in acting, then there was evil in poetry. If poetry had to entertain the crowd, then it must appeal to the populace, which is to say the lowest common denominator. And so it had to depict the lowest behavior. A frightful ancient logic anticipated the modern claim of Georges Bataille about William Blake, that he "managed . . . to reduce humanity to poetry and poetry to Evil."[15]

Augustine has supplied a missing link in Emily's argument that moves from fiction to sin. It is not that fiction itself is evil, but at its best it models and therefore inculcates evil behavior. Edmund suspected that his mother had a positive gift for storytelling. She told fiction at its best. In his memoir, he does not cite any examples of her work, but perhaps her heroes and heroines were indeed mischievous and naughty. In her self-judgment, Emily implies that fiction, as embroidery on truth, conceals a judgment on the world as it is, as God created it, and so masks an act of audacious pretension, the kind of act that turned Lucifer, the light-bearing angel, into Satan. In that case, authorship already models evil behavior. Augustine is distressed by egoistic and attention-getting behavior in human artistry, especially as it shows itself in crowd-pleasing rhetoric and eloquence. But unlike Emily, he does not dismiss all literary artistry out of hand. It is possible, after all, to tell fictions that have regard for truth.

As a biblical exegete, Augustine needed such fiction, for the Bible tells stories that to the early Christian mind could not possibly be factual, for example, the story of consuming sexual passion in the *Song of Songs*. This had to be a fiction. But it was fiction told with allegorical regard for truths about the relation between Christ and the church. The church father, Origen, earlier than Augustine, had already interpreted the story that way. The trouble with truthful fiction is that it cannot be the best fiction. For if fiction at its best depicts human behavior at its worst, then poets who picture goodness are not the best. Where biblical fiction is truthful, it fails as literature. This was a problem for Augustine from the start. He confesses that the Bible, at first sight, cuts a poor aesthetic figure next to Cicero.[16] His allegorical interpretations of the Bible can be seen as attempts to read into it an eloquence of complexity, even paradox.[17] What appears like bad behavior in humans is, read allegorically, an expression of divine goodness. It was only after centuries of medieval accretion to allegorical interpretation of the Bible that the simple sense of it could actually seem elegant, as it did to Calvin.

Allegory was Augustine's escape from the burden of sin that good stories carried. Allegory allowed a play on words of seeming sin and moral good that preserved both the moral and aesthetic worth of stories. But dual-mindedness always disturbs monotheism, which is ever tending toward the One. What saddled Augustine in the first place with the assumption that the best stories showed the worst behavior? Surely not the Bible itself, which, for all of the stories it tells, scarcely pauses to reflect on storytelling as such. The Bible prohibits graven images because it feared they would be worshipped, but it never prohibits stories, not even false ones. On the contrary, stories in the form of parables are indispensable teaching tools.

The Bible was only one of Augustine's teachers. Another major intellectual influence on him was Plato. Augustine himself credits Plato for his understanding of literature, most especially book X of the *Republic*, where Socrates famously decrees the banishment of poets from the ideal state. Emily Gosse and Augustine spoke out of religions that, though under siege, were long established. Theirs was the strength of inheritance. Plato's religious ground was much less firm. He was the founder of Platonic religion. Founded religions, such as Christianity and Buddhism, typically arise in protest against religious inheritance. Plato's inheritance was not simply Greek polytheism, it was Greek polytheism expressed in the words of what the ancient literary theorist, Longinus, would call sublime poetry. As one scholar observes, "The spiritual unity of the Greeks was founded and upheld by poetry."[18] The religion that Plato inherited, and rejected, was Homeric poetry.

Homer's epic poems are both religious and literary. They are foundational documents of Western literary culture. Among the ancient Greeks themselves, the *Iliad* and *Odyssey* were already "revered for their fineness as poetry."[19] Even Plato, their arch critic, admired them for their aesthetic excellence. But even before Platonic critique is brought to bear on them, their religious value is doubtful. Regarded from the standpoint of either Jewish or Christian values, the theme of anger that opens the *Iliad* and that supplies the motivation for so much of Achilles' behavior must trouble. The ordinarily moderate Maimonides, that paragon of medieval Jewish philosophy, judges anger one of the only two qualities (the other is pride) that can never be moral, even as compensatory counterbalance to another extreme emotion,[20] and in the medieval Catholic typology of sin, it counts among the most deadly. It is possible to read the anger in the poem, and the violence it spawns, as the backdrop that sets off in all the more striking relief the conciliatory scenes, most especially the final one between Achilles and Priam. And the poem has been read as an allegory of both Platonic and Christian religion. The scene in which the ordinarily distant Apollo, who so consistently "works from afar,"[21] reveals himself without disguise to Hector, in response to the stricken and bewildered hero's question, "Who are you, who speak to me face to face, O noblest of gods,"[22] must recall for Christian readers the annunciation verses in Matthew's and Luke's Gospel. But in general, the behavior of the gods does not inspire reverence, and that is one starting point for Plato's critique.

Plato is a key originating point for the conviction that was passed down all the way to Emily Gosse, that the false and the wicked correlate. Platonic religion shares with Christianity and Judaism the certainty that whatever is divine is good, therefore, divinity can never be responsible for excess or unjust suffering. But the Greek gods, as Homer portrays them, routinely harm each other, and human beings, from motives of spite, lust, and jealousy. His accounts of them are then assuredly false, but they also are wicked for modeling behavior patterns that corrupt human beings who hear about them.

That argument, as far as it goes, resembles twenty-first century concerns over admiring depictions of violence on television. But Plato's argument is against more than heroizing pictures of violence. It is not at all obvious that Homer admires the violent killings he portrays, or seeks to evoke admiration for them. On the contrary, it has been argued that Homer's detached and impartial hand in shaping the death scenes of the *Iliad*, which rival, in sheer gore, anything that can be seen on television today, works to evoke the horrors of war, violence, and heroic military action.[23] Violence as such is not the problem. Under certain circumstances, such as the suicide death of his teacher, Socrates, Plato understands and admires violence. The philosopher who suffers violence painlessly is a positive model. Plato's argument is not so much that Homer's stories of divinely inspired violence are wicked because they are violent as because they are false. In principle, false stories of divine goodness also must trouble Plato, though he does not consider that possibility. It is the falseness in stories that causes the greatest damage to their listeners, and now we are closer still to the mood of Emily Gosse.

The link of falsity to evil, in Plato, follows on the extraordinary bond he posits between metaphysics, epistemology, and ethics. They are related by an application of the principle that like attracts like, which extends across the boundaries of these philosophical disciplines and issues in the remarkable result that the higher portions of a human soul have less in common with its lower portions than with the higher reaches of reality outside it. The most philosophically mature human soul virtually detaches from its lower segments and assimilates to a metaphysical reality outside it, which supplies for it a new and better identity. The highest reality is the idea of the Good. The highest faculty of human apprehension is reason, which is always the agent, or subject, of knowing. By the exalted station that each of these occupies in its respective sphere, the Good in metaphysics, reason in epistemology, the two attract each other. The Good limits its accessibility to reason alone. Conversely, reason will have dealings with nothing but the Good. Imperfection can never be an object of Reason's apprehension. Marred realities do not lend themselves to being known at all. Imperfection as objective is always an object of misapprehension. As a lesser reality, it can only draw the attention of inferior, less truth-disclosing epistemological faculties. Conversely, those same faculties can only have what is less than the Good for their objects. By an extension of the principle that like attracts like, two things in mutual attraction become like each other. Reason knowing the Good becomes good. Imperfection and misapprehension, as mutually attractive, become like each other. The lesser faculties of the soul, which register imperfection, exhibit the imperfection they misapprehend.[24]

The trouble with fictional stories is that they are false. They do not describe anything that has actually happened (otherwise, they are history, a genre that, though extant in Plato's time, he does not consider). The soul that attends to fiction is morally infected by the falseness in the object of its attention. And so the problem with fiction is not simply that as public performance art in ancient Greece it had to appeal to the lowest common denominator of crowds. Even an audience of philosophers could be corrupted by fictional stories, since falseness activates the imperfections in those who behold it. The inferior parts of the soul that register falseness and imperfection outside it are constituted largely by undisciplined emotion and desire. They include such things as the disproportionate anger that motivates so much of the action in the *Iliad*. Plato implies that the best poetry appeals precisely to the burgeoning chaos of emotion that resides at the bottom of the soul. Those emotions must dominate if poetry is to register at all. Indeed, the greater the poetry, the more of those emotions it engages. This accounts for the striking claim that "the greater the poetical charm of them [i.e., passages from Homer and other poets], the less meet they are for the ears of boys."[25] Both the consumers and the creators of poetry are corrupted by the fictions they enjoy. "The imitative poet . . . is not by nature made, nor is his art intended, to please or to affect the rational principle in the soul, but he will prefer the passionate and fitful temper" (605). That the poet is what he is *by nature* locks him all the more irrevocably into his depravity. In preferring to depict "the passionate and fitful," he comes to exhibit them himself, so much so that Plato has Socrates adopt a mock discretion over his view of poets, "for I should not like to have my words repeated to the tragedians and the rest of the imitative tribe" (595). Should artists learn about how much literature Socrates would censor in the ideal state, then "we must beg Homer and the other poets not to be angry," (387) for that low emotion, later so vilified by both Judaism and Christianity, is just the one most natural to poets.

Plato had the same route out from this judgment on fiction that Augustine had, namely allegorical interpretation, but he chose not to take it. Plato did not trust that immature minds could discern the allegorical meaning in a story, and mature minds could rise directly, without the story, to whatever truth it allegorically told. Unlike Augustine, Plato was almost willfully blind to the lures of a story poetically told. A modern reader reacts with astonishment to Socrates' claim in book X of *The Republic* that "you must have observed again and again what a poor appearance the tales of the poets make when stripped of the colours which music puts upon them, and recited in simple prose" (601). The comment does not show the characteristic irony of Socrates, which might have undercut its seeming naivete, but it does show the religiously motivated asceticism that drove Plato, at least in this passage, to deliberately deny himself and others anything that blocks or postpones the vision of the Good. This is the asceticism that echoes in St. Augustine and, more pronoucedly, with a Christian turn, in Emily Gosse.

It cannot be our purpose here to evaluate Plato's critique of poetry but merely to identify him as a key originating point of a long tradition of religious censoriousness toward literature. Plato's idealism is simultaneously one of the most soaring and severe ever conceived. It surpasses both Jewish and Christian idealism by its sheer, uncompromising verticality. The idea of the Good does not condescend; it does not reveal itself to human beings in startling acts of self-disclosure. It occupies a pinnacle it never leaves. It is difficult to scale the very steep slopes that lead up to it. In one image, that of the famous "divided line," the Good resides at the top of a line that offers no scalable slope at all but is positively vertical. We who are wed to sensuality wallow at the bottom of the line and must be capable of the philosophical equivalent of levitation if we are to behold the Good. According to the myth of the cave, the shadows that constitute our everyday reality are not cast by the sun but by a fire burning behind us at the bottom of a cave, where we sit strapped. And so it is not as though to see our ultimate source of light we need merely to look upward. We must first burst the chains that hold us and then ascend out of a subterranean dimness, only artificially lit, that has been our home. The budding philosopher who escapes the cave does so at very great violence to some of his most natural inclinations. He must be compelled up the ascent to the sun outside. The Good is remote: "In the world of knowledge, the idea of the Good appears last of all, and is seen only with an effort" (517). Copies of it may be discovered and even fashioned in the world around us, but only with great difficulty. The overarching goal of *The Republic* is to model a state that would be a copy, in political reality, of the idea of the Good, but such a copy is highly volatile. Plato has no sooner laid out the plan for it than it evaporates from any real domain. We do not know "if the ideal ever becomes a reality" (534) and Socrates must concede that the true home of the ideal state is heaven (592). The ordinary world of sense perception already constitutes an immense distance from the Good. To fashion works of poetry whose sensual appeal holds our attention is to compound the distance that nature's sensuality already imposes between us and our goal. As a Christian, Emily Gosse could not so degrade the natural world, since God created it. But she could say that artistic refashionings of it constitute a pointless and distracting embroidery of what is already perfect in its simplicity. Emily is neither the first nor the last artistically gifted renunciant to condemn art for making a virtue of an obfuscating redundancy. A mere redundancy might be ignored, but one that pushes its claims on our attention, which only with great difficulty focuses on its proper end, is nefarious. It is the urgency of Emily's renunciation that she shares with Plato and with all others for whom the effortful claims of religion narrow the scope of acceptable activity.

Chapter 3

A Literary Critique of Religion
The Dantean Line

Ascetic censoriousness is not the only means religion has to subordinate literature. Religion can claim to be the historic origin of literature. Polytheistic religious rites provided the context and condition for ancient Greek drama; the Catholic Church in turn gave rise to the medieval forms of drama—the mystery, morality, and miracle plays—that laid the foundation for modern theater; the Bible itself becomes an instant source of literature through a slight turn of the interpretive lens through which it is read: from divinely revealed or inspired Word, to, as the eighteenth century would call it, an ancient compendium of the aesthetic sublime. Moreover, in the hands of some theorists, the grounding of literature in religion is more than merely temporal; it is logical. According to nineteenth-century romantic philosopher Friedrich Schelling, "Mythology is the necessary condition and first content of all art."[1] That dated, idealist-romantic claim resonates within the still-current theories of such literary myth critics as Northrup Frye, who, in telling us that "Greece and Israel have imposed themselves on our consciousness until they have become part of the map of our own imaginative world,"[2] is sighting beneath the modern fiction we enjoy whole, subterranean worlds of Greek and biblical myth. Novels that self-consciously pattern themselves on antique myths, such as Joyce's *Ulysses* or Mann's *Joseph and His Brothers*, are only the obvious examples of literature's grounding in myth, which, according to Frye, is so deep that it is not too much to speak of "the identification of mythology and literature."[3]

39

Of course, so deep a debt to mythology is not necessarily a debt to *religion*. When David Bidney warns us against reducing "myth to some other mode of cultural truth such as philosophy, religion, or history,"[4] he clearly differentiates between the two. Myth has been variously defined. In its simplest and earliest meaning, from the ancient Greek, it is a story about the gods. Modern theorists of myth have expanded that definition beyond its polytheistic context to include the stories Judaism and Christianity tell.[5] Myths so broadened in meaning are narratives set in a supernatural world, setting the bounds of our natural world, either its beginning or end, and providing a framework of values for living in it. Myths are habitable dramas with ready-made parts for humans to assume. Judaism, Christianity, and Plato are all mythic in this sense. But mythic stories, like all stories, lend themselves to interpretation. What the stories imply for human values and action may be ambiguous. The two creation stories of Genesis are a case in point. The fact of two is already an ambiguity. In the first creation story, of Genesis 1, a day of rest supersedes six days of creative activity. The creations of the active days are deemed good, but the final day of rest holy. Which value is to set the tone for human life: creative action or rest? The second creation story, of Genesis 2–3, is even more ambiguous. Does knowledge ultimately elevate or debase? Early Catholic and gnostic Christianity interpreted the serpent's role in the Garden of Eden in precisely opposite ways: as tempting to disobedience (for the Catholics) and as liberating toward enlightenment (for the gnostics). The interpretability of myth sets in relief how much religion differs from literature on its capacity for being identified with myth. Religion can never be identified with myth. For the very interpretability of myth calls forth from religion instruments of interpretation that narrow the scope of its meaning and determine its precise implications for human action. These constraining instruments are drawn from those features of religion—its ritual, law, and doctrine—that demonstrate how much storytelling fails to exhaust all that religion hopes to do. A religion's instruments of interpretation enable normative understandings of its myth.

But insofar as literature is not constrained by a religion's ritual, doctrine, or law, it is free to interpret the myths in its own way. And it is just here that the possibility opens up of a literary critique of religion. When Northrup Frye writes that "the writer or artist . . . may owe a loyalty to his own discipline and may have to defend that discipline against the concerns of society,"[6] he points to an autonomy that literature can claim to have over against religion. That claim of the literary voice to self-determination extends over the myths it inherits from religion. It may even extend beyond those myths, to the point of rejecting them and substituting new myths of its own. More radically still, granting a debt of literature to myth, it may be that myths co-opted by literature for aesthetic purposes, to unify plot, character, and setting, sacrifice their mythic status insofar as in the service of art they fail any more to model or indirectly prescribe human action, insofar, that is, as they now pour the full force of their power to unify not into human life but into the artwork, whose parts, thanks to the myth, cohere as a whole. A myth working so hard in the service of art may become something else, what Kant would call an "aesthetic idea," whose origins in the poetic mind owe nothing to religion at all but all to the private fantasies of the creative imagination. Literature in such a state has freed itself from religion entirely.

For literature to challenge religion so assertively, it must have developed a self-conscious awareness of its own powers over against religion. We do not find so striking a self-consciousness among the ancient Greek poets and dramatists. Prophetic and poetic functions were so intertwined for the early Greeks that it is difficult to separate them: the poet Hesiod presented himself as a prophet; the prophetic oracle at Delphi typically issued its pronouncements in poetic form.[7] Though Aeschylus, Sophocles, and Euripides all based their plays on myths they inherited, the earlier expressions of those myths had already been so inflected by literary voices, whether Homer's or Hesiod's or a lesser Greek poet's, that a self-conscious claim of literature to shape the myths in defiance of some alternative, religious interpretation of them lacks the basis for its own sounding. Institutional Greek religion was less concerned with norms for interpreting myth than with proper performance of civic rites that ensured the well-being of the city-state.[8] The Greek dramatists enjoyed considerable freedom of interpretation over the ancient myths; far from suffering restraints, they would have been expected to recast the myths according to insights of their own.[9] And, between the three of them, they do indeed shape the common core of myth differently. Unexpectedly, if ancient Greece is to show a literary voice laying claim to a body of myth that an oppositional religion differently interprets, it can probably do no better than to offer up Plato. Plato, interpreted as the poet he undoubtedly was, who denounced the inherited body of Greek myth and substituted new, philosophical myths of his own (or, as Milton puts it, in describing Plato, who "to fabling fell and smooth conceits"[10]), comes as close as ancient Greece can come to raising a protesting poet's voice against the interpretive authority of religion over myth; except that, in this case, judging from Plato's own dialogues on the trial and death of Socrates, it is not so much a priestly class as Athenian society itself that represents that authority in action.

Judaism comes much closer to fashioning a space that so differentiates the literary from the religious that the first can rise up in self-conscious rebellion against the second. It does so through the medium of the Hebrew language, which served for centuries in almost exclusively sacred contexts, except in medieval Spain and the modern era, when it freed itself to function in secular ways. As Robert Alter observes, it was precisely in secular settings, of poetry especially, that Hebrew became a vehicle through which literary artists could raise a prophetic voice of their own, often in stark contrast to and protest against the historic religion that shared the same language. The secular Hebrew love poetry of the Middle Ages, in its ambiguously homosexual and heterosexual expressions, marks the beginning of a literary, Hebrew voice sounding outside the bounds of Jewish tradition. Alter notes the particular case of the perhaps most celebrated poet of the Judeo-Spanish Middle Ages, Judah Halevi, who in one of his love poems, patterned on the Bible's Psalm 17, committed the "double blasphemy [of] substituting man for God in the biblical text and man for woman in the expression of passion."[11] This was hardly a prophetic act of poetic license; Halevi also was a devoutly Jewish poet. If a medieval Jewish poet strikes a prophetic pose, then it is most likely in defense of tradition, as in the case of Solomon ibn Gabirol, who, distressed by the claims of Arab poets for the surpassing beauty of Arabic, saw it "as his own personal prophetic mission" to demonstrate in his own poems the artistic potentials of biblical Hebrew.[12] It was only in the modern era that Jewish writers in Hebrew arose who so radically reinterpreted their inheritance of biblical myth as to place themselves both outside and against their tradition. Again, Alter is an insightful guide, this time to the work of the first great modern Hebrew poet, H. N. Bialik. In one of his best-known poems, *The Dead of the Desert*, Bialik envisions an array of gigantic, supernaturally preserved corpses of ancient Israelites who died in the battle, described in Numbers 14, to take the land of Canaan, after God had pointedly withdrawn his support for them. Bialik heroizes the dead, who even in death defiantly resist the assaults of nature upon them and the legacy of divine punishment they carry through time. As Alter describes it, Bialik evokes the world of the Bible precisely "to create a world antithetical to that of the Bible."[13] Bialik "deeply imagines a strong counterversion of the whole biblical episode, transforming it into an original myth" that "makes an implicit claim to displace the canonical text."[14] Here the poet does not simply reinterpret received myth but creates it anew.[15]

The break that separates the medieval Hebrew poet from the modern one is the Enlightenment and the persisting crisis of Jewish identity that followed in its wake. Part of what fed that crisis was the disjunction between the traditional Jewish religious identity, which kept Jews apart from the rest of society, and the new, secular one, which assimilated Jews to the nation-based, civic cultures that were opening up fast around them. The non-Judaic myths and values that Bialik and his more radical contemporary, Saul Tschernikovsky, expressed in some of their poems were simply the pagan, Greek ones that had already belonged for centuries to the heritage of Western Europe. Tschernikovsky, who translated Homer into Hebrew, made this most explicit in his poem *Before a Statue of Apollo*, where he paid his reverential respects to that divine Greek paragon of poetry and prophecy. The Jewish rejections of Jewish heritage in modern Hebrew poetry are inflected by an impulse, at once eager and doubting, to appropriate aspects of the pagan Greek traditions that since early rabbinic times Judaism deeply suspected. It was just the Jewish heritage of rejecting those traditions that allowed the embracement of them by modern Hebrew poets to constitute a revolutionary act. But then, the modern Hebrew poets are not so much fashioning a new myth as substituting one very ancient scheme of it for another.

That raises the further question of whether writers can really create myths at all. If "myths are not freely made, but represent a folk product expressing the collective labors, emotions, and geniuses of peoples,"[16] then poets merely express the myths that, at best, they carry subconsciously in their private psyches. But if we would look for a literary line of progression that begins with a myth received under religious sanction and ends in what seem to be poetic creations of an entirely new myth, understood to succeed the old, then we can probably do no better than a foursome of poets whose inventive boldness, with regard to

Christian myth, so markedly increases with each over his looming predecessor(s) as to constitute a virtual succession of continuous patrimonies: Dante, Milton, Blake, and Yeats.[17] This poetic line, which begins firmly rooted in Christianity, ends outside of it. The continuity of so religiously disruptive a literary line serves to instance the theme of this chapter: the literary critique of religion.

All four poets expressed through their poetry critiques of what they saw as abuses in the institutional church of their day, but the denouncements of clerical corruption in the institutional church are not the most interesting features of this line of literary critique. Institutional religion has always been prey to those who turn toward it a scrutinizing moral eye. Nor is such scrutiny of the church the exclusive province of poets. Ever since the Bible introduced a distinction between prophets and priests, the institutions of Judaism and then of Christianity have suffered critiques from within their very own ranks. The Protestant Reformation teaches that, if nothing else. The subtler critique that evolves over the six centuries that separate Dante from Yeats relates to the foundational stories on which Christianity rests, the figures, both human and divine that people them, and the values held to be implicit in them.

Dante's Christian credentials are impeccable. Though he was not a professional theologian, cleric, or monk, he was, by his own account, educated in the "schools of the religious,"[18] usually taken to be the Florentine convent schools of the Franciscan and Dominican orders. The most eminent theological spokesmen of the two orders, St. Thomas Aquinas and St. Bonaventure, are not simply speaking characters in the *Comedy* but influential presences in the structure and ideas most especially of the *Paradise*.[19] The analogous points of transition—from purgatory to heaven, Virgil to Beatrice, reason to revelation—are all grounded in the profoundly Catholic (and Jewish) idea, both medieval and modern, that natural states progressively approach supernatural ones. Biblical themes, symbols, and phrases weave throughout the poem. Dante's journey from Inferno to Paradise follows a biblical pattern that can be conceived in scriptural terms both Old and New: as both exodus from bondage to freedom and resurrection from death to life. The reigning idea of the Inferno, of *contrapasso*, that punishments are simply the intensified natural progressions of the crimes they punish, has precedent in the prophets, who taught, for example, that idolators punished by exile were in fact receiving precisely what they wished: cultural settings in which idols were norms. But perhaps the feature of his work that draws most deeply from Judeo-Christian tradition, and shows him most conspicuously its child, is the way in which actual, historical figures function symbolically for him. The realistic liveliness of his characters, and the sympathy so many of them win, owes partly to the fact that in his symbolic revision of them, Dante has not lost their historical grounding, so much so that it can become a challenge for scholars to determine the precise areas of overlap and difference between the actual Thomas Aquinas and the figure of him Dante constructs in paradise. Because it is a defining feature of Judaism and Christianity that God works in history, historical persons, in those religions, take on symbolic significance long before the Middle Ages conceived the fourfold method of biblical interpretation. The sense that readers of the *Comedy* have, that a historic Virgil underlies Dante's remake of him, is not so different from the sense that Jews who are celebrating Passover have, that a historical Egypt underlies the symbolic revision of it that they encounter in the Seder liturgy, or that Christians have, that a historic figure grounds the Christ they worship in the Eucharist.

And yet Dante's foundation in Judeo-Christian tradition is ambiguous enough to invite precisely opposite interpretations of how faithful he ultimately is to it. If Charles Singleton can claim, on the one hand, that "Dante sees as poet and realizes as poet what is already conceptually elaborated and established in Christian doctrine,"[20] then Erich Auerbach can suggest that the very sympathy Dante wins for his infernal figures, whose humanity is framed by God's eternal order, finally "turns *against* that order, makes it subservient to its own purposes, and obscures it."[21] In light of that obscuring, what first seems obvious about Dante, that, in Ernest Fortin's understated terms, he "was never fully integrated into the main current of Christian thought,"[22] suddenly seems a revelation of his deeper relation to the Church.

That Dante's *Divine Comedy* hangs in a balance that may tilt, alternatively, in the direction of either religion or literature suits it perfectly to ground a religio-literary tradition of anti-Christian protest. That hanging in the balance between religion and literature already opens a lens through which to interpret this highly interpretable and much interpreted poem. It is striking how easily the work lends itself to numeric interpretations.[23] At the simplest levels, each of the numbers

1, 2, and 3 points to a different interpretive scheme. Through the number 1, the poem appears as the highly ordered and integrated totality that especially draws the attention of critics such as Dorothy Sayers. The number 1 also highlights the express instances of singularity in the poem, which include Saladin, who, in Limbo, sits alone, and Dante himself, who, Cacciaguida advises, must take "thy stand apart."[24] Of course, 1 is the number of monotheism and the whole of three constituting the Christian trinity. Three is the more obvious number through which to read the poem, for both form and content: the three cantos, the terza rima, the trinity itself, images of which appear most expressly in Paradise but, at least according to one reading, in covert copiousness throughout the whole poem.[25] An image of three opens the poem—the leopard, lion, and wolf, who block Dante's initial way and provide the context for his need of Virgil—and closes it: the three differently colored, concentric circles that image forth the trinity. And yet, that climactic trinitarian image is only penultimate, ceding the place of final vision to the "novel wonder" of the shared space occupied simultaneously and miraculously by both the begotten circle of the Son and "our [i.e., the human] image" (Par. 33:136–137). Over that brilliant but impossible image of two-in-one, "vigor failed the towering fantasy" (Par. 33:142) and words failed the poem, for there it ends, as though that vision were a realization of apocalypse, halting any further possible motion. It is, all the same, a profoundly Christian image of Incarnation, already anticipated at the start of Dante's ascent through Paradise, at the level of the moon, where he appears to unite with its governing sphere. The image of two at the end of the poem contrasts sharply with the image of two for the whole of the poem, of a work hanging undecidedly in the balance between religion and literature. The one twosomeness anchors the poem firmly in Christianity; the other opens up a path to realms outside. That the figure of two can be so ambiguous is part of its nature. Ambiguity exists by its very etymology under the sign of two, as does Dante, whose birth sign was Gemini (the twins). And it is just the reading of the poem through the number 2 that situates it where it best suits our purpose: at a fork in the road that veers off one way in the direction of Christianity and in the other in the direction of a Christianity-critiquing literature.

By way of the number 2, wholes halve and polarities harmonize, even mutually identify. For Dante, as for Christians generally, Christ paradigmatically exemplifies the mutual identification of polar opposites, in this case of humanity and deity. Dante illustrates the idea most pictorially and most personally not through Christ himself[26] but through his representations of Christ: the Gryphon and Beatrice. The Gryphon that pulls the Edenic chariot is *"l'animal binato"* [bi-natured] (Par. 32:47), and Beatrice, the object of Dante's love, is both an earthly and a heavenly creature. Two works divisively in the case of the Gryphon's infernal analogue, Geryon, who is likewise double natured, but in an unconvincing, patchwork way, as signaled by its handsome human face misfitted to a venomous serpent's body, and likewise in the case of the schismatics of hell's eighth circle, where the punishment is to be split in half. The actions that accomplish these variations on two include reflecting and mirroring, in the case of the unifying movements, and suspension, hesitation, and indecision, in the case of the dividing ones. Thus in the final, trinitarian image of the Incarnation, the first and second circles, representing Father and Son, appear to reflect each other (Par. 33:118); and again, more complexly, in a picture that identifies movement with stasis and difference with identity, the Gryphon, itself unchanging, casts a wavering reflection of itself in Beatrice's eyes, which alternatively highlights first the one then the other of its two natures (Pur. 31:121–126; cf. Par. 13:55–60). Mirror imaging is a handy way to depict plurality in unity, like the multiple reflections cast by a single person looking into the kinds of curved, segmented mirrors found in department stores and old-fashioned fun houses. The many references throughout the poem, especially in Paradise, to mirrors and reflections (angels are mirrors [Par. 9:61], and so, Dante implies, are the paradisical lights, representing souls, that appear to him in the several heavens [Par. 18:1]), support the movement of two toward one that is so important to Christian doctrine. Dante's final picture of the Christian trinity is so doctrinally correct that the third circle, of the Holy Spirit, appears to proceed jointly from the other two, in harmony with teachings of the Western Church, and in contrast to those of the Eastern Church, which held and holds that the Spirit proceeds from the Father only.

The patchwork of Geryon and the sliced bodies of the schismatics are only the more pictorial representations in the Inferno of the number 2 working divisively. Much earlier in the poem than they, Dante introduces the case of the so-called neutrals: shades and angels that in decisive situations, from want of will, failed to ally with either of two opposing sides. These creatures inhabit an antechamber to hell, rejected by both heaven and hell for refusing to decide in either's favor. On the one hand, the principle of *contrapasso*, which is so biblically sound, condemns them to this space, as it eternally realizes their choice to hover in between. But on the other hand, neither the Bible nor Christian doctrine offers any warrant for this space. Nor is the quality here punished clearly a sin on biblical or Christian grounds. Hesitation in itself is clearly not a sin, even in Dante's own estimation. On the contrary, hesitation is the preferred act when, so Thomas Aquinas teaches (in Par 13:112–114), the mind has not seen through clearly to the worthiest of two options. On the other hand, in the context of Dante's journey, which proceeds under time constraints, of which his guides occasionally remind him (Inf. 20:124), hesitation may well be a sin, as Virgil indicates when, in response to Dante's request for clarity on the ominous wording inscribed over hell's gateway, he says, "Here one must leave behind all hesitation [*sospetto*],"[27] as though he knows that the sights in store for Dante will provoke him to stop and even, in one case, to turn around. But this realm troubles all the more if hesitation is a sin, for in that case in precise contradiction of one of the aims Dante is repeatedly given by his guides and admonishers for his journey through the afterlife, that he tell what he has seen for the benefit of the living, that they mend their ways, Dante's description of this realm provokes in the reader the exact sin it should be countering, namely, hesitation. The reader must hesitate between two alternate reactions that Dante himself sets up to the sinners held here. On the one hand, by their place in the ante-inferno, before a descent that symbolically signifies a progression of depths of sin, these souls are guilty of the lightest sin of all. And yet Virgil, whose appeal owes in part to his simultaneous detachment from the sinners he observes and respect for them, attesting as they do, by their sufferings, to divine justice, here, uncharacteristically, openly disdains the souls under his gaze. "Speak not of them" (Inf. 3:51), he says, nor does he talk *to* them, or encourage Dante to, and the two pass by these suffering souls, in marked contrast to those of the deeper regions, without a word exchanged with them. It is as though the shades in the antechamber are beneath contempt and, by extension, beneath even the souls buried down deeper than they, and so guilty of the worst sin of all: refusing to lend themselves as exhibits of divine justice, refusing to play at all the entire game of divine reward and punishment. In that case, Virgil acts the disgruntled team captain, disdaining those players who, for whatever reason, have chosen to sit this game out.

But if the sin punished here is refusal, then it is more than mere hesitation. That it does indeed have to do with refusal appears from the one sinner whom Dante allusively names in this realm: the one who fearfully made "*il gran rifiuto*" (Inf. 3:60).[28] At this juncture, the reader may become even more confused over the attitude most appropriate to the sin of these souls, for this allusion must call to mind Peter's threefold denial of Christ, which all four Gospels recount. Peter's denial reads as a refusal, under pressure of fear, to publicly own his master; by its threefold repetition, it is a "great refusal." And yet, because it is Peter, now in Paradise, who made the refusal, we know it is ultimately forgiven. And so the suspicion grows that, contrary to hell's gateway and its chilling inscription, hope does or can enter here.

That suspicion grows even stronger when the figure who, commentators largely agree, Dante actually meant by that allusion is more directly named: Celestine V, who reigned as pope for five months in 1294, and then, unprecedentedly, abdicated. Celestine, a Benedictine monk, founded a monastery and ably administered it according to rules of strict abstinence. It was late in his life, when, having lived some years as a hermit and acquired a reputation for great sanctity, he was chosen by a deadlocked college of cardinals to become the new pope. Celestine embodied in his personal life the very qualities Dante wished to see in the institutional church: material and temporal abstinence. Political machinations surrounding the papacy induced Celestine's abdication, the sin of which, in Dante's eyes, was the failure it represented to realize a golden opportunity to reform the church, and the path it opened to what Dante judged the further corruption of the papacy, in the person of Celestine's successor, Boniface VIII. Dante may be forgiven his failure to appreciate the great gap between personal and institutional goodness and the anger he felt over what, in Celestine's case, could be interpreted as a refusal to instance a possible and desirable incarnation of the personal in the political. But had not Dante himself, a poet fired by images of religious and philosophical purity, tried his hand at politics in Florence and failed at the same incarnation? It is much easier for Dante to imagine perfect heads of state and locate them in Paradise than perfect heads of church, most of whom, like Peter, are from the early church (see Par. 27:44) before it grew into the politically charged body it became. Perhaps the problem of Celestine is really the problem of the church as institution, which cannot but take on political hues that potentially conflict with spiritual aims and intentions, a problem Dante points at resolving when he locates in Paradise, Joachim of Fiore, the heretical prophet of the third, institutionless age of the church. Celestine and Joachim share the interest of the Spiritual Franciscans, that divergent group of medieval friars who perhaps strove harder than any other order in Dante's time to epitomize his ideal church of renunciant poverty and spiritual love. Joachim bequeathed a theology that the Spirituals eagerly embraced, because it served their doctrinal needs, and Celestine, in turn, as pope, patronized the Spirituals. How can Joachim be in heaven and Celestine in hell?[29] An infernal Celestine is so troubling that some commentators reject the received wisdom on the soul identified as the great refuser. It resolves the trouble to remove Celestine from that realm and replace him with, say, Esau, or Pontius Pilate, as some commentators do. But it equally resolves the trouble if Celestine is allowed to remain there, to perform the work of dismantling Dante's hell from within. Long before Blake, he is the first "no" to hell in all of its Dantesque finality. That Dante himself puts him there is his own act of undermining the divine order he ostensibly writes to serve.

The neutrals are not the only instances of a suspension within the divine order that moves to undermine that order. The sixth wrung of heretics has in common with the ante-inferno that it falls outside the schema of sin, based on Aristotle, that Virgil explains over the course of a wait in that same wrung. The very act of freely willed waiting, which is unusual in Dante's journey, manifests suspension in the plot. And heresy, like indecision, falls under the sign of two, since, etymologically, it derives from the idea of choice: choice for error in the face of doctrinal truth. It was Erich Auerbach who ingeniously deflected what hell intensified away from the sinner's desire to perpetuate sin, as Virgil would have it (Inf. 3:126), toward the sinner's personality in its full humanity. That deflection, practiced interpretively on the heretics Farinata and Cavalcante, wins so much sympathy for them at Auerbach's hands that, as already once noted, the divine order that punishes them there fails to persuade and ultimately founders on the reader's resistance to it. But a feature of this wrung requiring much less interpretive skill to fathom pushes just as hard against the grain of its location in hell; namely, that here, for the first time in hell, a space is opened for intellectual discourse. For it is just here that Virgil explains the *Comedy*'s typology of sin. This kind of speech, so frequent in Paradise, is rare here just because the atmosphere counts against it: hell is the place where, as Virgil puts it, "intellectual good" is lost (Inf. 3:18). But at least among the heretics, the atmosphere is not so poisonous to thought that intellect cannot operate there.

Of course, the Inferno's sanctum of reason is Limbo, Virgil's own realm. This wrung, too, like those of the neutrals and the heretics, lies suspended outside the Aristotelian typology of sin, though its suspension is so much more obviously between an inadequate, merely natural goodness and divine salvation. Virgil himself identifies Limbo as the place for souls "who rest suspended" (Inf. 2:52). The figure of suspension here is the pervasive longing, which stretches from this first wrung of hell indefinitely upwards toward a heaven never experienced but nonetheless known to define a blessed place of salvation, guaranteed by Christianity (Inf. 4:37, 61). The challenge that Dante's Limbo is to his heritage of Christian story and doctrine has been much discussed. It is intimately wed to the still-larger challenge posed to medieval Christianity by Dante's love of classical culture, which shows throughout the poem in so many ways: the epic structure, the invocation of muses, the conflation of pagan and Christian names for God, the depiction of creatures and rehearsal of stories from classical mythology, the Aristotelian underlay to the infernal typology of sin,[30] the very choice of Virgil as guide. Dante himself is troubled by the church's assent to the eternal damnation of virtuous pagans who, through no fault of their own, never heard the Christian message (Inf. 4:46–50; Par. 19:70–78). And the comfort he offers himself on that point, through the stories of the Emperor Trajan—whom God resurrected from Limbo so as, while living, to affirm the faith (Par. 20:106–117)—and of Ripheus—who, before the time of Christ, was granted a vision of the future Christian redemption and baptized by the three theological virtues (Par. 20:118–129)—has stimulated discussion on whether, in defiance of church teaching, Dante allows that Virgil himself might finally be saved.[31] Dante's own loyalties, divided between an antithetical pagan and Christian past, open up the richest opportunities for the number two, functioning divisively, to bifurcate the tenor of the poem so that one half stays within the church's fold, and the other ventures forth outside. Let us take up just one of those opportunities, suggested by Dante's double persona within the poem, as both poet-author and pilgrim-hero. The pilgrim is the Christian; the poet, if not quite pagan, chooses to classify himself with the greatest of the pagan poets (Inf. 4:88–102). In the contrast between the two, does the poet serve the pilgrim, or the pilgrim the poet?

In accordance with conventions of the classical epic, the overall conceit of the poem is that Dante the poet is recalling momentous events of the past. Where the poem departs from classical conventions is that the events recalled are from Dante's own experience. The juxtaposition of the two personas—of poet and hero—is sometimes so tight that the reader is lulled into conflating them. Consider, for example, the two neighboring tercets in Inf. 2:7–12, where Dante as poet appeals first to the muses, to help his efforts at recall, and then, directly afterwards, as pilgrim, to Virgil, to test his worthiness for the journey. Sometimes it is hard to know which persona is speaking. For example, in Par. 10:7, Dante directly addresses the reader, adjuring us to gaze with him at the high heavens. But we cannot be sure whether the position from which he invites us to gaze is the one the pilgrim holds, elevated to the fourth heaven (of the sun), or the one the poet holds, back here on earth, as he recalls that former elevation. Should we be reading ourselves into the poem as vicarious accompanist of the pilgrim, or accepting our place as the poem's earth-bound addressee, audience to the poet-author? The ambiguity is more than academic, for the resolution of it determines whether our act of admiration is ultimately religious or literary, for the universe itself, or for Dante's poetic evocation of it. When Dante tells us several verses later (Par. 10:25) that "I have set before thee; for thyself feed now," it surely appears that it is his own verse (and not God's universe) that he is commending to us.

One of the questions commentators raise about the *Comedy* is the extent to which Dante the pilgrim undergoes transformations that assimilate him to the regions he encounters in the afterlife and the souls residing there. It is clearly not part of the entry ticket to hell that Dante himself become evil; on the contrary, the visions allowed him there are meant to turn him away from sin. But the analog the pilgrim Dante experiences to the sufferings he witnesses in hell is fear. Fear dogs him the whole downward descent long, until at the climactic sight of Satan he falls into a state that mimics the sinful suspension of the neutrals: "I was not dead nor living" (Inf. 34:25). (Compare that to Dante's own judgment on the neutrals: even before dying, they "never lived" [Inf. 3:64].) The fear at that point was so great that it spills out beyond the actual experience of it into the recall of it: "With fear I bid my strain [*metro*] recall the marvel" (Inf. 34:10). Once again, pilgrim and poet work closely in step. But what sort of fear is it that allows Dante sufficient presence of mind to capture in verse what frightens him? This is fear at a distance, the kind of fear that later Enlightenment theorists of beauty would identify as a critical component of pleasure in the (aesthetic) sublime. What Dante discloses here is that not just readers of sublime literature delight in it, but authors of it too. The unexpressed delight Dante has in this recollection of fear is concealed beneath his evident success at setting it down in meter. That suggests that for us to share the actual fear Dante the pilgrim had before the vision of Satan, to experience that fear religiously as the emotional response to an overwhelming demonstration of divine justice, we, as readers, must leave Dante the poet's delight in the recollection of that fear and position ourselves with the pilgrim, at the depths of hell. But in so doing, have we really emerged from aesthetic experience into the religious? What tempers even that fear and inflects it aesthetically away from religion is that the whole downward descent, from top to bottom, is, as Virgil continually reminds us, "by destiny appointed" (Inf. 3:95, 5:23). That is to say, there is no real danger in the descent, since God guarantees it. More, the very sufferings that Dante witnesses are in an important sense unreal. The split, contorted, maimed, and bleeding bodies he sees are not actual bodies, for none of these souls has yet been reunited with its real body.[32] So both the torments Dante witnesses in the Inferno and his fearful reaction to them are as much semblances as his metered recollection of fear is a semblance of fear. Dante lets slip on at least one occasion that this is so when among the suicides in hell's seventh circle he "remained *as* (*come*) one assailed by terror" (emphasis added) (Inf. 13:45). It was not actual fear he felt but the likeness of it, just like what the tantalized moviegoer feels at the scariest parts of a horror film.

In Purgatory, Dante the pilgrim comes much closer to resembling the souls he encounters. The symbolic measure of this are the P's (for *peccatum*, or sin) traced on Dante's forehead by the angel guarding Purgatory's gate, which are subsequently brushed away by succeeding angels as Dante ascends the purgative slopes. But, as commentators note, Dante the pilgrim does not for the most part share in any of the purgative exercises of the souls there. The one exception comes at the last terrace. The fire that purges the lustful of their sin, at the seventh

terrace, serves also as the portal to the Garden of Eden. Dante does
indeed endure that penance and attests to his suffering through it (Pur.
27:49–51). But strangely, Dante the poet never recounts that the final
"P," for the sin of lust, was ever brushed away from Dante the pilgrim's
forehead. Dorothy Sayers indicates the spot where, "no doubt . . . the
last P is erased".³³ But her very denial of doubt awakens doubt. Perhaps
the final P, standing in metonymically for all the P's, still sits on Dante's
forehead to remind the reader that in fact his experiences here, too, as in
the Inferno, were at a distance. It was only the semblance of purgation
that Dante the pilgrim experienced. In consequence, so is the perfection that Virgil now attributes to Dante, by calling him "sovereign over
thyself" (Pur. 27:140), a semblance. Paradise bears that out. Dante the
pilgrim appears to be still tainted by sin, even in Paradise. Why else
would he have to be blinded in the eighth sphere, for what John Sinclair calls, in echo of Ulysses' sins (punished eternally in the Inferno),
"irrelevant curiosity"³⁴ about the soul of St. John, whether it ascended
to heaven in bodily form, as a medieval tradition taught, and why else
would Dante exhibit interest in whether the heavenly souls were satisfied with their stations and did not wish for higher posts (Par. 3:64–66)
if he himself was not still plagued by the sin that chiefly beset him,
namely, pride (Pur. 13:133–138)? as he himself later frankly admits
(Par. 16:6). Does Dante the pilgrim really exhibit the faith, hope, and
charity he claims to have during the theological interrogation in
heaven's eighth sphere? That interrogation, which tests Dante's hold on
the theological virtues, sparks as much disbelief as belief in the high
marks he receives, if only because the implicit conflation within the test
of knowledge of those virtues with possession of them is so absurd.³⁵
Dante was not that much a Platonist. Important as intellect is, it does
not accomplish the aims of religion without the practiced input of will
and the freely received infusions of grace.

  Why, then, does Dante claim for his pilgrim persona perfections
that, as poet, he subtly disowns? Perhaps because it so well serves the
story line of the poem if his pilgrim gradually assumes the qualities that
define the regions he observes, so that having begun in forested
despondency, perhaps even, Virgil suggests, in suicidal despair (Pur.
1:58–60), the pilgrim, having learned through his descent the qualities
to shun, progressively assumes the virtues he should have until by the
eighth heaven he has indeed acquired the very pinnacle of the virtues:
faith, hope, and charity. It serves the story line, which we, suspending

disbelief, are to follow, but the hint of distance that Dante, as poet, intrudes between Dante the pilgrim and the qualities he ostensibly assumes alerts us to the fact that what the pilgrim really models for us is not conversionary religious experience, as the plot would have us believe, but aesthetic experience: the pleasure, at once removed, in observing artfully presented suffering, purgation, and blessedness.[36] Dante's poetic skill at evocation testifies less to the greatness of God than of Dante himself, who by his words holds us spellbound, through his pilgrim, in the aesthetic simulation of religious experience.

This is hardly a novel interpretation. It is only a variation on that modern tradition of reading Dante bivalently, defined by such critics as Charles Singleton, who famously wrote that "the fiction of the Divine Comedy is that it is not a fiction," and Robert Hollander, who added that "Dante creates a fiction which he pretends to consider not to be literally fictitious."[37] Our interpretation is perhaps the inverse: the reality of the *Divine Comedy* is that it is a fiction. Dante creates a realism that he knows to be literally fictitious. He wants readers to share that knowledge to better appreciate his poetic skills. The *Comedy* so interpreted can at least supply an originating point for a tradition of reading poetry as religion's critic and successor. Hollander's arguments play, on different grounds, to the same purpose, for if, as he argues in the article of his just cited, Dante intends his poem to be read according to the "allegory of the theologians," then the *Comedy* twins the Bible and, as the later of the two, supersedes it. What title, we wonder, names the book that the universe becomes in that climactic vision, one of several, in the last canto of the poem, where all reality is "in one volume clasped of love" (Par. 33:86)? As much as it might be God's own book (the Bible) it also could be Dante's. This is the point at which to read Dante's own high claim for his poem, that it is a "sacred poem that hath made both heaven and earth copartners in its toil" (Par. 25:1–2), and for himself, that he is its prophetic author (Inf. 32:91–92, Pur. 32:103–106, Par. 21:97, 27:65–66). The plot of the poem supports the relation between poetry and religion that medieval theology established, namely, that religion (Beatrice) always surpass poetry (Virgil).[38] But if we are now accustomed to reading the plot self-underminingly, then we are not surprised when Dante announces his wish to return to his baptismal font, there to be crowned poet (Par. 25:8–9), as though to reverse established opinion on the relation between the two and position poetry to succeed and surpass religion.

It was Dorothy Sayers who paid Dante the compliment of being "simply the most incomparable storyteller who ever set pen to paper."[39] This would already raise suspicions in Emily Gosse over Dante's Christian trustworthiness. More radical praise comes from Peter Hawkins, who calls Dante's purgatory "this extraordinarily dense act of myth-making,"[40] more radical at least to the extent that myths surpass stories in weightiness. But Dante himself already gives an inadvertent premonition that beyond stories and myths he is beginning to create nothing less than new religion. In his earlier work, *On the Eloquence of the Vernacular*, he reflects on the nature of poetic authorship. The poet, he says, is a binder of words. And the verb he uses to express the binding is the Latin one: "*ligare*,"[41] which, according to some etymologies, gave the Romans, and ultimately us, the word "religion." If the poet, in binding words, is making religion, then no wonder Dante "was never fully integrated into the main current of Christian thought."[42]

But he has launched us on that other current we wish to pursue here, of Christian poetry's progress in distancing and supplanting Christianity. Our next stop is Milton. The titles of their two great epics fashion between them a continuous arc. We step from Dante's paradise, to which we have ascended from hell, into Milton's, who escorts us back out into the world we know. The epics have much in common. Like Dante, Milton locates himself and his poem in a dual biblical-classical heritage. Milton claims divine inspiration for his poem (1:6–17), as did Dante, and, like Dante, he understands what he has accomplished in poetry to be exceptional and unprecedented (1:16). Poetry itself is a sacred art, descending as it does, on Milton's account, from a primal muse, sister to Wisdom, who, according to Proverbs, even before creation "didst play in presence of th' Almighty Father" (7:30–31). The self-conscious awareness we found in Dante, in which he invites the reader to share, that he is aesthetically refashioning religious experience, appears in Milton too. For example, Milton mirrors his own role as epic poet in Raphael and Adam, who recount for each other, to their mutual delight, the different parts of creation history they separately know. Milton cues us to the fact that Raphael is fashioning the narrative for Adam's appreciation, by his prefatory disclaimer, that he will proceed by "lik'ning spiritual to corporal forms" (5:573). For example, Raphael imputes to God words he would never have actually spoken, in conversation with the Son, about the passage of time in days, "as we compute the days of heav'n" (6:685), for the Son would have implicitly understood that heavenly days were meant. The explanation of the days is there for the benefit of Adam, who would not have understood how a heavenly realm beyond the sun could measure the passing of days. For Adam, Raphael's "discourse is to my ear [sweeter] than fruits of palm-tree pleasantest to thirst and hunger both" (8:210–212), while for Raphael God has so formed Adam that "all comeliness and grace attends thee, and each word, each motion forms" (8:222–223). Since Milton has written both parts, the achievement is his own and the praise devolves to him.

But for our purposes, where Milton differs most interestingly from Dante is the greater degree to which he diverges from his inherited Christianity. Between Dante and Milton the Reformation occurs, which, precisely in its fracture of Christianity, sets up a new diversity of ecclesiastical norms for poets to challenge. Some of the purifications and purgations that Dante would have practiced on the church actually materialized under the guiding lights of Luther, Calvin, and George Fox. Indeed, their chastisements of church hierarchy surpassed those conceived by Dante, who never thought to dispense with the papacy as such (Par. 5:77) but only the corrupt pretenders to its throne. The church of Milton's time is so different from Dante's that Milton can be deemed broad-minded for tolerating all forms of Christianity *except* the papal kind (precisely Dante's kind). But of course the norm of Christianity against which this appears liberal is Puritanism, which had to contend with Catholics at one end of the Christian spectrum and Quakers at the other. Milton can be identified with Puritanism, if only because he most willingly served its government, under Oliver Cromwell, as Latin secretary, but his great poem, too, exhibits many distinctively Puritan ideas that would not have occurred to Dante—that hell is as much an inward state, residing inside of Satan, as an outward one, in which Satan resides (4:20,75); that the worship "God likes best" is rituallessly simple (4:738) and even spontaneous (5:148–150); and that idolatry, which hardly figures at all in the *Comedy*, is the work of devils still active in the world and so, even in its ancient forms, a danger deserving many verses of description (1:338–521).[43] At the same time, it is just because Milton, in other ways, dissented so ardently from Puritanism that he can receive the torch passed to him by Dante, of poetic protest and self-assertion against his church.

It is less to our point that Milton knew and admired Dante's work[44] than that he diverges from Puritanism more markedly, less ambiguously, than Dante does from medieval Catholicism. There is little disagreement among scholars that several of Milton's beliefs were openly at variance with accepted Puritan teachings, for example, his defense of divorce, of a precipitously Unitarian view of God and of free will. Interestingly, these views are not so overwhelmingly present in *Paradise Lost* to mark it un-Puritan, or at least the first two are not. Upon a casual reading, the poem, focused as narrowly as it is on Genesis 1–3, poses few overt challenges to Christian teachings at all, whether interpreted on Puritan or Catholic lines.[45] It is not so much the teachings of the poem that trouble a Christian sensibility as the characterizations. Readers have long noted the simplistic woodenness of God in contrast to the alluring depths of Satan. A comparison to Dante is here illuminating. Neither God nor Satan ever speak in the *Divine Comedy*. Neither receives anywhere near the characterization that Milton bestows on them. If we seek a precursor of Milton's Satan in Dante's *Comedy*, it is probably not to Dante's Satan that we turn. Irene Samuel suggests that one of the figures from the *Comedy* who most foretells the Miltonic Satan is Farinata, because of his contemptuous pride.[46] But such a precursor must give us pause, at least if we follow Auerbach, who in so humanizing this character wins from us so much sympathy for him. And if in search of Miltonic satans in Dante's *Comedy* we are pointed to the proudest characters there, who most reveal their pride in speech, rather than to the wholly mute and frozen figure of Satan himself then why stop with Farinata? He is hardly the only figure in the *Comedy* of the kind of pride that occasioned Lucifer's fall in *Paradise Lost*. Was not pride Dante's own special sin? How different is Dante the poet's tone toward Florence from Satan's toward God? Both loved the realms from which they were exiled, deemed their banishments unjust, and contemptuously dismissed the humiliating terms of reconciliation offered to them (1:263). Were they not both in their separate ways a "party of one," embarking in solitude on dangerous paths? Both exhibit a self-division over the loss of what their dignity prevents them from recovering, and both poeticize the self-division and in so doing win the reader's sympathy.

But we need hardly borrow from Dante for the sympathy Milton already amply awakens in us for Satan. It is no wonder the Romantics loved him, "spectacle of ruin"[47] that he was. From the standpoint of classical epic heroism, Satan can be appreciated for his faithfulness to his comrades and for his bravery in the face of defeat, of Death, of Chaos. To a modern sensibility, Satan is attractive for the soliloquies in which he exhibits such familiarly human polarities, such complexities of self-doubt.[48] But apart from all of these perspectives from which to appreciate Satan, Milton supplies his own. In a much-quoted passage from his famous plea for freedom of thought, the "Areopagitica," Milton confesses that he "cannot praise a fugitive and cloistered virtue unexercised and unbreathed, that never sallies out and seeks her adversary."[49] It is as though virtue is only as real as the freely willed resistance to temptations to abandon it. The whole of *Paradise Lost* can be read as an affirmation of faith in the face of acute temptations to abandon it, which were, in Milton's case, the failure of his political cause (through the Restoration) and the loss of his sight. Perhaps it is not so much the genus of virtue that Milton praises, as one Christian species of it, which Dante also praised, namely, faithfulness. But if so, then those touching scenes in which Satan exhibits a passing goodness—upon first seeing Adam and Eve, whom he "could love, so lively shines in them divine resemblance" (4:363–4), and later, on approaching Eve, whose "graceful innocence" left him "abstracted . . . from his own evil, . . . stupidly good, of enmity disarmed" (9:463–5)—point to more in Satan than a lost potential for goodness. They are *his* temptations, overcome, to abandon the evil to which *he* has sworn faithfulness ("Evil be thou my good," 4:110).

Temptation was clearly a central moral category for Milton. In a curious extension of the *contrapasso* principle, acts of resisting temptation become the salvific centerpiece of *Paradise Regained*, canceling the capitulations to temptation that focus *Paradise Lost*. Insofar as the capacity for being tempted is a defining mark of free creatures, it is hardly surprising that temptation looms so large in Milton's thought. It is, after all, the so-called free will defense that Milton marshals for his theodicy: If God created humans free, then they have the capacity to sin; if they can sin, they may sin, and if they do, the responsibility falls entirely on themselves. Multiple voices in *Paradise Lost*—God's (3:97–113), Satan's (4:42–43), Adam's (10:824–834), the narrator's (5:246–247, 10:1–16)—either absolve God of sin or firmly fix the blame for it on his creatures. Freedom does not simply supply the explanation of human sin; it entitles humans to the merit (or some of it) for the goodness they can claim. Resisted temptation ensures that goodness lived is freely chosen and not accidental or capricious. But temptations must attract, otherwise they fail to tempt. Insofar as Satan can tempt an Adam and Eve with whom we, the readers, identify, Milton must beautify him not simply for his human protagonists but for us too.

And so he does. Satan is, after all, a fallen Lucifer, "great in power, in favor and preeminence" (5:660–661), not simply in God's sight but also assuredly in Milton's (and so in ours). The office his very name indicates he filled was to bear light, which functions so critically in the poem as an emblem of goodness, and which Milton himself poignantly hymns at the start of book three ("Hail holy Light . . ."). Satan, whose face once shone "as the morning star" (5:708), preserves enough of his former beauty, or sense for it, to be repulsed by ugliness, as Milton makes a point of revealing in Satan's response to Death ("execrable shape" of "miscreated front" are Satan's terms of aesthetic disgust for Death [2:681,683]). The trick for Milton is to preserve for us enough of Satan's former Luciferan self to attract, while at the same time leaving us no doubt that Satan is, indeed, evil. Chiefly, two acts carry the evil: his temptation of Eve and his defiance of God. The trouble is, as we examine these acts more closely, the evil in them eludes. The role of tempter cannot itself be evil, not only because it is necessary but also because God and prelapsarian Adam also are implicated in that role. God may not himself tempt Adam, but he does intentionally subject him to trials, and trials are already halfway to temptations. God tries Adam with the idea that animals could be his fit companion (8:444–448), though indeed the whole of the human predicament, as God has constructed it, constitutes a trial (1:366), the beginning of which was to have placed a forbidden tree in the garden at all. Adam, for his part, draws so much attention to this tree in the first remarks we hear him make to Eve (4:419–433) that he seems to be setting up from the start what the sorry result will be. From the standpoint of plot, Adam's warnings to Eve against the tree, overheard by Satan, supply the knowledge Satan needs to hatch his scheme, but from the standpoint of character, Adam's obsession with the tree (half a speech worth) appears gratuitous, unless it has already begun to tempt him, and, by so inflecting his words to Eve, her as well.

We fully understand Satan's motive in tempting Eve: to have his revenge, if not on God, then on God's creation. Satan seeks revenge for the punishment God inflicted upon him. God punished Satan for rebelling against the divine order. But why did Satan rebel? Satan's heavenly state was the angelic counterpart of the prelapsarian Garden of Eden. Even the fallen Satan can admit how happily placed he was ("from what state I fell, how glorious once above," 4:38–39). As light-bearing angel, Lucifer would have enjoyed all the benefits of light, which, shining inward, as the blind Milton said, irradiates the mind (3:51–53). From that position of high understanding, what could have tempted him to rebel? If the temptation to Adam and Eve had to sur-pass the delights of the nearly perfect garden, marred, from the human point of view, only by the prohibition on the one tree, and if such a temptation could only be plotted by one as intelligent and mean-spir-ited as Satan, then how much more intelligent and mean-spirited would Satan's tempter have to be to lure him from the heavenly perfec tion he himself formerly enjoyed? Of course, neither the Bible, nor tra-dition, nor Milton supplies such a tempter. God is only registering that fact when he accuses Satan of being self-tempted (3:130), an attribu-tion that seems as off the mark, coming from God, as the one Satan later claims for himself, of being self-begot (6:860). For, as the Lord's Prayer indirectly teaches, temptation is something into which we are led by something outside ourselves, if only because whatever tempts us we must both desire and lack. And so Satan's act of rebellion remains, to readers, an enigma.[50]

This in itself would not trouble so much if it did not cut so against the grain of Milton's poem, which does, after all, intend to *explain*. In a poem that celebrates right reason and knowledge, such a gap in our understanding seems weighty indeed. Perhaps this is not a "knowledge within bounds" and we should read as addressed to ourselves Raphael's command to Adam: "beyond abstain to ask" (7:120–121), except that, with that reading, Milton furthers the burden of temptation he must hope his poem will quell. In shielding Satan's motives, Milton draws our attention all the more powerfully to them, and the fascination of Satan begins, counterproductively, to outweigh the evil of him. In fact, an explanation of Satan lies implicit in the poem, but it comes at the price of distancing Milton even farther from his Puritanism. The explanation lies in that rival religious impulse, which has accompanied our reflections from the start, and which, though friendly to Christi-anity in some of its forms, was not a friend to the English Puritans, namely, Platonism.

Platonism had in Milton's day a Christian revival in the persons of the Cambridge Platonists. But ever since the Renaissance, Plato and

Neoplatonism enjoyed an attention from intellectuals that they had not received in Dante's time. Milton read deeply and appreciatively in Plato's dialogues,[51] and so it is no surprise if the Platonic streams coursing through *Paradise Lost* offer themselves as interpretive schemes for reading the whole of the poem. Christianity, inflected by Platonism, moves to close the gap between faith and reason that in the hands of the Reformers and their Puritan descendants was so accentuated. But more significantly, in the context of *Paradise Lost*, a Platonic Christianity moves toward replacing will with reason in the ethical life. God himself sets the tone for this change when, according to Milton's Platonic conception (wholly absent in the Bible), he creates not simply by fiat but according to "his great idea" (7:557). Curiously, one feature God and Satan share is their high esteem for reason, as each derisively locates the other's strength in a reason-eclipsing power (1:247–249, 6:380–383). One of the distinctive teachings of Plato is that reason never chooses evil. The choice for evil is always by a lesser faculty of the mind than reason. A reason that allies so naturally with goodness obviates the need of will. Otherwise expressed, operative reason naturally chooses the good it beholds. This may be Milton's point when he has God say that "reason also is choice" (3:108), that is, the exercise of it entails the choice for good. When Milton attributes sanctity to reason (7:509), he speaks in the voice of Christian Platonism, and when he finds in reason the seat of love (8:589–591), he speaks in Plato's own.

Irene Samuel draws a suggestive parallel between Plato's account of the loss of human happiness and Milton's account of the fall.[52] The parallel is stronger than she suggests, as there is every reason to apply the metaphor of fall to Plato's account as well. In the *Phaedrus*, Plato pictures the fall of preembodied souls who have, for a time, enjoyed the vision of the good. The souls who lose sight of the supernal ideas "are carried round below the surface [of the upper world, where] . . . there is confusion and perspiration and the extremity of effort. . . . When she [i.e., the soul] . . . fails to behold the truth, and through some illhap sinks beneath the double load of forgetfulness and vice . . . she drops to the ground."[53] It is certainly possible to interpret Eve's act of eating the apple, and its immediate consequences, in these terms. The truth of which Eve loses sight is the distance that separates her from God; the ill-hap that befalls her is her encounter with Satan, and the fall to the ground is her bow to the tree after she has eaten from it. Confusion follows in the short term and extremity of effort in the long. Confusion begotten of ignorance is a fair précis of what Plato means by evil. If we ask, with Satan, "Can it be sin to know?" (4:517), as, on the Platonic reading, it assuredly cannot, then we must remember that the specific knowledge that this tree bears is of good and evil. Such a knowledge is Platonically impossible, because there is no reasoned knowledge of evil. Good and evil cannot be linked as joint objects of a single knowledge. On a Platonic reading, "knowledge of good and evil" must be read in parallel with "man of ill repute." It is not that knowledge has good and evil for its object. Rather, something masquerading as knowledge (what Plato would call "opinion," or worse, "ignorance") is simultaneously infected by good and evil, which is to say what masquerades as knowledge here is, by the confusion it harbors, itself really an instance of evil, pure and simple. This Platonic reading of the tree finds perhaps unexpected confirmation in the narration. Far from raising Adam and Eve to the level of God, the "fallacious fruit" (9:1046) reduces Adam and Eve to animal muteness (9:1064). If the fruit from the tree has cast a film over Adam's eyes, which Michael must remove for his clearer sight (11:412–413), then the tree has not imparted knowledge at all but ignorance and confusion. When Michael describes the giants of Genesis 6:4 as products of unions "where good with bad were matched, who of themselves abhor to join" (11:685–686), he too casts doubt that the tree ever combined in itself a joint knowledge of good and evil. Even God undermines the integrity of the tree when he implies that all along it had only evil to divulge: prelapsarian Adam had, in good Platonic fashion, both been and known the good, but in eating from the tree (which might have been called quite simply, the "tree of evil," except that then it might not have tempted) his former goodness is now "lost and evil got; Happier, had it sufficed him to have known Good by itself and evil not at all" (11:87–89).

But if a Platonic reading fits the fall of man, which really did not require any additional explanation, then how much more helpfully it fits the fall of Lucifer. It is Raphael who tells the story of Lucifer's fall. Raphael explains that after God begot his Son and proclaimed him King, Lucifer, "fraught with envy against the Son of God," "could not bear through pride that sight, and thought himself impaired" (5:661–662,664–665). If, taking our cues again from *Phaedrus*, we bring a Platonic reading to bear, then we need to find in Raphael's account an "ill-hap" occasioning a loss of sight of truth. The results in this case are somewhat startling, for the illhap can only be that God begot a son, and the loss of sight of truth, that this Son is indeed still one and the same as God. Satan's envy is sparked by his belief that he and the Son are comparable. He does not grasp the fine distinction over which the framers of the Nicene Creed labored, between that which God has begotten and that which he has made (i.e., created). Satan knew, at least at the beginning of his fallen state, that he was created by God (4:43). But even into *Paradise Regained*, he has not grasped the distinction between begotten and created Son ("The Son of God I also am, or was, and if I was, I am; relation stands; all men are sons of God"[54]). And so it mistakenly seems to him that the obeisance he now owes is "double" (5:783). That is the failure of knowing that generates the confusion that constitutes his fall.[55] Raphael's assessment of Satan's state, that he thought himself impaired, seals Satan in his confusion, for he was no more impaired by the Son of God than he had been by God himself, before the begetting.

Plato may explain why Satan rebelled against God, but he does so at this price: that Satan, Adam, and Eve are all absolved of their sin by the fact that they are victims of ill-haps over which they had no control, and of films that blinded their knowing vision.[56] (It is just because crime is essentially victimhood for Plato that he could project onto criminals a welcome of their punishment, insofar as it restored their reason.) On the Platonic reading, their choices, uninformed by reason, were not real choices at all but confused blunderings that, festering unchecked, constitute, in *contrapasso* fashion, their own punishment. If we advance farther down this road, then the very location of evil in Milton's theodicy shifts radically away from the freely choosing will toward something else, which the poem pictures in quite different terms—unheroic, unglamorous, pitiable at best, annihilating at worst, namely, chaos.

In some ways, Milton's chaos recalls Dante's circle of the neutrals, who seem, by their very location between good and evil, mired in a unique evil of their own. As in the case of the neutrals, so here, in the matter of Chaos, we are uncertain as readers what attitude to adopt. The personification of chaos inspires more pity than fear: "anarch old with faltering speech and visage incomposed" (2:988–989). He seems another order of being from the devils, playing to them a role like fate played to the mischievous Greek gods. This is especially true when Milton pictures, as one possible end for Satan, a continuous free fall through chaos, down "ten thousand fathom deep, and to this hour down had been falling, had not by ill chance the strong rebuff of some tumultuous cloud . . . hurried him as many miles aloft" (2:934–938). When Milton tells us that Satan stood poised "on the brink of hell," gazing "into this wild abyss" of chaos (2:917–918), we are suddenly unsure which way hell lies. Hell merely punishes; chaos threatens "utter loss of being" (2:440). Hell is, at least, an order. The hand of a personal God shaped it, as indeed it did Dante'e hell, and testifies still, however indirectly, to God's own order. Language has tricked us by redefining the term that Milton coined for Satan's palace, *Pandemonium*. In Milton's hell, Pandemonium is an ordered place where the devils hold respectful debate. But the term has descended into common speech as a fancy word for chaos. Language was perhaps carrying an intuition of readers when it effected that switch. The real evil of the poem, the part that, translated into the special effects of a modern horror film, would cause the greatest fright, is the nightmare of chaos that God has left untouched and that gives even Satan pause. And so if Satan rules an evil realm, then it must be a chaotic one. Even Milton conspires in the trick, for it turns out that Satan is not the ruler of hell after all, death is. And if any figure of the poem serves to identify images of chaos with those of evil, it is he, who "shape had none" (2:667) and at whose "hideous name," first resounding, all "hell trembled" (2:788).

If chaos draws evil's center of gravity away from Satan, then readers are free to indulge the attraction they cannot but feel for him. T. S. Eliot illustrates that indulgence when he pictures Milton's satan, in contrast to Dante's, a "curly haired Byronic hero," on which Irene Samuel drily remarks, "where in *Paradise Lost* Eliot found that curly hair on the scarred brow of Milton's Satan is a puzzle."[57] But Samuel misses the point that Eliot presumes: Milton invites us to picture Satan in the most dashing ways we can. His physical appearance must match his eloquent speech and the poetic imagination he exhibits uniquely of all the characters in the story he fashions to seduce Eve (9:568–601). Critics have noted how much that capacity of Satan assimilates him to Milton himself,[58] which suggests that Dante and Milton further have this in common, that up to a point they both inhabit Milton's Satan.

It seems unlikely that Milton himself would ever have admitted that. However much the beautified Satan and the Platonic theodicy (subordinate though it be to the free will defense) cohere in Milton's poem, Satan does not remain the attractive being Platonic thought allows him to be but is robbed of his beauty and his elegant speech by the end. Milton would not have tempted readers to believe that poetry could serve evil's interests. Having succumbed to the confusion consequent on their unknowing act, Adam and Eve are given the counsel by which "shalt thou lead safest thy life, and best prepared endure thy mortal passage when it comes" (11:364–366). The final verses of the poem might suitably end a bedtime story. With their simple and understated assurance, they simultaneously invite both the pages of the book and the reader's eyes to close, as though to foretell, after the horror of death's punishment, "a death like sleep, a gentle wafting to immortal life" (12:434–435). Satan for his part will not be redeemed from his confusion. He will succumb to the annihilation he only narrowly escaped in chaos' realm.

That is not the ending that Blake envisioned for Satan. In Milton's last image of Satan, Eliot's "byronic hero" has been reduced to "a monstrous serpent on his belly prone" (10:514). In Blake's hands, the satanic serpent is redeemed, at least according to the picture he presents of it in his apocalyptic poem *Jerusalem,* where it takes its place, now "wondrous" and "clothed in gems & rich array" (*Jerusalem* 98:44), among the reintegrated elements of a formerly self-divided reality. This is not the only revisioning of Milton to be found in Blake. Of all of our poets, perhaps none is more intimately related to any of the other two than Blake to Dante and Milton. Like them, he saw himself a prophet, a "Voice of one crying in the Wilderness,"[59] in the hallowed line of John the Baptist, calling his hearers to "Mark well my words, they are of your eternal salvation."[60] And like Dante and Milton, he understood himself to express his prophetic vocation in artistic feats hitherto unrealized: in Blake's case, "a method of Printing which combines the Painter and the Poet . . . [that] exceeds in elegance all former methods."[61] To most modern readers of Blake, the great artistic talent concealed behind that, by Blake's own standards of religio-moral judgment, rather modest self-assessment surpasses his much more grandly self-proclaimed prophetic gifts. The engraved books he bequeathed to posterity consummate a unique marriage, beyond that of heaven to hell in the early prophetic work on that theme,[62] of art to poetry. Toward the end of his life, Blake accepted commissions to illustrate other poets' works, including both Dante's and Milton's. Blake was not uncritical of Dante. He was appalled by the spirit of punishment that pervades the *Inferno.* Still, Margaret Bottrall's assessment, that "no poets could be more dissimilar than these two,"[63] seems extreme, given their shared gifts, especially compared to Milton, for pictorial imagination. But it is of course Milton who was the much greater inspiration for Blake. Blake not only illustrated *Paradise Lost*, he authored and richly illustrated the poem *Milton*, "the only extended literary work in English . . . that features a poet as protagonist and title character."[64] In a climactic moment of that poem, Blake pictures Milton joined to him in the most intimate way possible, "entering" him (Milton 21:4) by way of his foot, an imaginative image that cannot but evoke for readers familiar with both Milton and the Bible Raphael's description of angelic intercourse (*Paradise Lost* 9:620–629) and a traditional interpretation of the "feet" attributed to the angels attending God in Isaiah's heavenly vision (Isa. 6:2) and why they must be concealed, namely, because they are sexual organs. The point of that union is that now, through Blake, Milton can correct the error that he, along with Dante and most of Christendom, taught, namely, that God excels at providing space for punishment. Blake is the medium for Milton's redemption from error. Once again we encounter the poet's self-conscious awareness of his artistry and the invitation to us, the readers, to appreciate the import of it, in this case that in some sense Milton is writing the poem that Blake named for him. The metaphor, if extreme, is undeniably apt. From the standpoint of the rights poetry has been claiming, to dislodge Christianity from its traditional moorings and interpret it anew, Blake can be read as an intensification of Milton, taking Christianity even farther outside itself. The intensification proceeds on two tracks, of continuation and reversal.

Platonism was the congenial context for Milton's beautification of Satan. The Platonic stream flows through Blake's work too, amplified by the Neoplatonic mysticism Blake absorbed more directly from his favorite mystics: Paracelsus, Jakob Boehme, and Emanuel Swendenborg.[65] But quite apart from mysticism, Blake participates in the deep Platonic skepticism toward the five senses and their capacity to deceive. The eyes are "This Life's dim Windows of the Soul."[66] He asserts the existence of a "real and eternal World of which this Vegetable Universe is but a faint shadow,"[67] and he rehearses the central Platonic myth, and more assertively than Milton, for Blake's suspicion of the senses extended to the buddings of modern empirical science, represented in Blake's work by the consistently disparaged Isaac Newton (in contrast to Galileo, whom Milton invites graciously into his conceits), and even to nature as a whole (which, for Milton, joins with God to "bid the same" as God [*Paradise Lost* 6:176]). Eternity, in contrast, is the location where "all things acted on Earth are seen in the bright Sculptures of Los's Halls,"[68] a romantically (artistically) inflected vision of the world of ideas, or, the place where "Forms Eternal Exist For-Ever."[69] As in the Platonic scheme, evil is the chaotic result of occluded vision.[70] The Tree of the Knowledge of Good and Evil, which, on the Platonic reading of Milton, is already morally stained, even before its fruit is tasted, passes into Blake's work an overt portent of evil, so much so that, unlike the satanic serpent, it is expressly excluded from Blake's apocalyptic vision of the final redemption.[71] Blake parodies the tree in two poems from *Songs of Experience*, *The Human Abstract* and *A Poison Tree*, the titles of which are as revealing for our purposes as the poems themselves. The problem with the tree, on a Platonic reading of Milton, was that it seemed to harbor what was in fact an impossibility. Its deceiving nature illustrated the very evil of which it claimed to give an improving understanding. Milton would not say as much, but Blake does. This tree, watered "with soft deceitful wiles," "bears the [fatal] fruit of Deceit."[72] Milton could not say as much because it would too much impugn his God, who after all created it. But Blake does not shrink from the obvious conclusion that the creator of the tree must himself be flawed. Like the flawed demiurge, creator of the world, in Plato's *Timaeus*, Blake's creator-god, Urizen, is a limited being who makes the fateful error of divinizing limitation. Blakean Eternity is a place of differentiable deities, reciprocally integrated as mutually enriching contraries. In the Blakean pantheon, Albion, in one of his expressions, is Urizen's father. Error begins in Albion's act of "turning his eyes outward [away] to self, losing the divine vision" of integration.[73] That loss of vision is the beginning of creation. Where biblical creation begins with light, the Blakean counterpart originates in darkness. Creation is itself the fall, as Blake, parodying refrains from Genesis, calls each of its aeonic days "a State of dismal woe,"[74] and the result, a world of "vast enormities: frightning; faithless."[75] The climactic result is the very chaos with which Genesis 1 begins.

When Urizen admits "I have erred,"[76] he completes Blake's overt articulation of the Platonic theodicy that runs underground in Milton. Error inciting chaos is the Platonic story of evil. Error originates in heaven; the world we inhabit, perceived through our bedimmed senses, is the resulting chaos. Chaos, which in the reason-hungry Milton resides unaccountably between hell and earth, receives in the reason-doubting Blake an explanation. Of course, what Blake gains over Milton in clarity and consistency he loses in fidelity to the normative

Christian story. Against the backdrop of a fully articulated Platonic theodicy, Blake can now intensify Milton's beautification of Satan. It is surely no accident that more references to Satan occur in Blake's poem *Milton* than in any other of his works. But the Satan of that epic is not Milton's. Milton's Satan steps into Blake's oeuvre as the wittily irreverent Devil in *The Marriage of Heaven and Hell* (hereafter MHH). It is precisely in that work that Blake made his now-famous claim that Milton was "of the Devil's party without knowing it."[77] The critical consensus on this work, that it parodies mystical philosopher Emanuel Swedenborg's *Treatise Concerning Heaven and Hell* (1784), implies that some of the outrageous claims in it—"Sooner murder an infant in its cradle than nurse unacted desires" (MHH 10:67)—are to be taken lightly. But the celebration even here is less of desire than of the energy that motivates it—precisely the energy that in Blake's view, shared by many, Milton exhibits in his portrait of Satan and lacks in his portrait of God. When Blake groups under a section titled "The Voice of the Devil" a claim about the Bible, that it errs when it teaches that "God will torment Man in Eternity for following his Energies" (MHH 4), he certainly expresses, via the Devil, a view of his own. In the one illustrative portrait this book contains of a devil, he does indeed appear to be, according to T. S. Eliot's Miltonic imaginings, curly haired and, in addition, sweet faced.[78] All that marks him as devilish is the light flourish of his little bat wings. But the more important beautification of devilishness is in the text, where Blake subsumes under hell's good graces the very process of his artistry: "printing in the infernal method, by corrosives, which in Hell are salutary and medicinal, melting apparent surfaces away, and displaying the infinite which was hid" (MHH 14). The marriage of poetry and art in engraved books, which Blake took, in his own estimation, to new heights of elegance, is at heart the devil's work. We do indeed behold books of cast metal arranged on shelves in the infernal library (MHH 15).

In Blake's later works, fiery creativity becomes an identifying feature of the life force, or zoa, called "Los." Los not only loses the moorings in devilishness but assimilates to a Christ figure. In contrast, the role of Satan is taken up by that chaos-inducing figure of error, Urizen (*Milton* 10:1). Milton, insofar as he identified with the Urizenic God of *Paradise Lost*, must acknowledge his own satanic tendencies and renounce them, as indeed he does in Blake's own poem for him. Western literary tradition had recognized a distinction in roles for the evil angel: under the name Satan he acted as accuser and adversary, as the Hebrew origins of his name would imply, while under the name Devil (which derives from the Greek translation of the Hebrew *satan*), he served mainly to tempt.[79] That might account for the two figures of the "evil one" in Blake: the witty, attractive Devil, who properly tempts us to recognize the transforming powers of our own energy, and the cold and hypocritical Satan, who works to repress and punish it. Part of the point of *The Marriage of Heaven and Hell* is to highlight and affirm such concentrations of contrariness: "without contraries is no progression" (MHH 3). Dante and Milton might agree, at least insofar as their epics harbor counterveiling tendencies both toward and away from Christianity, but neither formulated such bivalence the way Blake does, as a point of principle. Blake's principled bivalence has an epistemological ground that carries Christianity to its margins and beyond.

Though Blake would not have known about the philosophical developments in the Germany of his day, he is strikingly in tune with them, for the central point of the critical idealism evolving there was that the world we behold with our senses is partly constructed out of our own minds. Blake expresses this idea through one of the stories he tells in the *Marriage of Heaven and Hell*, about an angel and a narrator who impose on each other their respective visions of the world. Each does not simply hear the other's rendition of reality but is caught up in it, is actually there, much like Alice in her looking glass. The point of enmeshing each of the characters, unwillingly, in the other's vision is to demonstrate that the mental construction of reality is not solipsistic but involves us all. Blake's assumption is that, ultimately, reality is our friend. This is Blake's counterpart to the Kantian dictum that reality does partly supply itself to us. The rest we must construct ourselves. But it is possible to construct reality with fidelity to its givenness (and get it right), or not (and get it wrong). It is for this reason that Blake can aphorize: "A fool sees not the same tree that a wise man sees" (MHH 7:8) (Where a fool sees wisdom in the Tree of the Knowledge of Good and Evil, the wise man sees ruin). And it is for this reason that he can picture Milton quite literally resculpting the body of the vindictive and error-prone Urizen, shaping it more humanely (*Milton* 19) than he had in *Paradise Lost*.

It is just at this juncture that we catch our first glimpse of Blake reversing a Miltonic idea, for a consequence of Blake's idealistically attuned epistemology is that "where man is not, nature is barren"

(MHH 10), whereas in Milton, it was already a premonition of the Fall, that Eve can ask with seeming innocence about the stars, "Wherefore all night long shine these, for whom this glorious sight, when sleep hath shut all eyes?" (*Paradise Lost* 4:657–658), which opens her, later, to receiving the infernal suggestion that the moon shines "in vain, if none regard" (5:43–44). All of *Paradise Lost* was, from Blake's point of view, an epic of healthy desire's restraint (MHH 5), an outcome that Blake takes up as his charge to reverse. Blake reaches back farther, to reverse Dante, when he brings Milton back from the dead to atone for his sins rather than projecting himself, now living, into the afterlife, as Dante does, to learn in advance the lessons of sin. Blake's reversals of Milton are more evident than the continuations, but as Blake himself would admit, the reversals gain their force and propulsion just from the contraries they reject and so, indirectly, they count as much for intensifications of Milton as the continuations do. This applies to the whole of Blake's "makeshift mythology"[80] and its "host of outlandishly named figures,"[81] for as *Milton* teaches in its preface (and as Milton must come to learn), the mythologics in which we couch our teachings should precisely *not* be Greece's or Rome's, those very cultures that held Dante and Milton so much in thrall, for these were "Stolen and Perverted" from "The Sublime of the Bible" (*Milton* 1). Blake was enough the heir of Dante and Milton to feel their need to set the Bible's stories within and against an alternative mythical system. The alternative system supplied the play for the ambiguities that the two older authors unconsciously exploited. That Blake constructs his own mythology for that purpose constitutes a dramatic illustration of his teaching that bidden as we are to construct our reality, we do so with conscious and careful attention to the harmonies latent between it and us and not be sidetracked (as the Greeks were) by false and destructive ideals of heroism. Our final question for Blake must be: Where does the Bible contextualized by his mythology leave Christianity?

The critical cultural change that intervened between Milton's time and Blake's was the Enlightenment, which inflected Christianity in new ways. Rationalizations of Christianity, under the aegis of seventeenth- and eighteenth-century Deism, muted the particulars of Christian myth and ritual and pushed the religion toward universal abstractions. At the other extreme, emotionally charged sects that dissented from the established Anglican Church took shape in the form of the Ranters, a pantheistic group that dispensed with all norms of authority save inward religious experience, and the Diggers, a group that called for a radically communalistic Christian life. In Blakean terms, the church had suffered a division into its own spectre (rational abstraction) and emanation (emotional personification). Some commentators observe that Blake's own roots are in the radical dissenting sects, though Blake notes with appreciation the appearance on the English church scene of John Wesley (*Milton* 22:61), who falls in between the established Anglican Church and radical dissent and may better represent contraries held in balance. But Blake was not a Methodist. Perhaps by this time it comes as no surprise that commentators on Blake divide as much as those on Dante and Milton, on the issue of the authenticity of their poet's Christianity. If one commentator can say of Blake's use of Christian terms that he "frequently employs them in a manner which, from the orthodox point of view, simply does not make sense,"[82] another finds that his admittedly "radical Christianity was only an extreme form of Protestantism."[83] Blake himself was as little a churchgoer as Milton became toward the end of his life. Though differently grounded, his critiques of the institutional religion of his day are as scathing as Dante's or Milton's. Religion and its priestly representatives undermine the creative tensions within the contraries of life (MHH 16–17); curse joy (MHH 9); bind desire.[84] One of Blake's favorite images for religion is a net; like a spider's web, it is spun for the purpose of trapping and killing. And yet, especially in his later poems, Jesus figures as a key salvific presence.

If Dante had inaugurated a "party of one," that in succeeding centuries Milton and Blake assumed, then all three poets may be understood to have anticipated the modern, Barthian distinction between Christian religion, which they rejected, and faith in Christ, which they espoused. But Blake's Jesus differs from Milton's, who in turn differs from Dante's. Dante's Jesus was the second person of the trinity, coequal with the father and spirit. Milton's was the Son of God, subordinate to the father. Blake's Jesus moves to replace the father, who, having become hopelessly entangled in Urizenism, now more closely resembles Satan. This would make Blake a Swedenborgian, itself an expression of Christianity at its most marginal. But Blake, who for a short time allied with Swedenborg, came to reject him too. And if we can pinpoint the lever that, as it acquired weight in Blake's mind, magnified the space between him and Swedenborg, then we may settle at last on an evaluation of Blake's Christianity. That lever was the Imagination.

To measure the importance of imagination to Blake, we need only observe that in the scales of the philosophical balance, it weighs as much as the Understanding—that indispensable tool of reality's ordering—did in Kant's epistemological scheme. Where Blake departs from Kant and allies so intimately with the German Romantics is in choosing imagination over reason as the operative mental faculty in ordering the world. That "real and eternal world" of Blake's, cited earlier is, in context of the quote, and over against both Plato and Kant, precisely the world of the imagination. The imagination is that activity of mind that pares from what the senses perceive all that obscures the underlying harmonies of reality. The imagination is in precise analogy with those corrosives of the printing process that "display the infinite which was hid." It is through his imagination that the prophet Isaiah, reenvisioned by Blake, can claim, "my senses discovered the infinite in every thing" (MHH 12). It is just here that Jesus enters, for the import of such a redemptive act, functioning so immanently in this world, invites from the Christian storehouse of terms no less a designation than Jesus. And so it comes as no surprise when Blake explicitly identifies the human imagination with "the Divine Body of the Lord Jesus" (*Milton* 3:3–4).

It also is just here that the breach with Christianity, even in its most radical forms, begins to open, for the reenvisioned prophet Ezekiel, elaborating on what Isaiah has said, implies that the source of Isaiah's insight was Poetic Genius (MHH 12). The prophets were, of course, poets. Blake's suggestion that poets are the great adepts at exercising imagination sparks little protest from Christianity, but if Jesus is the name for imaginative acts, then the conclusion implied, that he manifests most fully in poetic creativity must give the religion pause, for now there seems little ground for distinguishing the collective company of poets and their poems from Jesus,[85] as indeed Blake implies when, in a much-quoted passage from Henry Crabb Robinson, he asserts, "He [Jesus] is the only God. . . . And so am I and So are you."[86] (This was how Milton's Satan thought.) Would Blake have been so generous in sharing with his friend the status of God if Robinson had not been himself a writer and if not a poet at least a connoisseur of poets?

Blakean poets are the alchemists of the modern age, charged as one critic observes, with "transforming religion back into poetry."[87] Perhaps the heaviest of Blake's critiques of religion is that its rituals, laws, and doctrines are all fabricated encrustations over what "the ancient poets" knew, that "All deities reside in the human breast" (MHH 11). Blake, much more than Milton (and certainly Dante), emphatically discards what had been Christianity's instruments for interpreting its own myths and professes to reveal its gospels for what they first and foremost were: "labours of art" (*Jerusalem* 77) and "Jesus and his Apostles and Disciples [as] Artists."[88] Blake has all but substituted art for Christianity and poets for priests. The substitution is fully realized by the last in this poetic line of descent: William Butler Yeats.

If Yeats is, as one critic avers, the "last of the great Romantic poets,"[89] then he is already used to serving as an end point. It is not that poets after him do not also press poetry into spiritual offices that burst the bounds of Christianity, but that this is no longer an original gesture. Certainly Yeats is deeply grounded in his poetic predecessors, but tradition for him is no longer what it was for them—the Christian tradition—but rather the aesthetic tradition of poetry that they themselves helped define, "an infallible church of poetic tradition."[90] When Yeats comments on Blake's interpretations of Dante and Milton, allying himself with Blake's "little-understood philosophy rather than one incorporate in the thought and habits of Christendom"[91] (i.e., Dante's and Milton's), he both arrays for us, one final time, this foursome of poets in the line of descent and signals the break with Christianity that happens toward the end of the sequence. Unlike the interpreters of his predecessors, few critics worry whether or not Yeats falls within the Christian fold. It is not simply that his deepest proclivities are out of sync with Christianity[92] but that, as Austin Warren implies, religion in his hands no longer had any function except to serve the expressive needs of poetry.[93] Yeats admits as much when in his own mythic creation, that personality-typing, history-dividing, geometry of the cosmos called *A Vision*, he reports a key statement of one of the spirits who dictated it to him and his wife: "We have come to give you metaphors for poetry."[94]

Yeats stood as grounded in Blake as Blake had in Milton. He may not have penned a poem in Blake's name, but early on in his career, in 1893, he did issue, in collaboration with a friend, a new edition of Blake's poetry. "My mind had been full of Blake from boyhood up," Yeats tells us in his *Vision*.[95] Certainly Yeats follows in the spirit of Blake when in that *Vision* he conceives by powers he attributes to spirits beyond a mythology to structure his poetry. Yeats interpreted Blake's own mythology in the most sympathetic terms: Blake was the prophet of a new religion of art for which there was as yet no undergirding mythology, and so he was forced to create one.[96] The problem is that such a personal mythology baffles other minds. Could Yeats have had Blake in mind when in an early poem he pleads for distance from approaching spiritual insight, lest he "learn to chaunt a tongue men do not know"?[97]

Yeats' *Vision* may be "rich, confused, and baffling,"[98] but its sources in "the Upanishads, Buddhism, the religion of Platonism, the Jewish Kabbalah, and the Neoplatonic tradition of alchemy" are all nicely summed up for us by F. A. C. Wilson in the phrase "the tradition of heterodox mysticism."[99] Indeed, no one acquainted with the recently promulgated Myers-Briggs Personality indicator will find at all foreign the large section of the *Vision* devoted to personality types. And it is just here, where Yeats grounds his mythology in extra-Christian religious tradition, that we pick up a thread continuing from Milton and Blake, namely, the Platonism. Wilson believes that "almost all of Yeats' work could be said to . . . derive from Platonic sources."[100] References to Plato in Yeats's work range from such overt citations as we find in *A Vision* to the Platonic year and in several poems to Plato himself (*What Then*, *The Tower*, *The Delphic Oracle upon Plotinus*) to such subtler incorporation of Platonic ideas as we find in *Vacillation*, where the part of the soul is to say "Seek out reality, leave things that seem" or in *Among Schoolchildren*, where Yeats invokes the image from the *Symposium* of primordially bisexual beings. Yeats himself credits Plato with the first philosophical use of his favorite symbol, the gyre,[101] but that very symbol points to a break Yeats made with Milton's and Blake's use of Plato to ground a theodicy of chaos-inducing error. Yeats subscribes to a quite different theodicy, whose ancient roots are in the heretical Bible book of Ecclesiastes: Evil contextualized by cycles finds a place that mutes its own evilness. Part of the point of *A Vision* is to divide history into ever-repeating cycles of twenty-eight stages that incorporate alternating times of growth and decay. The distress that marks the end of an old cycle is, from another perspective, the birth pangs of a new one. This constitutes an intensification of Blake's principle that progress depends on tension between contraries. Both Blake and Yeats were apocalyptists, but whereas the contraries within Blake progress toward a single climactic apocalypse, whose issue is a final and consummate peace, the apocalypse within Yeats is cyclic, coming at the end of each respective age, whose midpoint locates a peace that in the end is only passing. The Yeatsian contraries do not resolve in any ultimate redemption; they reemerge toward a state of decay, taking the form, say, of that famous beast, composite of contraries, half lion and half man, that "slouches towards Bethlehem" in the poem *The Second Coming*. We are enmeshed in the cycles. Where is the way out that Plato promised?

In his essay, "The Need for Audacity of Thought," Yeats offers the curious observation that "Christianity must meet today the criticism, not, as its ecclesiastics seem to imagine, of the school of Voltaire, but of that out of which Christianity itself in part arose, the School of Plato."[102] Here he formulates most concisely what has been our assumption from Milton on: that Plato is the poet's friend in the progressive undermining of Christianity. But with Yeats, the relation with Plato changes. And the key to the change lies embedded in the Yeatsian shift in theodicy. Yeats may have inherited from Blake a theodicy-grounding Platonism, but once that theodicy is abandoned, the point of the Platonism itself gives way. And it is precisely that lead that Yeats unexpectedly follows, for the references to Plato in the poems are not uniformly positive. Consider *Vacillation*. What vacillates here are the narrator's loyalties to, on the one hand, a Platonic picture of reality that looks beyond the senses, and, on the other, an artistic view of reality that looks precisely to the senses that are, after all, the necessary condition of art. The Platonic Soul of the poem *Vacillation* may commend the reality of the unseen, but the counterveiling poetic Heart in the poem will not abandon the sensual medium of its creativity. As though to complete our own cycle, which began one chapter ago with the Platonic rejection of Homer, we are now, through this poem, returned via Yeats to the arms of Homer, who, according to the Heart (who appears to speak for Yeats and who has the last word in the dialogue with the Soul) "is my example and his unchristened heart." In the concluding line of this poem, the famous Platonic picture of poetry banished by a religiously inspired philosophy is reversed: it is now the Homeric narrator, identified with poetry, who banishes religion, represented here, as Dante might have done, by a historic individual, the nineteenth-century philosopher of mysticism, Baron von Hügel. Lest we miss the reversal, Yeats highlights the Platonic underlay when he banishes the religionist "with blessings on your head,"[104] just as the Platonic philosopher, too, had dismissed poetry with hopes that a defender would one day represent its case.

But then Plato is no more the poet's friend than Christianity is. Rather, the two are grouped together under the rubric of religion and jointly banished. We can hear the poet's perhaps surprising rejection of Plato in the words of the poem *Ego Dominus Tuus*, vs. 47–51:

> . . . art
> Is but a vision of reality.
> What portion in the world can the artist have
> Who has awakened from the common dream
> But dissipation and despair?[105]

The poet has usurped the place of the philosopher as the waking seer of reality, but part of what the poet sees is precisely the sensual world that Plato rejected and all of the dissipation and despair of what the senses disclose. For the poet, Plato represents nothing more than a pointless self-denial, so much so that he finally assimilates to little more than "the first Christian".[106] The double banishment of Plato and Christianity is a further intensification of Blake, who valued Jesus enough to conform him to his own mythology, while Yeats implies that even the tradition of heterodox mysticism, under which he might have, with effort, subsumed Christianity, is too religious for his tastes and might as well be exiled too. It is not that no religion at all remains, but what remains is the pure form of what Blake had veiled with his idiosyncratic mythology, to say nothing of his residual attachment to Christian symbols, namely, the pure religion of art.

Remembering the lessons of Hawthorne, we might suppose a religion of art to sacralize ambivalence, and that is certainly the tendency in Yeats if we follow the suggestion of Margaret Rudd, that "Yeats substitutes vacillation for belief."[107] The religion of art must sacralize ambivalence, torn as it is between this dual office of the senses: to breed dissipation and despair, on the one hand, salvific art, on the other. But the religion of art, even when it was first conceived by the early nineteenth-century German Romantics, did offer up moments of realized redemption from the otherwise pervasive tensions between spirit and sense. And Yeats does too, never so movingly as in his perhaps best-known poem *Sailing to Byzantium*. In *A Vision*, Yeats tells us that "if I could be given a month of Antiquity and leave to spend it where I chose, I would spend it in Byzantium a little before Justinian opened St. Sophia and closed the Academy of Plato."[108] The time is as significant as the place. If the poet is to succeed the Platonic religionist, then the times of the two must overlap, at least a little, to make the succession clear; Hagia Sophia should have been built, but not yet opened, so that the poet can maximally appreciate its artistic splendor, without the distracting clamor of the worshipping hordes. As in Hegel's idealist system, so in Yeats's cosmic ideas manifest at lesser levels of history and personality. Byzantium is the historic period that for Yeats embodied the idea of the momentary truce of embattled contraries. It certainly helped Yeats so conceive the Byantine Empire that he had, by his own admission, so little head for politics,[109] and so much for art, for it was the art of the Byzantines that captivated him. Yeats simultaneously compliments the Byzantine artists and locates them in his artistic genealogy when he observes, about their depictions of Satan, that he is "always the half-divine Serpent, never the horned scarecrow of the didactic Middle Ages,"[110] and, he might have added, never out of sync with the vision of the beautified Satan on whose behalf Milton and Blake so labored. But the Byzantine artists had in any case a talent still much praised for capturing the mood of eternity. A famous textbook on art comments about a Byzantine mosaic of the Emperor Justinian, "The dimensions of time and earthly space have given way to an eternal present amid the gold translucency of heaven."[111] Yeats himself witnessed comparable mosaics at the Church of S. Apollinare Nuovo, in Ravenna, Italy. And the innovation of those mosaics, that they adorned the walls, and no longer merely the floors, as had been the custom, partly inspired the picture Yeats paints in his poem of "the sages standing in God's holy fire, As in the gold mosaic of a wall." And yet, from the standpoint of reconciled opposites, Byzantium offered up a still greater artistic treasure, the Church of Hagia Sophia, built under the reign of Justinian between 532 and 537. The great domed church is itself an architectural resolution of opposites between angular and curvaceous forms. The basic, rectangular plan incorporates a nave, at whose center is a square upon which rise the arches that support the dome. What allows the dome to rest on the oppositional form of the square is another artistic innovation: spherical triangles, called "pendentives." These pendentives take the form of a cone or gyre, and so supply Yeats, perhaps even without his knowing, with a prototypically Byzantine affirmation of the harmonizing potentials of his geometric shape of choice: the gyre. The affirmation comes at the price of Christianity itself, its doctrine and stories, for whom the sacred shape is the cross, and it illustrates the extent of emancipation from Christianity that

Yeats seeks for art: even liturgical art, seen through the poetic eye, was to advance from being "a beauty that would be sanctified" into "its own sanctity."[112]

No one who has ever thrilled to the opening scenes of the 1939 classic film *The Wizard of Oz*, based on the book by Frank Baum, can doubt the redemptive use of gyres, at least within the world of art. The gyrating tornado both fills Dorothy's wish to transcend the rainbow and rids another people of a wicked witch. The figure of a circle moving through a continuous path of ever-increasing, or decreasing, diameters stimulates the imagination toward ideals of unity: if the gyre is sensate, then it can observe whatever is at its center from all possible angles at once and so acquire what is, in effect, an absolute view of it; or, whatever is at the center, can regard all that passes it along the ever-changing diameters as part of a single whole, as indeed Dorothy may regard the pieces of her life swirling around her in the tornado. But most importantly, at least for this poem, is that any discrete individuals, caught up in the gyre, are united with each other in a single figure. It is to this unifying office that Yeats puts the gyre of his poem. Those sages, fixed in an eternity of mosaic art, gyrate down to the narrator and catch him up into their world. Only in that way can the sick heart of the aging narrator attain an integrally sensual release from the despairs of sensuality. That the sensuality of the sages is the glittering stone that constitutes them, and not any living, fleshly being that the stone figures might represent, Yeats indicates by reversing the natural direction of his metaphor. It is not the mosaic sages who stand as in a holy fire, it is the enfired sages who stand as in a glittering mosaic. The metaphor reaches from the fleshly to the artistic and so locates the mosaic as the desired fulfillment of Yeats's longing.

> Players and painted stage took all my love
> And not those things that they were emblems of.[113]

These verses, from *The Circus Animals' Desertion*, written twenty years after *Sailing to Byzantium* and after the advancing old age of the earlier poem had given way to the borderland of the poet's own death, capture most simply and poignantly the consolations of the religion of art, which seems never to fend off fully the resiliencies of despair. It is no accident that Yeats's choice for the religious figure he took the poet to supersede was not the prophet, as in the case of predecessors, but the priest.[114] The priest is, after all, the consummate mediator; his office is wholly exhausted by that role, unlike the prophet, who also motivates change. The poet as priest does no better than "to partake of two worlds, to vacillate between them and express the poignancy of vacillation."[115] If the poet seeks a continuous stasis, then it may matter less that his products offer listeners islands of redemption, ever on the point of submerging, than that in the creative process itself he assimilates to God.

Part 2

Theoretic Concerns

Chapter 4

Creation and Creativity

The Platonic tradition of asceticism toward art and the poetic line of *Religionskritik* define only the extremes of challenge that Western literature and religion have posed to each other. Within the extremes lie many instances of accommodation and synthesis. One form these instances take is analogy. The very idea of analogizing constitutes a meeting ground between religion and literature, since they both practice it. Literary metaphor is a species of analogy, and both monotheism and Platonism require analogy if they are to speak of God at all. But the analogies between religion and literature are most evident when literature is abstracted from its genre within the arts and taken for a representative of art as a whole. For the arts in general press forward from their separate domains at least three themes—creativity, beauty, aesthetic experience—that find in religion natural analogs: the creation of the world, the beauty of holiness, and religious experience. The three artistic ideas follow in a natural order: each indicates an object of critical attention in logical sequence: the artist, the art object, and the audience. And it is already a sign of possible imperfection in the analogies that the religious ideas do not necessarily match that order. The beauty of holiness refers preeminently to God, who should lead the religious sequence of ideas. But the nature and history of the analogies favor the arts in this case, for only one of the analogies has been dignified with the epithet "the great analogy,"[1] based on its distinguished pedigree within the history of ideas, the one between artistic creativity and divine creation. And so it properly heads the list.

But religion will not concede to the natural order of art's ideas without a protest. By wrenching creation out of its natural subordination to God within the harmony of religious ideas and shifting it to the front of the sequence, art confronts us head on with what, on the face of it, is one of the most difficult beliefs within monotheism: that God, the all-good and all-powerful, created the world. Judaism, Christianity, and Plato all agree that the world was made by God. But it is not the first thing they would tell us about themselves. Except for that minority of religious souls who come to their faith either by the classic proofs for the existence of God, which take their bearings from the most general features of the world, or by that worldly optimism that Leibniz typified (and that Voltaire parodied), when he said that this is the best of all possible worlds, the world as we know it is too troubling a place to serve as chief portal to either monotheistic or Platonic faith. Revelation is the typical point of entry to Judaism and Christianity; creation is a presupposition of revelation that surfaces in the logic of belief only later. That creation is indeed embedded within doctrines of revelation points up how much, with the notion that God created the world, we have entered the realms of faith.

God, after all, is the agent of creation. His counterpart in art is the artist. Emily Gosse would not simply deny any analogy between God and the artist; she would not accord the artist a status from which the comparison could arise in the first place. The very idea is too presumptuous for words. Ancient and medieval theologians of her ascetic bent might acknowledge the basis for the comparison, but only so far as to render intelligible and pointed their vigorous rejection of it. Thomas Aquinas denied that any creature could create.[2] Literature was not above returning the favor, as R. G. Collingwood reminded us over sixty years ago, when he allowed that the "odium theologicum" was such a force among aesthetes that some of them would not import into the sacred precincts of art a word so tainted with religious associations as "creation."[3] Both sides had grounds for stretching the distance between them, over the issue of creation and creativity, to the maximum. The monotheistic God was, virtually by definition, incomparable. When the Jewish liturgy repeatedly poses, in its "Mi-Khamocha" prayer,[4] the rhetorical question, quoting Ex. 15:11, "Who is like you O Lord?" it does not expect to be answered: the Human Artist. Even the Platonic creator god, who resides in the hierarchy of being somewhere short of the highest pinnacle, occupied by the idea of the Good, was, according to Plato, "past finding out."[5] Art, from its side, has inherited from Kant and his romantic successors the notion that artworks are unique and artists persons of genius. They have no need to borrow from what in the Kantian system is in the end the mere postulate of God, a dignity that their native genius already imparts to them. And yet, by a peculiar dialectic, the incomparability of God and the uniqueness of the artist become a new basis of analogous comparison between them, through the concept *creatio ex nihilo*, as we shall shortly see.

Between the Bible and Plato, and the religious traditions descending from them, teachings on creation extend over a wide range. The point of origin for these teachings are, respectively, Genesis 1–3 and the dialogue, *Timaeus*. Ancient Jewish and Christian Platonists, such as Philo and Justin Martyr, were quick to see the striking similarities between the two texts,[6] so much so that it was a commonplace among educated Jews and Christians to attribute Plato's teachings precisely to Moses. The two accounts of creation resemble each other structurally by comprising, each of them, two distinguishable creation stories. We have that understanding, about Genesis, from the higher biblical criticism, which sought to distinguish between the different authorial voices of the Bible; and about *Timaeus*, from Plato himself, who about halfway through the dialogue has the narrator announce "a new beginning of our discussion of the universe."[7] Even the change in the content of the stories, as they move from first to second, is analogous. The second story in both cases elaborates on the human element within creation. The creator of humanity in the second creation stories is characterized differently from the creator of the world in the first ones: in the Platonic story, as plural and lesser (gods); in the biblical story, as more personable and approachable. The second story, in both cases, introduces sources of imperfection for what appears to be perfect in the first: human disobedience in the one case, matter and its receptacle, in the other. Creation falls or experiences an exile in the biblical account, whereas in Plato's, creation is imperfectly constituted from the start, by the very conditions of it, namely, the world of sensation and the spatial context for its existence, both of which receive upon them the harshest Platonic judgment possible, that they deceive, the sense world by misleadingly appropriating for itself names that belong to the eternal world of ideas, and the receptacle of space, by lending itself to a "spurious reason" within us that mistakes space for being.[8] But for our purposes now, the most important commonality between the stories is that they all either openly state or else imply that God created the world from some kind of preexisting and formless matter. From that common point of origin, which Philo and Justin Martyr both noted, the biblical and Platonic traditions veered in different directions: the biblical tradition toward the teaching that God created the world from nothing; the Platonic tradition, that God emanated the world in an act of self-expression. Both views developed out of philosophical or theological problems in the original texts. The theological problem for biblicists was that the "tohu va-vohu" (Gen. 1:2)—the unformed nature of the world—that preceded creation seemed to compromise divine omnipotence, while the philosophical problem for Platonists was how, assuming the originating givenness of ideas and the world of sensibility, the second derived from the first. But the consequence of these elaborations was this range in religious teachings on creation, that, under God's agency, it: either happens from nothing, or emerges from a prior chaos, or emanates from within God.

Arrayed in that sequence, like three dots along a straight line, the three views suggest a movement between four different sets of opposed ideals: freedom and necessity; will and reason; miracle and explicability; purposiveness and propulsion. To speak generally, Neoplatonic emanation is reasoned, necessary, explicable, and propulsive; *creatio ex nihilo* is freely willed, miraculous, and purposive. Creation as the ordering of a prior chaos exhibits a mixture of the two families of values and can incline either way, which helps explain the contrary directions in which Genesis 1–3 and *Timaeus*, as examples of this type, evolved. The two opposing ideals of each pairing may be in conflict, but they do not necessarily exclude each other. The purposive God who wills creation from nothing and the one who orders a prior chaos may both proceed according to reason, and if they do, they may or may not work from a preexisting pattern of ideas. Plato's God clearly does, and the ideas he copies transcend him; the God of Genesis 1 does not necessarily work with a pattern, but if he does then the ideas of it are his own. When the book of Proverbs, writing as though to interpret Genesis 1, hymns a female personification of wisdom, whom God made "at the beginning of his work" (Prov. 8:22) and was with him at the beginning of creation, "rejoicing before him always" (Prov. 8:30),[9] it implies that wisdom offered the patterns on which God created the world, a suggestion made explicit by a later, rabbinical interpretation of Proverbs that identified the Torah with wisdom and set it in overt analogy with an architect's drawings.[10] Much later, the same idea appeared with a Platonic resonance in Milton, as we have already seen (*Paradise Lost* 7:557), but then Milton was simply benefiting from a Judeo-Christian tradition of Platonism that read the eternal ideas as God's. Only the emanational God of ancient Neoplatonism, whose creative activity is propelled of necessity from within him, needs no pattern to intentionally copy, at least according to Plotinus, the chief spokesman for Neoplatonism, since what God emanates is, by the universal laws of emanation, already "a kind of image of the archetype from which it was produced."[11]

The purposive and propulsive views of creation generate an additional spectrum of evaluations of creation's product, namely, the world. The God who creates from nothing produces a world that is purely and simply good, as Genesis 1 states. The God who emanates the world generates a descending sequence of images of himself, each stage of which is further removed from himself and consequently less good. The God who orders a prior chaos demonstrates his goodness through the sheer act of shaping a formlessness that was implicitly bad or at least imperfect, but the product of his work need not be as good as he is, depending on the malleability of his material. In the second creation story of *Timaeus*, Plato indicates how resistant to order sensible matter can be. And the goodness of the creation that the God of Genesis 2 fashions is already in doubt, even before the human act of disobedience, through the sheer existence within it of the malicious serpent. And so like creation itself, the worthiness of its product, the world, also moves along a spectrum of value that extends from the goodness implied by *creatio ex nihilo* to the moral diminishment that emanation entails.

Such a range of religious views on creation lays the foundation for an abundance of analogies with aesthetic theories of artistic creativity. The very word "poet" reaches over to religion for an analog in God, since its etymological descent from the Greek verb *poiein* implies a maker, and we know from the Nicene Creed of Christianity that God is "maker of heaven and earth." Judaism and Christianity (if not Platonism and its descendants) reach back to the arts through the goodness they pronounce on the created order, which finds its reflection in a common assumption of aesthetics, that products of artistic creativity are uniquely valuable.[12] Secularism has conferred a particular dignity on the ancient, monotheistic concept of creation. The monotheisms have sometimes grouped their theological concepts under the three key headings of creation, revelation, and redemption. Of the three, only creation has found its way into the secular world as a prized value there going under the name of "creativity." It is a high and common compliment to be called creative, but revelatory and redemptive are quaintly peculiar attributes of praise, apply as they might, in secular translations, to teachers in the first case and to any kind of service provider (e.g., librarians) in the second. If the concept from religion that receives the most hospitable welcome in the secular world is that of creation, then the arts may well turn out to be the part of that world that is friendliest to religion.

The originating sources of the religious creation stories, in the Bible and Plato, contain theories, or at least preludes to theory, of human creativity that implicitly compare it to God's. The Bible has little to say about human artistry. It implies a negative judgment on writing when, in Ecclesiastes, it laments that "Of making many books there is no end" (Eccles. 12:12). But it lays a foundation for even more tension with visual art when in the second of the Ten Commandments it mandates that "You shall not make for yourself a graven image, or any likeness of anything that is in heaven, . . . earth . . . or water (Ex. 20:4). The Bible never anticipated that such images, understood as art, would draw the religious veneration they do as exhibition pieces in the museums of the modern world; but it did know, within its own ancient context, that such images could attract an interest and even a veneration that was inconsistent with its monotheism, and so it prohibited making them at all. It is all the stranger that in that same book of Exodus, shortly after the Ten Commandments appear, several chapters of commandments are given for building a visually splendid structure, called the "tabernacle," or *mishkan*, meaning the place of dwelling of God's presence. This is the formal location for worshipping God that the Israelites were to use as they wandered through the desert. And this tabernacle does indeed include images of things of the natural world. The appointments of the tabernacle are listed in Ex. 31:7–11. They include the ark of the covenant, which is to hold the inscribed version of those very Ten Commandments just given, to be located in the most sacred part of the structure. The ark is an elaborately constructed box overlaid with gold and topped with two carved creatures, called *cheru-bim*, who between them create a seat upon which God's presence is understood to descend. Scholars debate how these creatures looked, but at the very minimum they had faces and wings (Ex. 37:7–9). The same creatures are pictured in the curtains that form the walls of the tabernacle (Ex. 36:8). Also, the menorah, a seven-branched candlestick, is explicitly patterned on natural objects, especially flowers (Ex. 37:17–20).

By its resemblance to elements within God's creation, the tabernacle, which is a work of human hands, begins to instance a human analog to the biblical accounts of divine creation, especially Genesis 1, interpreted as the rabbis did, as the execution of a preexistent plan. The tabernacle is a fashioning of preexisting materials: the metals, skins, and woods that God commands the Israelites offer up for its creation (Ex. 25: 1–8). The Bible underscores in the most elaborate way that the tabernacle is built according to plan: chapters 25–30 of Exodus supply the plan in the form of commandments from God, while chapters 35–39 narrate the actual construction. The second set of chapters virtually repeats, down to the smallest detail, what is given in the first. If we accept a principle of rabbinical interpretation, that the Bible is never needlessly repetitve, then we may suspect that the point of the seeming redundancy is to underscore how much the construction of the tabernacle did indeed follow a plan. The rabbis themselves discerned enough additional analogies between Genesis 1 and Exodus 25–39 to set the two accounts of creation, the one divine and of the world, the other human and of a building, in explicit parallel. For example, they heard in the blessing Moses pronounced on the builders of the tabernacle, after it was finished (Ex. 39:43), an echo of the blessing God gave the seventh day, which marked the completion of the six days of creation (Gen. 2:3). And so we appear to have in the Bible itself, not long after the story of the world's creation, an account of human creativity that Jewish tradition takes as analogous to God's.[13]

But we would be hasty to judge this the kind of analogy that art would wish. The narrative of the tabernacle's actual construction does not follow immediately on the plan given for building it. In between occurs one of those biblical stories that has enduringly troubled Jewish tradition, that of the Golden Calf (Ex. 32). The story narrates an instance that, for Judaism, became paradigmatic of violating the second commandment's strictures against image making. The placement of this story, in the midst of the tabernacle's, is not without logic: they are both stories of image making after all. The difference between the *cherubim* and the calf is that the first were made according to explicit divine command, the second out of sheer human initiative. A more careful reading of the second commandment—"You shall not make *for yourself* a graven image" (Ex. 20:4)—suggests a distinction between forbidden images, made for human satisfaction, and sanctioned ones, made for God's. The very name of the man who oversees the building of the tabernacle, Bezalel, connotes a similar distinction. Bezalel is "filled . . . with the Spirit of God, with ability and intelligence . . . to devise artistic designs" (Ex. 31:3–4). But he is one who stands, according to one interpretation of his name, Be-zal-el, in the shadow of God. He does not invent but rather executes designs given by God. Moreover, the shadow in which this artisan stands does not simply serve to subordinate him to God; it also envelops him and his work in a tone of suspicion. For the English word "devise" translates the Hebrew word *lachashov* that throughout Hebrew scripture often carries connotations of malicious, foresightful plotting (e.g., in the story of Esther, it is Haman who devises evil against the Jewish people). It is as though the patterned planning Jewish tradition saw as God's work in Genesis 1, becomes, in its human analog, something that borders on scheming. The hovering of that connotation over human creativity may explain the strange disclaimer of Aaron, who oversees the making of the Golden Calf, that, having cast the peoples' gold ornaments into the smelting fire toward the construction of the idol, he merely witnessed, without effecting, the actual emergence of the calf, which simply "came out" (Ex. 32:24); he may have made the calf, he seems to say, but he did not perform the "devising" that would have simultaneously admitted it to the realm of human artistry and him to the realm of Bezalel—a case of Bezalel gone wrong.

In a religious document that prizes obedience as much as Exodus does, any human initiative that offers as much scope for disobedience as image making must be suspect. Among all of the things the ancient Israelites are commanded to be, creative is not one of them. We already know that poetic creativity does not fare much better in Plato's ideal state than sculptural innovation does in the Bible's. Even Plato's praise of poets, in *Ion*, is barbed. For there he says, in evident agreement with the Bible, that "all good poets . . . compose their beautiful poems not by art but because they are inspired and possessed."[14] But that they are possessed while they are inspired inflects their creativity in ways that are as troubling, by Platonic standards, as Bezalel's talents are by the Bible's. The Platonic poet's inspiration requires him to be out of "his wits."[15] The loss of reason to the poet that such possession entails is a strong contrast to the specialized expressions of reason that the creator gods exhibit in fashioning the human body, for example, in shaping the bowels to discourage gluttony.[16] Indeed, the *Timaeus* is structured as a tribute to the powers of reason: it situates itself as successor to the discussion of the ideal state in the *Republic* and as prelude to the discussion in the *Critias* of the Athenian state. *Critias* depicts the realization of the *Republic*'s political ideals. *Timaeus* accounts for what must occur in between what the other two dialogues describe, namely, the creation of the habited, material world. There is no room in the sequence of dialogues for witless creation. In the Platonic system, the loss of reason to the poet is as much an implicit judgment on him as in the Bible's, the potential for image making to become idol making is on all artists.

If we seek on art's behalf less ambivalent analogies between the creativity it displays and God's, we do better to look to modern theorists of art. We anticipated one of these analogies already, between artistic creativity and *creatio ex nihilo*. It was Immanuel Kant who most explicitly invited this comparison when he specified originality as one of the features of creative genius. As Stein Haugom Olsen notes, "Prior to the late eighteenth century there was no premium on novelty in art and literature."[17] One of the demands that modern aestheticians make of art objects is that they be or exhibit something entirely new.[18] Novelty moving toward the most extreme instance of itself would have no explanatory causes or antecedents, would appear to rise up out of nothing. And when Monroe Beardsley, reflecting on the freshness that art objects bring to the world, allows that "something like a miracle occurs"[19] in making them, he points us back to Genesis 1. But the feature of the story that rises to complete the analogy with miracle is not the ordering of a preexistent chaos but the miraculousness of the ordering: the fact that it occurs through the sheer utterance of language. Bible critics have long noted that the God who creates simply by speaking is indeed a novelty in the context of the ancient mideastern creator gods. But even within the bounds of the Genesis story itself, language does appear ex nihilo, without any explanatory or causal precedent. That is all the better for the analogy to art, for there is indeed an art for which the claim has been made that, within the context of language, it creates ex nihilo, namely, poetry. When a poet conceives a new metaphor, by juxtaposing two hitherto unassociated words or sets of words, she fashions something new that was not implied, predicted, or caused by what was already given in the language. Creative speech comprises meanings that "appear to be created ex nihilo," says Carl Hausman.[20] Metaphors, as the paradigms of creative speech, are indeed "miniature examples of works of art."[21]

Part of the difficulty with creation out of nothing is that the originality of the product is in tension with its intelligibility. If whatever is intelligible is subsumable under categories that logically and conceptually precede it, and if what is created out of nothing submits to no such categories, then the product of *creatio ex nihilo* appears unintelligible. This is a cruel fate to fall to the world, though not an improbable one. If the world can receive such opposing interpretations of it as we find between the Judeo-Christian and Platonic traditions, then perhaps it is indeed unintelligible. If we can conceive it, on the one hand, with Plato, as a live organism with an animating soul of its own (Plato calls it a god) and, on the other hand, with Judaism and Christianity as an inanimate product only parts of which, selectively, receive a soul, then perhaps we are divided over the categories we think most appropriate for understanding it. When Kant tells us that the very idea of the world as a whole transcends the powers of our understanding to grasp it, and will lure us, if we follow it, into a tendency we would not expect of reason, toward treacherous self-deceptions, he merely encapsulates for us what the divergencies between the biblical and Platonic views of the world already suggest, that the world we inhabit is more mysterious and less responsive to our scrutiny than we may suppose. Hausman proposes an ingenious solution to the problem of originality's intelligibility, which might well have won Kant's approval, namely, that a true originality uniquely instances the concept that renders it intelligible. A poem is, as much as the world itself, a unique instance of its subsuming concept. In accordance with the analogy between religion and art that *creatio ex nihilo* would shape, both the art object and the world are in consequence assimilated to God, for one way of supplying meaningful content to a term that resists it as much as "God" does is to circumscribe the subsuming concept of divinity by the single instance of it that God provides. If a concept is present, then intelligibility is too. But if the instance is unique, then it is also original. In this way, intelligibility and originality are reconciled.

But the price of the reconciliation may be too high for art. Though the concept of *creatio ex nihilo* is not strictly scriptural for Judaism or Christianity, by the Middle Ages it was standard doctrine for the philosophically informed within both religions.[22] God's creative act, if it is indeed ex nihilo, is free, miraculous, and original: free, because unnecessitated and uncaused by anything that preceded it; miraculous, because inexplicable in terms of its antecedents; and original, precisely because unprecedented. Jews and Christians (if not Platonists) rest comfortably with all of those aspects of divine activity. And modern theorists of art are hardly lacking who happily apply each of these qualities to human artistry.[23] At the same time, some aestheticians may sense that, as one philosopher observes, the same qualities transposed to the creative acts of artists produce claims for art that are "frankly exorbitant"[24] or, more to the point, simply false to their creative experience. Monroe Beardsley is not alone when he argues in his seminal essay, "On the Creation of Art," that "creation is a self-correcting process, in which the artist constantly redirects his aims."[25] Such a view implies that the material of the art object plays a part in its own fashioning, contributes to the final form toward which it moves, and so precludes that it arises ex nihilo out of the artist's genius. It is just this dialogical resistance of the material of art that breaks down the analogy to *creatio ex nihilo*. If divine creation is unimpededly free, then human artistry must contend with foilings, blockages, and redirectings.[26] These may loom so large in human artistry that it ceases to seem like creation at all and more like selection among alternatives presented by the material at hand: a view of art that finds the Platonic creator god(s) a more congenial analog.

The Greek gods were already much more assimilated to human nature from the start. Plato's creator god follows suit. Through the sheer fact that he is given the materials of the creation he effects, he is already more like a human sculptor than the monotheistic god of world-creating speech. And Plato, the master dialogist, is not blind to the potentials for dialogue between god and his material, which must give consent[27] to his actions upon it. Suspicious of art as he was, Plato nonetheless offers an account of the world's creation that is remarkably akin to some modern theories of human artistry. If the art object judged

by modern standards is a self-sufficient whole, then so was Plato's created world.[28] If the artwork, in the relation of its parts to its whole,
resembles a natural organism, a corporeal being exhibiting intelligence,
then so was Plato's world "a living creature,"[29] imbued with reason.[30] If
the artwork is unique, then so was Plato's world "solitary."[31] The
modern voice that speaks in these analogies with Plato belongs to the
author of what has been called "perhaps the finest extended account of
creativity in the philosophical canon,"[32] namely, *The Critique of Judgment*, by Immanuel Kant. It should not surprise us if Plato, that ancient
idealist, who supplied Western philosophy with if not its finest then
certainly its first[33] account of creativity, should find his natural counterpart among modern aesthetic theorists in the father of German philosophical idealism, for it is the same kind of thing that animates Plato's
god, when he creates the world, and Kant's artists, when they fashion
their artworks, namely, ideas. The chief difference between the Platonic
ideas that motivate the creator god and the aesthetic ideas that motivate
Kant's artists is that the first are in heaven and the second on earth,
where they reside in artistic human minds.

Kant himself defined aesthetic ideas in contrast to rational ideas.
He grounds his understanding of rational ideas, quite soundly, in science. Rational ideas occur at the extreme application of science's
inductive method, beyond the bounds of science. These are the ideas
we arrive at when we abstract from the many instances of individual
things around us to the most encompassing notions available to us. In
a variation on the ultimates conceived by Descartes and Spinoza, who
proceeded deductively, rather than inductively, three ideas emerge to
fill these maximally encompassing roles: self, world, and God. Self is
the idea that encompasses all of our inner feelings, thoughts, and
desires; world encompasses all impressions we have of the things outside us; and God is the idea that intelligibly connects the other two,
ensuring that, ultimately, if moral law prevails in our self, then happiness will prevail in our experiences of the world. If rational ideas are
the end points of abstraction from the particular to the general, then
aesthetic ideas are just the opposite. These are born as abstractions in
our mind and move from there to expression in concrete things. But
whereas the concrete things that spark rational ideas are in nature, the
end points of aesthetic ideas that show themselves in the external
world are art objects.

Prima facie, the rational ideas seem closer than the aesthetic ones to Plato. It is, after all, among the rational ideas that Kant's idea of God resides. But part of Kant's point is that the rational ideas lack objects. Rational ideas are reason's extensions beyond the limits of representation and conceivability. Nothing in our experience corresponds to them, and we can claim no knowledge of what they presume to denote. They therefore stand in need of careful circumscription—the critique that critical philosophy supplies—lest they presume to give more than they truthfully can. For, like sirens, these ideas play to reason's desire to know the ultimates but, in fact, left unchecked, they supply nothing but delusion. Nothing could be further from the role and intent of the ancient Platonic ideas.

The aesthetic ideas, in contrast, are not tempters, nor unlike the rational ideas do they pull away from nature toward an unknowable and unreachable transcendence. Rather, the sensible world is their destiny. Like the Platonic ideas and unlike the rational ideas, they have expressions of themselves in the sensible world, but they inhabit it in a unique and Platonically resonant way: as finite locations of infinity. All Kantian ideas partake of infinity. The rational ideas are infinite in the sense that no itemization of finite instances of things exhausts their scope, but each rational idea merely seems to instantiate its infinity in a single object—the aesthetic ones actually do. Kant famously calls the aesthetic idea a "presentation to the imagination that prompts much thought, but to which no determinate concept can be adequate, so that no language can express it completely and allow us to grasp it."[34] It is here that the aesthetic ideas show their affinity for the Platonic ideas. When Socrates finds that in trying to articulate the idea of the soul, he must have recourse to metaphors, such as that of wings, because his "theme [is] of large and more than mortal discourse,"[35] he sounds like Kant telling us about aesthetic ideas that burst the bounds of finite, articulable concepts and show themselves instead in the indefinitely long strings of associative images they provoke. And, reciprocally, when Kant says of the aesthetic ideas that "they do at least strive towards something that lies beyond the bounds of experience,"[36] he echoes a bit of the longing that the old Platonic ideas inspired, redirected now to a place Plato would never have thought appropriate: the art object.

By their transcendence of merely "mortal discourse," both the higher Platonic ideas and the Kantian aesthetic ideas generate metaphor. But where the Platonic ideas are merely difficult to see with the mind's eye, and appear to the philosopher only after the rigorous training described in *The Republic,* the Kantian aesthetic ideas are overtly paradoxical. An aesthetic idea behaves like a rule for the artwork it inspires, but unlike most rules it cannot be generalized and applied toward the creation of multiple expressions of itself. Whatever an aesthetic idea inspires is original. A copy of an artwork is not the artwork itself, at least not in the same sense as the original. A copiest studies the original for as much of it as he can reproduce. It is the original artwork itself that guides his reproduction rather than the aesthetic idea that animated the original work. But what sort of rule is it that determines the creation of a single, unique thing? The question rises of its own if Kant's aesthetic theory is laid against the backdrop of his moral theory. Part of what determines the goodness of a good will is the generalizability of its behavior, that is, the fact that the behavior it inspires in a unique instance is generalizable (Kant would say conceptualizable) as a rule to follow in like instances. If generalizability pertains to the very essence of rules in ethics, then how can it not only not apply to the rules that govern artistic creation but be positively proscribed in that case? That is the paradox of aesthetic ideas: their ruliness is a seeming only, just like the more famous "purposiveness without a purpose"[37] that, at the level of Kantian art appreciation (rather than creation), characterizes objects that are judged beautiful.

Part of the reason Platonic ideas escape this paradox is that they are under no burden to explain the creation of unique, sensual objects. On the contrary, part of their purpose is to explain the reality of classifiability in our world. The Platonic ideas may have originated as explanations for commonality among sensual objects, but the direction of the attention they evoke is always heavenward, even in the case of the most sensually compromised of the high ideas, namely, beauty. Under the philosopher's gaze, individual instances of beautiful things dematerialize before the idea they copy. Plato had little enough concern for art objects let alone any originality they might display. It was just to his purpose if the eternal ideas the creator god copied when he made the world allowed for multiple sensual instances of themselves. But suppose the Platonic ideas were adapted toward explaining the creation of sensual objects that were original—one object, uniquely, to each idea? They might well be on their way, in that case, to becoming Kant's aesthetic ideas. The aesthetic ideas are the old Platonic ideas, transposed earth-ward and secularized.

Art may find in Kant an aesthetic parallel to Plato's cosmology, but it will not find in him a particularly strong advocate. Kant, like Plato himself, was much more impressed by the beauty of nature than of any-thing shaped by human hands, and he had less use for the artist's admitted genius than for the scientist's knowledge.[38] The overall urgency of Kant's thinking is in any case away from either art or science and toward ethics. In Kant's romantic and idealist descendants, we do indeed find champions of art who analogize it fully to divine creation. The world itself becomes an explicit art object, each work of art itself a self-contained world.[39] But if *Timaeus* is the ancient, cosmological counterpart to these modern aesthetic theories, then we are not lacking alternative theories whose inspiration draws more from the Bible. In Genesis, creation rises, quite independently of ideas, on a chaos that is progressively ordered and filled with clearly identifiable components. That the spoken word is the means by which the chaos is ordered and filled already invites from the world of art a juxtaposition with the process of literary creation. And one of the most prominent analogizers of literary creation to divine creation, on the model of Genesis 1, is Mircea Eliade, a comparative religionist who displayed in his own career the talents of both the religion scholar and the novelist.[40]

For Eliade, the idea of creation is a magnet that draws and sub-sumes under itself all other theological categories. Creation is the order that results from the appearance within chaos of a center, from which things that previously conformed to no standard of value now take their measure. The appearance of the ordering center is revelation. If, over time, the order begins to fray, then redemption is the renewal or repeti-tion of creation. The application of this view to the biblical creation stories requires selective reading. The world of Genesis 1 may have been fashioned from chaos, but its linear progression does not easily conform to the circular shape suggested by Eliade's image of a center. More problematically still, the climax of the biblical creation story is not the center of the new world, whatever that might be (humanity?), but a location outside the ordering process entirely: a place of rest from ordering. Perhaps this is why Eliade augments the story with his find-ing from Psalm 89, of Rahab, "a promordial monster,"[41] who had to be slain before creation could proceed; where chaos resides in the figure of a monster rather than in an amorphous formlessness and void (as Genesis 1:1 would have it), its destruction holds the place of a potential center from which a new order can arise; just as, in the Mesopotamian creation myths, to which Rahab unexpectedly assmilates the biblical creation story, the body of the god that personified chaos becomes a structure in the new world order.

But Eliade does not need Rahab's help. The rabbis already oblige his theory through their own interpretation of the biblical tabernacle as a repetition of divine creation. The analogy is not lost on Eliade, who shifts the tabernacle center stage. Sacred buildings are the paradigmatic repetitions, on the human scale, of a divinely produced model on the cosmic scale: "altars and sanctuaries represent an *imago mundi*, a miniature cosmos."[42] The ancient tabernacle was indeed a center for the wandering Israelites, and its successor, the Temple, more of one still, since the tribes were obliged by biblical law to pilgrimage there three times a year.

The Bible itself does not analogize the tabernacle to creation, and if the rabbis later do, then it is under the aegis of aggadah and its penchant for metaphor. When Eliade says that "the discovery or projection of a fixed point—the center—is equivalent to the creation of the world,"[43] he may mean for the equivalence to be taken literally. And yet he sometimes also encloses the human act of creating on that model within quotes, as though to suggest a metaphor.[44] He may indeed intend for play within his use of the term, wavering between a literal and metaphorical understanding of the equivalence between human creations and divine orderings, for then he is already opening up the way to further analogy with aesthetic creativity—if only because his metaphorical speech, if we follow Carl Hausman, is already an act of literary creation. That Eliade's talent for metaphor would show itself more fully in several lengthy novels is perhaps evidence for Hausman's suggestion.

Either way, the defining role that Eliade assigns creation within the framework of religion invites a natural and an easy analogy with the arts. Eliade puts it succinctly: "Cosmogony is the paradigmatic model for all creating."[45] His comments on the ancient tabernacle open up an application of this idea to architecture, and in other essays he interprets Asian sculpture through a cosmogonic lens.[46] But literature, too, Eliade's own art, is a creative endeavor fashioned after the model of cosmogony. For Eliade, the novel is modernity's successor to myth.[47] And myths, like all of the other categories within Eliade's religious universe, take their significance from creation: they are recountings of origins. A member of an oral culture who hears a myth recounted feels transported to the beginnings of time, of history, of his own people. Novels approximate what myths formerly accomplished. In the otherness of the time to which novels transport their readers, they simulate, even if they do not strictly duplicate, the primordial time that myths evoke. The space of the novel is an imaginary universe founded by the author. If novels simulate the created universe, then they, like the universe, must have their centers. It is these that literary critics help uncover for readers, the same way religions pinpoint the revelations that center the world for their practitioners. "This is why a writer or a literary critic is usually better prepared to understand the documents investigated by the historian of religions than, say, a sociologist or an anthropologist."[48]

There is perhaps no more apt illustration of that claim than the literary critic (and one-time pastor in the United Church of Canada), Northrup Frye. The particular religious document that Frye so passionately investigated was the Bible. Eliade and Frye shared a concern with encompassing patterns within their respective areas of inquiry, primal religions for Eliade, Western literature for Frye. They were both systematizers, searching for archetypes, understood in their most etymological sense, as orginary and ruling themes, symbols, motifs, or myths that crossed cultural lines, in the case of primal religions, or the works of different writers, in the case of Western literature. The kinds of archetypal themes they discovered in their respective domains were similar, for example, the purifying powers of water, which Eliade found across the religions and Frye across differently authored stories within the Bible.

Frye builds on an insight he inherited from one focus of his scholarship, William Blake, who dubbed the Bible the great code of art. Blake's point was that much of Western literature and art was informed by ancient, biblical symbols that his contemporaries were already beginning to forget. Frye wished to uncover the biblical themes that held what he believed the key to unlocking the structure of Western literature, especially for moderns who, while continuing to enjoy the classic novels, poems, and stories of the ages, had all but lost touch with the Bible. But as he explains in his introduction to *The Great Code: The Bible and Literature*, he found that the great sprawl of the Bible was already a centuries-spanning work of literature in its own right, needing an eluciation of its archetypal themes and the structure they build.

COLORADO COLLEGE LIBRARY
COLORADO SPRINGS, COLORADO

Creation was simply one biblical archetype among many, for Frye, unlike the definitive pillar of religion it was for Eliade. And though he does not hear the echo of Genesis 1, that the ancient rabbis did in the story of the tabernacle, ears for that kind of associative resounding— *resonances* is his term[49]—throughout the books of the Bible are what Frye cultivates in himself and his readers.

The Great Code is primarily a work of biblical interpretation. In a later work, *Creation and Recreation*, Frye explores more fully whether and how Genesis 1–3 provides an archetype for human creativity. Frye shares in Eliade's assumption that has one of its grounds precisely in this story, that creation defines itself against a backdrop of chaos. But he draws out the further implication of this view, less commonly stated, that except by confronting chaos there can be no creativity. (The implication of that limitation on creativity is part of what moves theological interpreters of the stories toward *creatio ex nihilo*.) And he implies that this is part of the message we receive from such products of literary creativity as "Don Quixote and Captain Ahab and King Lear,"[50] chaos confronters all. What draws Frye's further attention in the Genesis creation stories is their assimilation of chaos to nature under the figure of the cycle. Bible critics have long noted the linear progression that characterizes Genesis 1. The advancing line implied by the story, culminating in human beings and then the Sabbath, already repudiates the motion in which nature most typically moves, that of the circle or cycle. Gen. 2–3 simply intensifies that repudiation when it opts to villainize a creature that by shedding its skin in regular cycles dramatically epitomizes the natural order. It is that order, too, that the story rebukes when it derives the first female from the first male, in direct opposition to nature's rule. The cap on this analysis is the explanation of death that Gen. 3 provides. Death is the indispensable marker for cycles in nature's realm, for in the various shapes it takes it marks the transition from one cycle's end to the beginning of the next. So understood, death is a necessity, not an evil, and no more in need of explanation than, say, language, which is an indispensable condition of both stories that is never explained. The predicament of death that Gen. 2–3 presupposes is part of the larger problem of nature and the uncontrollability of its cycles. From the standpoint of anything riding a cycle about to close, the future is dissolution, or chaos. The first story comes in answer to that fear by reading onto nature an artificial structure of linear progress that culminates in a sanctuary of supernatural rest. The trouble with these

COLORADO COLLEGE LIBRARY
COLORADO SPRINGS, COLORADO

stories is that however much they allayed the fears of their original tellers, their effect now on readers and hearers is precisely to inhibit any confrontation with chaos, and so any expression of creativity.

Blakean that he was, Frye cannot help but turn the tables on the sunny optimism of Eliade's analogizing of human to divine creativity. Divine creativity, as we have it from the Bible, works in precise opposition to human creativity, which must free itself from the biblical models of chaos-subjugation before it can even begin to find itself.[51] But it is not as though human creativity is thereby any less analogized to divine creation than it was in Eliade's account; it is just that the analogy is, along Blakean lines, inverse or "devilish." "The encounter of God and man in creation seems to be rather like what some of the great poets of nuclear physics have described as the encounter of matter with anti-matter: each annihilates the other."[52] But of course what passes for divine creation in the Genesis stories is, on Frye's account, itself a creative (and fictional) response by humans to danger and fear. At our three-millennial remove from the origin of those stories, we can appreciate the creativity they express. But our admiration for them must not take the form of internalizing the structure they implicitly commend but rather of emulating the self-subjection to chaos that they presuppose. Only then will we find our own creativities stimulated.

The last of the ancient cosmogonies to find its analog in modern theories of artistic creativity is neoplatonic emanation. And here our choice for spokesman is the Oxford scholar of history, R. G. Collingwood (1889–1943). Though known principally for his *The Idea of History*, Collingwood also bequeathed to posterity a major treatise on the philosophy of art, *The Principles of Art*, first published in 1938. Collingwood himself would reject any suggestion of affinity between his theory of artistic creativity and Neoplatonic emanation. He allies his own theory with the biblical view of divine creation, which he pointedly contrasts to a Neoplatonic one he implicitly rejects.[53] But this self-evaluation of his own deepest religious affinities seems tendentious, inflected perhaps by a residual commitment he felt to Christianity.[54] In fact, it is the parallels within his theory of art to Plotinus, not the Bible, that stand out, especially on an issue central to them both, namely, expression.

The very idea of expression has a distinguished philosophical pedigree that allies naturally with monism (rather than monotheism). It is one means by which seeming plurality can be explained in monistic systems, whether Spinoza's, Hegel's, or Hinduism's. To take the case of Spinoza: There is only one reality, called Substance, in Spinoza's monism, but it shows itself on three distinct levels—substance proper, attribute, and mode—of progressively decreasing being. It is just when two of these levels share a quality that the lesser level can be said to express the greater one. For example, substance exhibits three chief qualities: it is eternal, infinite, and conceived through itself. But the attributes of thought and extension also are infinite and self-conceived. In so being, they express substance. The attributes, as lesser levels of reality than substance, relate to substance as expressions of it. Expression relates the attributes to substance closely enough to draw them to the brink of identity with it but simultaneously allows them enough distance from each other to be distinguishable. This is a tension within the expressing relation that Spinoza himself never overtly articulates, but that his interpreters do, for the attributes within Spinoza's system lend themselves to being seen as either subjective interpretations of substance or as objective realities. If they are subjective interpretations, then their distinction from substance elides; if they are objective realities, then their distinction from substance endures. That Spinoza allows for either view of the attributes may be his indirect statement of the paradox of expression: that whatever two things are related by this relationship course back and forth between identity with each other and separation. They simultaneously attract and repel each other.

It was that dynamic between an entity and its expression that Hegel articulated more directly in his *Phenomenology of Spirit*. Hegel's addition to Spinoza's substance was to set it in a relationship with itself of ever-increasing self-consciousness. The premise of Hegel's *Phenomenology* was that any distance between subject and object constitutes a problem for knowledge, for any medium between subject and object introduces the possibility of error in what the subject perceives of its object. It is only when the distance between subject and object is reduced to nothing that the subject can claim certain knowledge of the object. But in that case, the subject and object are identical. The process by which consciousness becomes aware that its object of consciousness is also its own self is just what Hegel traces over the course of his long and complex book. Subject and object are two seemingly distinct realities that are actually identical. Hegel needs a relationship between them that allows for enough distance between them to account for the seeming distinction between them, while simultaneously drawing them into a proximity so close that they identify with each other. And it is just this kind of approach-avoidance relationship between two things that expression supplies. The expressing relation appears quite early in the book, at the point that Hegel discusses the concept of force. Part of the appeal of Hegel's analyses is that they match imprecise concepts from our everyday speech, such as force, to precise, hopefully clarifying locations in his phenomenology of ideas. Force is the stage in the phenomenology that follows immediately in consequence of the "thing of many properties." Just before consciousness hits on the idea of force, it is struggling to understand the relationship between the singularity of any given object and its plurality of qualities (what Spinoza might have called substance and its attributes). What Hegel allows, which Spinoza does not, is for that static situation of a single object with its many qualities to transform into a relationship of movement, between force and its expression. A first-year student of physics may well wonder whether the equation, $f = ma$ [force = mass x acceleration], supplies the thing of force itself, or a measurement of its expression. It is just when the student grasps that force and its expression are precisely the same that she begins to understand the scientific presentation of this idea. Hegel says it too: "Force, as actual, exists simply and solely in its expression."[55]

The relation that Hegel found between force and its expression or Spinoza between substance and attribute is very similar to the relation Collingwood posits between emotion and art. This similarity comes as no surprise, especially insofar as Collingwood acknowledges his debts to Hegel and Spinoza.[56] "Artistic activity," says Collingwood, "is the experience of expressing one's emotions."[57] Like Spinoza, who distinguished between levels of reality at which substance exists, Collingwood distinguishes two distinct levels of emotion: an unconscious psychic level and a conscious level at which the experiencer of the emotion first becomes aware of it. Emotion at the first level only preexists. It is just when it moves to consciousness that it first comes into being. The key claim of Collingwood is that an emotion so converted to consciousness that has come into being is simultaneously expressed. That is, an emotion exists in its expression, or, as Collingwood puts it, an emotion is "endowed at birth with its own proper expression."[58] The parallel to Hegel's claim about force just quoted, is very close indeed. If expressing emotion constitutes artistic activity, then we have here an account of artistic creation: Art occurs when emotion unself-consciously experienced becomes self-conscious and, ipso facto, expressed.

   This will seem too broad of an account of art, admitting too much
to its ranks. But Collingwood allows that much more does indeed
count for art than we are ordinarily prepared to admit (and also much
less). Like most monists, Collingwood disputes the seeming appearance of things. To begin, he identifies art proper with artistic activity.
And artistic activity occurs within consciousness as preconscious emotion enters consciousness. What we deem works of art (paintings,
scores, sculptures, novels) are really the material by-products of art,
itself an imaginative experience that occurs within consciousness. This
would seem to make us all artists, except that our socializations typically atrophy our capacity to become aware of our emotions. In fact,
emotion at the preconscious level accompanies all of our sense experience. Colors, shapes, and sounds all carry emotional resonance that in
modern cultures we fail any longer to perceive. Children and artists are
able to tap that emotional resonance and raise it to the level of consciousness within themselves. The pictures they paint, the music they
compose, and the language they speak, in consequence of that, are all
merely extensions of that consciousness-raising, which itself is the
imaginative activity that constitutes art proper. Collingwood carefully
distinguishes art proper from what simulates it: artefacts produced with
the intention of arousing certain emotions in observers (this is magic),
or artefacts produced with the intention of affording observers a channel for discharging their emotions (this is amusement). Art proper
requires a preconscious, preexisting emotion that whoever has it raises
to consciousness within herself. The receipt of that experience by others
is irrelevant to its status as art.
   The viability of this account as art theory is less significant for us
here than its congruence with the religious account of creation we find
in the work of third-century Neoplatonic philosopher Plotinus. Like
Spinoza many centuries after him, Plotinus distinguished between
levels of reality, which he called "hypostases," meaning foundations.
The hypostases of the One, Intellect, and Soul followed one from the
other in that order, in a descent that somewhat parallels the decrease in
self-sufficiency within Spinoza's monism from substance to attribute to
mode. Each hypostasis in the series stands to its predecessor as an emanation of it. And what Plotinus says of emanation assimilates it quite
closely to what Spinoza, Hegel, and Collingwood say about expression.
Whatever emanates stands to what emanates it in a relationship that is
simultaneously of identity and difference. Each hypostasis is simultane-

ously "in identity with its prior" and "lower" than it.[59] Part of what makes each hypostasis higher or lower with respect to the other is the one-sidedness of the dependence between them. The emanating hypostasis "is immanently present throughout"[60] what it emanates, but not vice versa. The emanatee is, alternatively, an image, an utterance, offspring, circumradiation, or an overflowing of the emanator,[61] but the relationship is not reciprocal. All of the dependence is of the lesser hypostasis on its predecessor(s). "Things engendered tend downwards."[62] The ultimate issue of downward emanation is the material world. That emanation is a process by which that world comes to be is what makes it a creation theory. That the source of the emanation, the Plotinian One, descends from the Platonic Good makes it a religious creation theory in the Platonic line.

Plotinus's valuation of the product of emanation, with respect to what emanates it, is precisely opposite to Collingwood's valuation of the product of expression, with respect to what it expresses: in the first case, a lesser hypostasis; in the second, artistic activity. Art is an improvement on the unself-conscious emotion it expresses; intellect is a decline from the One that emanates it. But within the framework of this inverse evaluation of the products, respectively, of emanation and expression, the processes themselves are remarkably similar. Both processes are grounded in a kind of propulsive necessity. Artists are so attuned to the emotional content of their experiences that they suffer an "oppression" from it until it is expressed. The oppression propels them to artistic activity, which secures for them "a new feeling of alleviation or easement."[63] Though the One, in Plotinus, could never suffer from oppression, it too operates under necessity, as though from sheer affluence and effluence of being: "All beings, coming to perfection, are observed to generate; they are unable to remain self-enclosed."[64] Emanation, like the emotional resonance of sensory data in Collingwood, is pervasive and at the point of its readiness to appear (when an object has reached its perfection, in the case of emanation; when an emotion has shown itself to consciousness, in the case of artistic creativity) is irrepressible. From this follows another commonality between Collingwood's expression and Plotinus's emanation: neither is planned or directed toward a preconceived goal. Ends subordinate to themselves whatever moves toward them, which makes them unthinkable indignities for the One[65] and, for artistic creativity, compromises that debase it into craft.[66] Or, if any end is implied, it is an entirely self-directed and self-contained self-knowledge. What the artist accomplishes with his artistic activity is a self-awareness that eludes nonartists (though art products can spark self-awareness of emotions, and hence artistic creativity, in the viewer, who becomes thereby an artist also).[67] The Plotinian One is above knowledge, but the Intellect it emanates becomes a way for self-knowledge to occur within being. For when the Intellect contemplates the One, a kind of ideation occurs that foretells Hegel's: The ideas beheld by Intellect are both the active subject and passive objects of its intellectual activity, so much so that its knowledge is a self-knowledge.[68] These ideas, constituting self-knowledge in the Intellect, become the patterns for objects in the material world. The anti-climax of these objects within Plotinus's theory of creation has its counterpart in the near-dismissiveness that Collingwood sometimes directs toward the actual, material products of artistic activity.

Plotinus shares in that aesthetic. For him, as for most ancient and medieval thinkers, the *idea* of beauty surpasses art. It is the idea embodied in an artistically rendered statue that makes it beautiful; the beauty of the idea precedes and outshines the statue itself.[69] Philosophical idealists are rarely the truest friends of art. This becomes more patent in Collingwood's case within the larger context of his work, where art, following Hegel's account of it, appears beneath religion and science in the hierarchy of human intellectual achievement.[70]And yet an admitted disciple of Collingwood, Dorothy Sayers, does find a higher dignity for art in her analysis of its relation to religion, only the religion in this case is Christianity. That is not so surprising; Christianity, with its centering doctrine of Incarnation, provides, at least prima facie, a more hospitable context for art than the Platonic tradition can.

Sayers, whom we have already encountered as an interpreter of Dante (whom she also translated), modestly prefaced her essay, "Towards a Christian Aesthetic," with these words: "It will be immediately obvious how deeply this paper is indebted to R. G. Collingwood's *Principles of Art*."[71] The one contribution she allows she may make over and above Collingwood is to relate his aesthetics to the the Christian doctrine of the Trinity. The Trinity is, in formal, catechetical terms, a mystery of the Christian faith. The word "mystery" may work as more than a facile pun when it links this high Christian doctrine with the Lord Peter Wimsey novels for which Sayers is best known.[72] When philosopher John Hospers alludes, in a seminal essay, to "a mystery wrapped in an enigma,"[73] he is sharing his view of human creativity, but he might just as well have been describing the Trinity. And so the Trinitarian God of Christianity seems perfectly poised, especially at the hands of a mystery writer, for illuminating analogies with human artistry. On the other hand, to pursue these analogies in the context of Collingwood's aesthetics will seem an unexpected diversion toward Christianity of what has been a (Neo)platonically inflected philosophy of art. But the turn Sayers gives Collingwood's aesthetic will seem less strange in light of a curious fact in the history of ideas: that the same Greek term that some Neoplatonic theorists used for emanation—*probole*—appears as well in early Christian theology as the designation for the act by which the second person of the Trinity (the Son) emerges from the first (the Father).[74] The classic formulation of the Trinity—three persons in one substance—asks for a relationship among the three that both preserves the distinction of each of them while simultaneously identifying each with the one God of monotheism. This is just the kind of difference-in-identity that the expressing relation, as we have already encountered in Spinoza, Hegel, Collingwood, and Plotinus, is designed to support. Emanation is just the ancient form of the expressing relation that some theologians of the early church imported into Christian doctrine to explicate the Trinity.

The trouble is that emanation theory imported into the Christian doctrine of the Trinity no longer works in the service of creation theory but is now confined to the inner workings of the deity, whereas what we want from religion is an account of creation that somehow parallels artistic creativity. But this is just what Sayers proceeds to supply. Sayers assumes what Eliade would later make explicit in his own theorizing, that the defining attribute of deity is creativity.[75] If God is a Trinity, then each of the persons within it must contribute to God's creative output. Sayers highlights the language of the Nicene Creed that assigns to each of the persons a different creative function: the Father is maker of all things; the Son is that by which all things are made; and the Spirit is giver of life. Not only the persons of the Trinity, in their relation to the one God of monotheism, illustrate the expressing relation, but their creative actions also are set in such intimate proximity to each other that they too interrelate through a kind of expressing. And it is here, through Sayers, that Collingwood is joined to Christian Trinitarianism.

In the title of her book on aesthetics, *The Mind of the Maker*, "maker" applies jointly to God and human artists, for Sayers's thesis is that the creative process is virtually[76] the same in both cases—an idea is actively realized in such a way as to affect beholders of that realization. That affecting receivability of the realized idea is its power. And so an artist's trinity, of Idea, Activity, and Power,[77] emerges in parallel with the godly one, of Father, Son, and Spirit. Sayers is more original, with respect to Collingwood, than she might have us believe. Emotion is not the indispensable catalyst for Sayers that it is for Collingwood; it appears, rather, at the end of the cycle of creation, in the receivability of the artwork. The catalyst for art is rather the Idea. In her preference for Idea over emotion at the origin of creativity, Sayers betrays her doctrinal conservatism. For whatever occurs first in the artist's trinity will find its analog, within the divine Trinity, in God the Father. And within a classical Christian view of diety (as opposed to a view informed by process philosophy), emotion is too volatile and changing to claim the divine Father for its analog; this is so true that, as over against the Platonic theory, which posits a kind of dialogue between the maker and his responsive material, Sayers presumes an Idea that is, like the God of medieval theology, impassible and unchanging.[78]

But these differences with Collingwood notwithstanding, the way Activity manifests an Idea, for Sayers, is very similar to the way art manifests emotion, for Collingwood. In both cases, what is expressed is first known only in its act of being expressed: "The writer cannot even be conscious of his Idea except by the working of the Energy which formulates it to himself."[79] This is Collingwood's claim, with Idea substituted for emotion, and Energy substituted for artistic activity, or art proper. Sayers's further reflections on Power would commit her more fully to a role for observers in the creation of art, except that the receptor of an artwork can be the artist herself, so much so that with Collingwood Sayers can allow the artwork to exist in its perfection wholly in the artist's mind. It is just her Christianity that pushes her toward the incarnation of the artist's Idea in observable materials, for "it is the nature of the word to reveal itself,"[80] where word here is the second person of the artist's trinity, which is, by definition (and hence, by nature) a *manifesting* Activity. And so it is, not surprisingly, her Christianity that allows her, unlike the Platonists, to attribute to the art product a worth that exceeds the mere Idea it manifests.

A difficulty with Sayers's theory is a tension in her presentation. She wants, on the one hand, to adduce human artistry as an illuminating metaphor for divine creativity, which otherwise surpasses our comprehension. When the Creed tells us that the Father makes all things, and the Son is that by which they are made, it gives us the barest formula. It is only when we set those actions of making and accomplishing in analogy with having an Idea and realizing it in Activity that the creedal statement acquires substantive meaning for us. But, on the other hand, Sayers wants to say that an independent examination of Trinitarian teachings on divine creation, based on nothing but creedal formulas, shows them to perfectly mirror our understanding of human artistry. In this case, it is as though the Creeds on their own terms imply that the Trinity actively creates out of preexistent ideas within the Godhead. But surely the Nicene Creed is not so philosophically explicit—at least Sayers fails to make the case that it is. In a question-begging sleight of hand, worthy of one of her own fictional perpetrators, she transforms her metaphor of divine and human creation into a discovery of independently existing similarities between. Sayers cannot first analogize divine to human artistry and then claim to discover how similar they are. This explains the distress that nags the reader over Sayers's ultimate claim: Does the writer's trinity define (in human terms) or copy its divine counterpart? But this may be a petty quibble. What Sayers's work really serves to show is that it is possible to intelligibly intermingle Trinitiarian formulae with a Collingwoodian aesthetic of expression. To the extent that Trinitarian teachings are creation doctrine, Sayers does indeed harmonize a Christian theory of creation with an aesthetic theory of human creativity.

Chapter 5

Beauty

From out of their respective contexts of religion and art, creation and creativity build bridges of analogy to each other. Beauty, in contrast, suffers from one modern interpretation of it that so rigorously confines it to the arts that its analogy in religion all but disappears. That interpretation owes a great deal to Soren Kierkegaard. Kierkegaard, who famously delineated the three stages on life's way, separated aesthetics from religion by the stern-faced middle of the three: ethics. It is not simply a case of "either/or" (rather than both/and) between the stages of life, for the aesthetic life might transform to the moral one, and the moral to the religious, but beauty itself provided no direct entree to God. Perhaps Kierkegaard expresses this judgment on beauty no more amusingly than in his essay, "On the Difference between a Genius and an Apostle," where already in the title he acknowledges the romantic ideal of the artist in the very act of satirizing it, and where he chides all seekers of eloquence in the rhetorical climaxes and flourishes of St. Paul's letters:

> St. Paul has not to recommend himself and his doctrine with the help of beautiful similes; on the contrary, he should say to the individual: "Whether the comparison is beautiful or whether it is worn and threadbare is all one, you must realize that what I say was entrusted to me by a revelation, so that it is God Himself or the Lord Jesus Christ who speaks, and you

111

must not presumptuously set about criticizing the form. I cannot and dare not compel you to obey, but through your relation to God in your conscience I make you eternally responsible to God, eternally responsible for your relation to this doctrine, by having proclaimed it as revealed to me, and consequently proclaimed it with divine authority."[1]

If the call of religion is to eternal responsibility, then the implication here is that attentions to beautiful form are inevitably, from the standpoint of what is most important, irresponsible.

But Kierkegaard notwithstanding, beauty has connected art to religion, only not in the way that creation and creativity have. It is not here a case of analogizing two distinct concepts from religion and literature but rather of analyzing how one concept insinuates itself with them both. Beauty simultaneously tantalizes and troubles both religion and literature, though not for the same reasons. The problem of beauty is twofold: first, of meaning, and second, of value. Unlike creation and creativity, which, mysterious as they may be in origin, are nonetheless recognizable when they do present themselves, beauty is elusive in its very nature. It wants definition. Part of the distress beauty causes literary theorists is over that definition, which remains contested to this day; while religions, for their part, pace Kierkegaard, are unsure whether the lure of beauty, however defined, serves their own highest ends or not.

It is a simple matter to amass citations from both the religious and literary realms that testify to the ambivalence each evidences over this second in line of the aesthetic categories, after creativity and before appreciation, that we consider here. Ever since Cervantes introduced into *Don Quixote* the character, Chrysostom, the shepherd, who died from despair over the beautiful Marcela's indifference to him, beauty has been building a mixed legacy in the world of novels. Even a responsive

> beauty troubles the senses, for all that it concerns the spirit, it breeds in one a sort of despairing happiness, leads to a contemplation that never wholly finds its object, but is worth a world of kisses.[2]

But let us confine ourselves to two authors we have already studied, Homer and Milton, who span between them the rise and fall of the epic poem and the classic representatives of beauty each proffers: Helen of Troy and the biblical Eve. According to Homer, conflicting claims, by Greeks and Trojans, to Helen and her beauty caused the Trojan War. Helen married the Greek Menelaus, but she abandoned him for the Trojan Paris. At the beginning of the *Iliad*, Helen reviews the Trojan troops while the "elders of the people"[3] gaze upon her. These onlookers, weighty with experience and wisdom, resemble the choruses of the later Greek plays, who, as spectators on the action, provide a distance from the tragic events to unfold that works to comfort and reassure the audience. In this case they pronounce on Helen's "terrible" beauty, which will occasion so much suffering. And as though to heap on the beauty itself the full responsibility for the suffering to come, they excuse both warring sides for their murderous behavior, for, in the face of such beauty, "there is no blame."[4]

And now Milton shows us the other side of beauty, which works against the evils of life. In *Paradise Lost*, Milton retells the story of the Garden of Eden but elaborates with much of his own imaginative detail. Satan has no role in the biblical story, which casts as tempter merely the snake, who entices Eve to eat from the tree God has forbidden her. Milton projects Satan into the snake, through whom he addresses Eve. As for Eve, she is "divinely fair, fit love for the gods" (9:489), though the Bible itself withholds all comment on her appearance. Eve's beauty, when Satan first sees her, "overawed his malice," so much so that he "abstracted stood from his own evil, and for the time remained stupidly good, of enmity disarmed" (9:460–465). Satan, who at Milton's hands makes a sympathetic appearance here, seems even to correct the ancient judgment on beauty that Homer passed when he reflects that Eve's beauty is "not terrible" (9:490), except, inversely, for him, by temporarily robbing him of his malice. The contrast between Homer and Milton is all the more striking for being unexpected. In light of our second chapter, we might have expected the literary affirmation of beauty to come from the pagan Homer and the judgment from the Christian Milton.

In fact, Milton's tribute to beauty owes more to the Greek tradition than to the biblical one. It is only in the Greek translation of the Bible, which renders the Hebrew *tov* as *kalos*, that we are given the option of translating the "good" God pronounces on creation as "beautiful." If the Hebrew Torah were our representative of Western religion's teachings on beauty, then we would have to say that religion here spoke more with Homer on Helen than Milton on Eve. The Torah speaks of beauty sparingly. Few characters are specifically called beautiful, though those who are include matriarchs Sarah, Rebecca, and Rachel, as well as Joseph and Moses. Nature itself is hardly ever overtly beautiful, though the trees of the Garden of Eden, which preceded nature as we know it and so count for supernatural, are "pleasant to the sight" (Gen. 2:9). This is not so surprising in light of the horror the entire Bible shows of any tendency to worship nature. And this might explain Torah's laconic references to human beauty, too, when it stops, as it occasionally does, to consider it. Torah is much more comfortable with beauty when it appears in ritual contexts. That some of these objects, for example, the menorah, are patterned on flowers suggests that only a natural beauty tamed by divinely prescribed ritual meets with Torah's full approval. Among the ritual objects that Torah explicitly calls beautiful are the vestments the priest, Aaron, wears (Ex. 28:40), which gives biblical warrant for the textile arts within both church and synagogue. It is in the context of ritual that a verse from the Psalms appears, which even D. H. Lawrence appreciated: "Worship the Lord in the Beauty of holiness."[5] Lawrence commented that he was not sure what the beauty of holiness was, but "if you don't think about it—and why should you—it has a magic."[6] In fact, in its biblical context, the verse means simply to worship God in the context of the beautiful objects he prescribed for his sanctuary.

What draws to that verse from the Psalms the aura of elusive meaning that Lawrence sensed in it is the possibility of reading it as a reference to beauty in God's own being. Though anthropomorphisms of God abound in Torah, one human attribute that it never directly ascribes to him is beauty. Only one remarkable passage goes so far as to suggest an image for divine beauty: a paved work of sapphire stone that was heavenly in its clearness, which appears to the elders of Israel in one of the few visions of God that the Torah discloses (Ex. 24:10). But the Hebrew is clear that this is a simile: What the elders of the people saw, in seeing God, was "as it were" sapphire stone. The verse also positions the sapphire at God's feet, an anthropomorphism that suggests that the vision of beauty beheld is really subordinate to God himself. The passage indirectly indicates how remarkable this vision was when it stops to note that it occurred without harm, for in another passage, the Bible declares that no one can see God and live. Perhaps the Bible here parallels the *Iliad* by intuiting a potentially terrible beauty in God.

But, then, what is beauty? This is the first question that literature and religion must put to this idea before poets can claim to have captured it in their work, or theologians to have evaluated its bearing on religious life. After we have determined what constitutes beauty, our question to religion and literature becomes this: How does the achievement of beauty in artworks relate to the contribution (if any) of beauty to the religious life? This question entails another: Is beauty identifiable with qualities that characterize both artworks and God?

Though the philosophical discipline that explores such questions, namely, aesthetics, is no older than the eighteenth century, philosophical reflection on beauty dates back to ancient times. The distinction between modern and ancient reflection on beauty is that the one self-consciously isolates it for its bearing on typologies of creative and original artworks, while the other embeds it in other philosophical and theological concerns, which might only incidentally include the merits of what were understood in any case less as artworks than as technical accomplishments of craft. But for our purposes, even purely theological understandings of beauty are illuminating. As entrées to the question of beauty's meaning, we take four philosophers who reflected on it in contrastive ways: Plato, Aristotle, Burke, and Kant. Plato is already one of our spokesmen for religion, but in his quest for a definition of beauty, he serves also as a philosopher. To each philosopher, we then put our second question, about the import of beauty for literature and religion, which subsumes within it the further question of whether beauty is ascribable to both artworks and God.

If Plato inaugurated the tradition of an ascetical critique of art, then we might not expect him to show much interest in beauty. But Iris Murdoch, who is as worthy a modern spokesperson for Plato as we can hope to find, reminds us that Plato was surrounded by the high-water marks of ancient Greek beauty, in both sculpture and drama, which cannot but have moved him.[7] In fact, Plato esteemed beauty highly as an abstract idea, not as an expression in artworks. If "true beauty" inspires human activity of any kind, then it is not artistic efforts but the virtuous, moral life.[8] Plato defines beauty as that which all beautiful things have in common, which is, according to his theory of ideas, their participation in the idea of beauty. He suggests a progression of beauties that ascends from physically beautiful things, such as faces and bodies, to beauties of the individual soul (in virtue) to those of the state (in its institutions and laws), to those of knowledge or science, culminating in an idea of absolute beauty that is seen to be what underlies all of the beautiful things in the series, entitling them to be called beautiful in the first place.[9] If we ask for a further definition of this absolute idea, Plato responds by trying, through his language, to position us to actually see it in an intellectual vision, "pure, clear, and unalloyed" and "simple and divine."[10] Those last two descriptives are the most significant—"simple," implying that it cannot be analyzed or reduced to other terms, so we must not expect a definition, and "divine," implying that here at the upper reaches of Plato's thought there can be no conflict between beauty and religion. If, in Platonic religion, what holds the place of God in the monotheisms is the Idea of the Good, then divinity and beauty are companions in the upper reaches of reality. They exist in intimate, mutually informing proximity—the idea of the Good causes all beautiful things and is itself beautiful.[11]

Where beauty and goodness differ is in the ways they are copied in the world of the senses. Virtuous behavior exhibits both goodness and beauty, but beauty enjoys the additional option of incarnation in the appearance of physical objects, especially human bodies. Beauty is an effluence of particles reaching the soul from without and transforming it.[12] The power of beauty to communicate over distance, imparting something of itself to those who see it, helps explain how it functions religiously, as a way to the Good:

> Sight is the most piercing of our bodily senses; though not by that is wisdom seen; her loveliness would have been transporting if there had been a visible image of her, and the other ideas, if they had visible counterparts would be equally lovely. But this is the privilege of beauty, that being the loveliest she is also the most palable to sight.[13]

Beauty, unlike wisdom, is literally visible to sight, as well as, in its celestial form, to the eye of the soul. It is the only celestial form of which this is true. By that double visibility, it uniquely links the world of sense to the world of forms. If preborn souls in their heavenly travels beheld the form of beauty, then anyone who now "sees the beauty of earth is transported with the recollection of the true beauty."[14] If ideal beauty and goodness are celestial neighbors, then the soul, beholding one, sees the other too.

The Platonic notion that beauty approximates the divine carried over into Judaism and Christianity. In Christianity, the doctrine of the Incarnation provided a ready means of ascribing beauty to God, through the person of Jesus of Nazareth. Though, like Eve, Jesus receives no physical description in the Bible, Platonically inclined theologians found in the second person of the Trinity a ready subject of beauty. The erotically charged biblical book, the *Song of Songs*, became one avenue of articulating that beauty. Chapter four of the biblical poem is most explicitly a tribute to beauty in the physical appearance of the beloved: "Behold, you are beautiful my love, Behold, you are beautiful! Your eyes are doves" (Song 4:1). The sensuality of the book is so marked that it troubled the first-century rabbis of Judaism who formulated the canon. What convinced them to include it, according to Jewish teaching, is that its author was reputedly King Solomon, the wisest man of ancient Israel. Neither Jewish nor Christian commentators, though, allowed the erotic beauty to go uninterpreted. For the third-century Christian allegorist, Origen, the *Song of Songs* is a mystical love poem between Christ and the soul, or else Christ and the church. According to Origen, Christ addresses the soul with the words from Song 4:1. And in response:

> the soul is moved by heavenly love and longing when, having clearly beheld the beauty and fairness of the Word of God, it falls deeply in love with His loveliness and receives from the Word Himself a certain dart and wound of love.[15]

The beauty of Christ simultaneously charms and smites, in illustration of that dual nature of beauty we found adumbrated between Homer and Milton, though the wounds of love here recall as well the Crucifixion. More importantly, in imitation of the Platonic descent of beauty, the beauty of the Son, through whom all things were made, extends to constitute "the beauty and grace of all things."[16] Eastern Orthodox Christianity best preserved this tradition of beauty within the Godhead. Within the Orthodox liturgy, Christ is praised as "the supremely beautiful, possessed of a beauty above all the children of the earth."[17] Judaism, too, found a place for beauty within the being of God. Beauty is one of the ten *sefirot*, or emanations, of God within Kabbalistic mysticism. Kaballah arranges the sefirot in a pattern of relationships, in which some form pairs of balanced opposites, while others stand without opposition.

Beauty is one of the unopposed sefirot, sitting at the center of the pattern that interrelates them all. In the diagrammatic depictions of the sefirot, connecting lines illustrate how each relates to the others. From its location at the cener, beauty is the only one of the ten that connects by unbending straight lines to all the others, as though to suggest a mediating power to beauty within the economy of the divine being.

There was another side to the Platonic view of beauty. The bridge that beauty provides from the world of sense to the world of forms within Plato's system may uniquely position it to aid the Platonically religious life. But the bridge also can be a trap, for the sensuous forms of beauty can hold their admirers captive, so that their further ascent is blocked:

> The lovers of sounds and sights, I replied, are, as I conceive, fond of fine tones and colours and forms and all the artificial products that are made out of them, but their mind is incapable of being or loving absolute beauty.[18]

The reference here to "artifical products" suggests those very arts that Plato critiqued so heavily, as we already know, in the *Republic*. Beauty as an immaterial and indefinable ideal that draws attention away from sensual experience offers little scope for literature to exemplify it. And yet, through at least one of his dialogues, the *Phaedrus*, Plato opens a way for beauty to if not manifest in literature at least inspire it. The *Phaedrus*, which gives us some of Plato's most religiously tinged thoughts on beauty, is chiefly a dialogue on rhetoric. And we already know from Augustine that in the ancient world no great divide separated writers and declaimers of poetry, as Socrates himself suggests when he classes orators with "Homer and the other writers of poems."[19] The trouble is, as the worth of rhetoric unfolds, it appears to have nothing to do with the beauty (the "finish and tournure"[20]) of language but rather with its truth. This would reduce rhetoric to philosophy, except that language, in its very quest for truth, must sometimes have "recourse to fiction," "poetic figures," "exaggeration," "fancies," and parable.[21]

The necessity of figures and fancies derives from the inability of language to literally describe the highest truths, as Socrates indicates in his rhetorical question, "I want to know whether ideals are ever fully realized in language?"[22] What Plato openly allows to answer to this problem is not so much poetry as myth: "tolerably credible and possibly

true though partly erring myth" and "stories which though not wholly
destitute of truth are in the main fictitious."[23] Since all language of the
ideal fails to truly and fully describe, stories and myths fare no better in
that regard than other ways of speaking. But myths do serve better than
other linguistic forms as a "medicine or preventive."[24]An example of a
mythological preventive is the famous noble lie.[25] But a medicine,
unlike a preventive, is administered to one already suffering. The greatest suffering the soul can know in Plato is distance from the good. Natural beauty is the beginning of one cure for that. But Plato comes
within a hairsbreadth of implying his whole construct of the ideal state
is a myth when he suggests its power for good is independent of
whether or not it will ever describe a political reality.

> In heaven . . . there is laid up a pattern of it, methinks, which he
> who desires may behold, and beholding, may set his own house
> in order. But whether such an one exists or ever will exist, in
> fact, is no matter; for he will live after the manner of that city,
> having nothing to do with any other.[26]

Socrates had situated the laws of the state in a progression of beautiful
things culminating in the abstract ideal of beauty, but now Plato suggests that such a description of those laws as he has offered in the
Republic may substitute for the actual state itself. And the description
can occupy the place that an actual republic might hold in the ascent to
beauty. But then, like all the other things on that ascending ladder, the
description of the ideal state is not really about that state at all but
about the form at the top of the ladder that all the wrungs anticipate. If
the story of the *Republic* is not really about the polis but about an
abstract ideal that it indicates, then Plato has fashioned an artificial
form in language that is deliberately multivalent or ambiguous and that
succeeds in one of its meanings not so much by describing as by becoming translucent before a reality that cannot otherwise be indicated.
Plato knew about allegory, and that the epics of Homer could be interpreted by way of it, but he denied himself and his ideal state that
option, as we saw, for fear that readers could not properly appropriate
the allegorical meanings. But now he appears to invite an allegorical
reading of his own *Republic*.

Plato has already suggested, from the standpoint of his religious-
ness, that poetry is at its best when it is inspired, that is, when the poet

is merely a conduit for supernatural forces beyond him. That, too, is a kind of translucency of the poet's mind, through which energies from heaven pass toward fashioning something earthly (a poem). Platonic allegory is just the reverse of that, a translucency of language through which earthly sight can pass toward a vision of something heavenly (a form). The appeal of this to religion is obvious. Plato fueled a facility with allegory that Jewish and Christian writers of the ancient and medieval worlds developed to the fullest, but allegory also was a bequest to literature. Perhaps the *Song of Songs* illustrates, at least insofar as that biblical book in its innocent sensuality claims first a place in poetry and only secondarily a place in religion, precisely through such artful interpretations of it as Origen (and the rabbis) conceived. But beyond that, we have the instance of "the greatest of all allegorists,"[27] Dante, who marks the emergence of this form from out of exclusively doctrinal uses. From Plato's point of view, the secularization of allegory deprives it of its highest references, including the idea of beauty. But in the hands of some literary theorists, allegory, freed of its religious ties, comes into a beauty of its own. Dorothy Sayers may be right, that "allegory, of late years, has been suffering from what is popularly known as a 'bad press.'"[28] But, Robert Lamberton, paraphrasing French critic Jean-Claude Margolin, draws our attention to "the element of mystery involved in the experience of allegorical art, the enigmatic surface that appears to be referring to something beyond itself."[29] In Margolin's own words, there is

> ce plaisir délicat de l'allégorisme, fait de dépaysement, de gout de l'inconnu, du sentiment de participer plus ou moins à la creation, de l'incitation à la reverie.[30] [the delicate pleasure of allegory, comprising a sense of estrangment and of the unknown, the feeling of participating more or less in creation, and the inducement to dream]

Northrup Frye echos the image of the enigmatic surface when he locates the meaning of a poem at least partially in its texture: "the word texture, with its overtone of complicated surface," speaking to a latent multiplicity of meaning.[31] If we follow Frye, the company of allegorists expands to include not just Dante and his literary descendants but any creative writer who suggests to his reader that "'by this, I *also* (*allos*) mean that,"[32] which readily admits Hawthorne to the group, as we saw in chapter 1, but most other writers besides. In Frye's analysis, what makes an expanse of writing literature is that it takes more of its meaning from the self-contained interrelation of the words themselves, which he calls the "centripetal pull of the words," than from any outward reference, or centrifugal force, they exert. And it is just words functioning centripetally in this sense that yield, simultaneously, ambiguity of meaning and "pleasure, beauty, and interest."[33] But the practice of allegory, in Frye's hands, expands beyond the confines of literature to the criticism of it: "All commentary is allegorical interpretation,"[34] insofar as any critical comment on a work of literature associates an image in it with a concept. Then, insofar as criticism raises our awareness of beauty in literary works of art, allegory does too.

To be sure, Frye's is an extreme instance of a voice speaking on behalf of allegory's contribution to beauty in literature, but perhaps no more extreme than Plato's, on behalf of Platonic religion, when he extols the power of beauty to raise our sights to the vision of the Good. What joins the two is their shared estimation of language's capacity for accommodating dual or ambiguous meanings in one flow of words. In both cases, the religious and the literary, beauty's ability to fill its communicative office owes in large measure to the inherent ambiguities of language.

One problem with Plato's view of beauty is that it seems to purchase the harmony between religion and beauty at too easy a price, by abstracting the beautiful to such a degree that it loses the content in it that we prize. It loses definiteness. If part of the problem of beauty was its want of definition, then Plato has skirted the problem by elevating beauty to a point beyond definition. It fell to Plato's successor, Aristotle, to characterize the beautiful in the way that we have come to associate with classical civilization, in terms of, to quote the philosopher himself, "order and symmetry and definiteness."[35] By his definiteness, Aristotle sensualizes beauty in ways that Plato largely resisted. Out of his critiques of Platonic religion, which turn on the theory of forms he rejected, he also inflects that religion in a new way. Aristotle rightly charges Plato with failing to account for the presence of change and movement in our world. Reasoning that what Plato took for the underlying reality or substance of things, namely, their forms, could not account for change as we know it unless it itself in some way acted, he activated substance. And reasoning farther from the highest movement we know, namely, that of heaven, to its cause he deduced a first cause

"which moves without being moved, being eternal, substance, and actuality."[36] Aristotle carries over from the forms their immateriality, eternity, and substantiality, but, with the addition of actuality, transforms
them into something new: "something which moves while itself [is]
unmoved, existing actually, [and that] can in no way be otherwise than
as it is."[37] He preserves a sense of the sublime stasis of the forms by
having the famous "unmoved mover" act effortlessly, and without delib-
erative intent, drawing all that it affects toward it. A constellation of
values gathers around what is now the Aristotelian God, almost all of
which recall Plato: primariness, necessity, intrinsic desirability, goodness, ultimacy among objects of thought. The Aristotelian God is the
Platonic Good imbued with an effortless action that affects all things.

An important feature of the Aristotelian God from our perspective
is its beauty.[38] This too carries over from Plato. But the basis of beauty's
applicability to God is different in Aristotle. Aristotle has brought to
the philosophical deity a definiteness it lacked in Plato, through its now
more evident relationship to the world of change. Change arises
through the attraction God ceaselessly exerts on all that is not God.
Plato's hierarchy of beauty suggested as much, but the only change it
accounted for was in the beholder, whose attentions were gradually
drawn upward. Each instance of beauty in the ascent of beauty
remained statically and unaccountably where it was. By situating God
as the final cause not only of the beholder's attentions, but of the objects
he beholds, those objects too are given a reason to change. It is by just
this importation of definiteness into deity that it takes on the features
of Aristotelian beauty. For Aristotle, this new definition in the relation
between God and the world also can be described in terms of completion. As the final cause of all things, God is also their completion.
Indeed, an Aristotelian might say that the new definition Aristotle has
brought to the relationship between the philosophical God and the
world is itself a completion of Plato.

The notion that definiteness could be a defining mark of beauty
already pulls it down from Plato's highest reaches of abstraction. The
danger of ascribing such a beauty to the philosophical God is that it,
too, experience a loss of height. Aristotelians might consider that a
price worth paying for a God intelligibly related to the world. But they
might also say, in anticipation of later apophatic thinking within the
monotheisms, that the definiteness they have purchased for God
applies precisely and only to his relation with the world, and not to God

himself. No such apologies for definiteness are needed, however, with respect to the new range of applicability it gives beauty to things of the world. Aristotle never imagined that definiteness alone made something beautiful. His definition of the concept allies it immediately with order and symmetry, themselves a kind of definiteness. Order and symmetry receive further refinements through the examples of beauty that Aristotle says they provide. For example, the design in animals, which displays organization fitted to a purpose, is beautiful,[39] suggesting that beautiful order is harmonious (not coercive). But for our purposes, it is the manifestation of order in proportion that is most critical, for it opens the applicability of beauty especially to literature.

Aristotle himself supplies the application of his theory of beauty to literature in his seminal work, *The Poetics*. The concept of imitation so central to that work is itself an instance of proportion, in this case between reality and its reconfiguration in literature. In Aristotle's own example, just as, in reality, "a creature of vast size" becomes too indistinct (indefinite) to qualify as beautiful, so tragic drama "must be of a length to be taken in by memory."[40] Or, again, characters must be "like the reality" and "appropriate,"[41] a term that itself defines beauty in *The Topics*[42] (and that bears a suggestive, if not an etymological, similarity to proportion). But then, having fattened Plato's lean abstraction of beauty on a diet of definiteness, Aristotle has effected a most easy harmony between religion and literature through the applicability to each of qualities that unfold out of beauty's new girth. Through the concept of activity, he even suggests an analogy between them. For just as in the *Metaphysics* he activates the Platonic ideal of reality, so in the *Poetics* he weights the plot line of dramas, rather than, say, their presentation of character, with the greatest import for their success as works of art. Perfectly realized actuality is to God what plot line is to drama.

Like Platonic beauty, so too Aristotelian beauty bequeathes a portion of itself to later Christianity. The exemplary Aristotelian within medieval Christianity was Thomas Aquinas (1225–1274), who shares Aristotle's commitment to the definite. The Aristotelian marks of beauty—completeness, proportion, harmony, and symmetry—appear within Aquinas's account of beauty too.[43] Aquinas echoes Aristotle's appreciation of the beauty inherent to the all-causing and to thought that takes deity for its object ("Beauty, pure and essential, dwells in the contemplative life"[44]), but he includes among the features of beauty two that Aristotle did not mention, namely, brightness and clearness.[45]

These more distinctly visual features of beauty, which recall Plato more than Aristotle, render beauty even more immediately sensual, which offers up the opportunity for Aquinas, as it did for Origen, to admit beauty into the Godhead by way of the uniquely incarnated Second Person of the Trinity. For within the Trinity, the Son exhibits all the definitive marks of beauty: completion, by virtue of the fact that he shares the perfect nature of the Father; proportion, since he is the "express Image of the Father,"[46] and brightness, since he is the Word that enlightens the human intellect.

The element of brightness that Aquinas imports into beauty might give us pause, especially when color unexpectedly proffers itself to illustrate: "Things are called beautiful which have a bright color."[47] What might Aquinas have been imagining, the colors of ecclesiastical vestments or of stained glass windows (such as L. P. Hartley pictured for us in his novel)? If we think Aquinas begins to build here another kind of bridge to the arts than Aristotle conceived, then we probably are wrong. He is certainly not opening up an appreciative path to secular literature, as we already know from chapter 2. Aristotle's own application of his beauty ideal to literature did not carry over to Aquinas or to the Western Christian Middle Ages.[48] But Aquinas does bridge us forward in time to the modern world, for one of the instances of beauty we have from the modern philosopher, Edmund Burke, is precisely "clear and bright" color.[49]

Enormous intellectual and social change separates Aquinas from Edmund Burke (1729–1797), the great English conservative best known for his book *Reflections on the Revolution in France* (1790), in which he denounced that social upheaval. His *Philosophical Enquiry into the Origin of Our Ideas of the Sublime and the Beautiful* dates from 1757. The two books, on politics and aesthetics, are more related than appears on first sight. The chaos of modernity is the incitement to both, on the social and political levels in the later book, and on the intellectual and aesthetic levels in the earlier. It was the "confusion of ideas" surrounding our notions of beauty that, according to Burke's preface to his book, stimulated him to write it.[50] Beauty had fallen indeed from Aristotle's time if, in contrast to the clarity and definition Aristotle brought to the idea, it now suffered from "extremely uncertain and indeterminate" talk about it.[51] For Burke, what had muddied the aesthetic waters was an excess of figurative speech about beauty (for which Aristotle and the thinking he inspired might be held partly responsible). Burke has little use for the classical view of beauty as harmony or proportion. In the chapter, "Proportion Not the Cause of Beauty in Vegetables," he observes that those most beautiful representatives of plant life, the flowers, are often not proportionately structured. He asks, "How does the slender stalk of the rose agree with the bulky head under which it bends?"[52] And in the chapter critiquing harmony as beautiful, "Fitness Not the Cause of Beauty" he observes, "On that principle, the wedge-like snout of a swine, with its tough cartilage at the end, the little sunk eyes, and the whole of the head, so well adapted to its offices of digging and rooting, would be extremely beautiful."[53] If the abstract notions of proportion and fitness so miss the mark of beauty in these humble instances, then how much more confusion can they be expected to cause when they are taken for marks of beauty in intellectual or spiritual referents?

To reclarify the concept of beauty, Burke proposes to restrict its application to the purely "sensible qualities of things."[54] "By beauty I mean that quality or those qualities in bodies by which they cause love."[55] Thomas Aquinas, who was as guilty as anyone of inappropriately extending beauty's reach, nonetheless properly redirected our sights this way when he instanced brightness as a type of beauty and even more so when he suggested that "the beautiful is that which pleases on being perceived."[56] Burke puts it this way: Beautiful things cause love in us, simply from "the direct force which they have merely on being viewed."[57] The value of this definition for Burke lies in its empirical testability and in his confidence that we are, most of us, moved to feelings of affection and kindness by the same kinds of qualities in sensual objects. For that commonality of response in us becomes the foundation for the sense we have that we do participate in a broadly embracing community of taste. But the price of the clarity in Burke's definition of beauty and the community of taste it justifies is a subjective sensuality that has devastating implications for both God and literature, at least insofar as they aspire to beauty. For as Burke himself allows, God is not "presented to the senses,"[58] and, even if he were, it is doubtful he would, on the religious terms of either Judaism, Christianity, or Platonism, affect us exclusively or even predominantly with feelings of affection. As for literature, if Burke's own analysis of it is right, then it does not move us through our senses, not even by way of sensual imagery.[59] What Burke has in mind by qualities in things that induce feelings of affection in us are most restrictedly sensual indeed, such as, besides brightness to sight, smoothness to touch and sweetness to taste. It is no accident for Burke that we speak of our judgments on beauty in terms of taste, for this should itself remind us of the humble origins of all of our aesthetic talk in "that most ambiguous of all the senses."[60]

But the implications of Burke's aesthetic for literature and God are devastating only if they do indeed aspire to beauty. If we are seeking bridges that beauty builds between them, then their shared failure to instantiate beauty becomes itself a commonality. Beauty in this case unites religion and literature by the similarly shaped hole it leaves in both of them. And yet it is not as though beauty in another guise does not fill the hole, for it does, under the name of the sublime. This is a concept with ancient roots indeed in the Greek philosopher, Longinus, who wrote *On the Sublime*. Longinus differs from our other philosophers in that he is less interested in sublimity as an abstract concept or as a quality in things than for its expression in oratory and literature. He defines it as "excellence and distinction in expression."[61] Sublime language goes beyond merely interesting, pleasing, or persuading us: it must amaze us. And part of the amazement it induces rests on the weighty thoughts it must carry. To illustrate his point, he cites, in chapter nine, passages from the *Iliad* that describe battles between the gods or acts of divine grandeur, such as the sea god, Poseidon, performs in his wrath. Uncharacteristically for an ancient pagan writer, in the same chapter he even cites as illustrative the opening verses of the Bible. "Let there be light, and there was light" is sublime, by the transition it makes, through sheer spoken fiat, from a state of originary darkness to light; this too must amaze us.

It was in part that biblical reference that recommended Longinus to eighteenth-century aestheticians, who soon saw that, in Longinus's terms, "the Bible was the richest treasury of the sublime,"[62] filled as it was with such passages as the parting of the Red Sea and the giving of the Ten Commandments. Burke inherited and contributed to this seventeenth- and eighteenth-century tradition. He built on both Longinus's and the Enlightenment's interest in the Bible's renditions of the aesthetic sublime. With them, he defined the sublime in terms of the emotions of pain, danger, and terror it provokes in us, but "at certain distances," which so preserve our safety that we respond to it with delight.[63] And he drew on the Bible, chiefly the book of Job, to illustrate. But if the Bible is sublime, then surely by implication God is too. Burke raises this consequence gingerly, sensing perhaps a blasphemy in citing "that great and tremendous being as an example in an argument so light as this."[64] But God does exemplify several of the features that Burke associates with the sublime: power, infinity, vastness, magnificence, and a forcefulness that, certainly on the biblical account, induces terror. The safety that in the purely aesthetic case comes from a certain distance from the perceived danger, depends, in the case of God, on his presumed qualities of mercy. But literature also participates in the sublime. It does so through the association that words make with emotions. Among the arts, literature exhibits an abstraction from the senses that locates it beyond the reach of Burke's so sensual theory of beauty. If Burke were Platonically inclined, then he might think that words touch our senses through mental images of sensual things they evoke. But Burke, who is so much the eighteenth-century psychologist in aesthetics, anticipates twentieth-century theories of language when he insists that words communicate independently of mental images. But he remains enough moored to psychology not to be able to allow that words, so freed of images, can communicate anything with clarity. This does not mean they fail to communicate at all, for if we distinguish, as we should, "between a clear expression and a strong expression," then we understand that words are expressions that communicate not with clearness but with strength. But then Burke has positioned language in general, and literature in particular, to function in the service of the sublime, one of whose defining features is its strength of power. And it comes as no surprise that all of Burke's instances of poetic language come from sublime (rather than beautiful) verses.[65]

From Plato through Aristotle to Burke, beauty undergoes a course of progressive subjectification. Platonic beauty was an abstract idea existing objectively but at great remove from us. Perceiving it is as difficult as perceiving the divine. Aristotle, who rejected Plato's theory of objectively existing abstractions, brought beauty closer to us, in the objects around us. Finally, Burke brought beauty closer to us still by defining it in terms of its psychological effects on us but in the process undermined its claim to any objective existence. The fate of beauty over this line of development resembles that of knowledge at the hands of the British empiricist philosophers. And just as objective knowledge found its rehabilitation in Immanuel Kant, so did beauty under his analysis stay the course of subjectification that had progressed so far with Burke. In Kant's hands, beauty recovers its applicability to both religion and literature.

Kant famously characterized beauty as "purposiveness . . . without the presentation of a purpose."[66] It is just by sharing a concept of purpose that teleology in nature and beauty in art can be the otherwise improbably paired subjects of Kant's third critique. It is one of the fascinations of the Kantian system that the aesthetic idea of purposiveness finds its ground in a scientific concept of cause and effect. An object has a purpose if it has an effect, the concept of which figures in its cause. Aristotle would have called the Kantian purpose of an object its final cause. We can think of many objects that fit this description, for example, the objects of human technological production. Toasters toast bread, and the idea of toasting bread must have figured as a cause in the creation of the first toaster. The object and the end it serves fit together intimately. Generally, objects with purposes they so aptly fit have an effect on our lives—to clothe, feed, house, amuse us—the concept of which does indeed figure in their cause. If someone had not had the idea of the end in view that they serve, then they would not have come into being. Many other causes must be factored in, besides the concept of the end in view before the object actually comes into being. But the concept of that end is part of the causal chain.

It is out of this concept of purpose that Kant teases the idea of beauty, for suppose the effect of an object, the concept of which figured in its cause, were that very object itself. In this case, the particularly intimate fit is not between the object and an end it serves outside of it but between the object and itself. We say, colloquially, "suit yourself." And we mean, if you want to do that, then do so. That is, let your acts harmonize with your desires. Kant allows that, apart from human willing and acting, objects can also exhibit this particular self-suitedness. Beautiful objects suit themselves in this double sense: they exhibit harmony within themselves and, in consequence, they are freed from serving a purpose outside of themselves. To judge a thing beautiful, we must perceive both of these features of an object: its internal harmony and its freedom from subjection to ends outside of itself. Kant calls purpose that has become self-referring or reflexive "purposiveness," rather than "purpose," because it departs from our ordinary idea of purpose as an external end served. But by the same token, he calls it "purposiveness" (and not some other word unrelated to "purpose") because he derives this idea from our concept of purpose. And if we perceive purposiveness in a thing as being simultaneously freed from any subordination to external purposes, then we are perceiving an essential feature of beauty.

Kant's treatise on beauty is called *Critique of Judgment*, because he considers beauty in objects to be, in part, a function of judgments we make about objects. We perceive beauty in objects when we judge them a certain way. We must judge them as purposive without a purpose, as though to imply that this constitutes one way of judging an object that is open to being judged in other ways too, through which we would miss the beauty of the object. And Kant does want to allow for this multiperspectival viewing of things, between which we can switch back and forth. His example is a clearing in the forest. We can judge this clearing in either of two ways: either as an object with a purpose outside of it to, say, shape a space for a country dance, or, as an object with a purpose inside of it, that is, as an object that exhibits self-suitedness and freedom from any ends outside of itself. Viewing it that second way is to begin to see it as beautiful. At the same time, this does not allow for pure relativism in judgments of beauty, since presumably not everything we encounter can be judged self-suited. Some things seem only suited for how they play into other things, or seem positively ill suited.

We see Kant's dependence on past theories, most especially on the ancient and medieval idea that beauty is harmony. But Kant is not making that simple identity. For one, the harmony is perspectival; it depends on our judging objects a certain way. On the other hand, the harmony is tied to objectivity through the concept of purpose, which Kant defines in objective, cause-effect terms. By these refinements, Kant is able to locate the concept of beauty where we intuitively feel it belongs, not with our scientific concepts of cause and effect, as Plato might do, or with our subjective concepts of pleasure and pain, as Burke might do, but uniquely on the boundary between subjectivity and objectivity.

But now we are on the verge of a paradox in Kant's theory. To judge an object beautiful is to judge it as one whose purpose feeds back into itself rather than outward toward another thing. And in so judging it, we must disregard its relation to other things, in particular, whatever position it might hold as the effect of a cause. Insofar as we admit causal concerns into our judgment of the object, we lose the beauty in it. But it was precisely from causal considerations that Kant generated his idea of purpose in the first place. And so when Kant turns the concept of purpose back on itself, to give self-directed purpose, he converts an idea for which causation was definitive into one from which it is necessarily excluded.

This paradox underlies the peculiar phrase: purposiveness without a purpose. Kant formulates the paradox in other ways. To think causally is to think scientifically. It is also to conceptualize, to place things in categories. We must be thinking this way to generate the idea of purpose at all and from there the idea of purposiveness. Conceptualization is presupposed but necessarily unrealized in judgments of beauty. This accounts for another way Kant presents the judgment of beauty—as one that harmonizes with our power of concepts without, however, being a conceptualization. The self-suitedness of an object harmonizes with its suitedness to an end outside of itself in that they are both cases of suiting or fitting together. But the other fitting, in the case of an object judged to have a purpose outside of itself, is judged scientifically, in terms of cause and effect, while the self-fitting, in the case of an object judged beautiful, is judged in terms of its unique independence from all causes and ends outside of itself. A beautiful object exhibits the suitedness that an effect exhibits when seen in conjunction with its cause, but it is simultaneously judged free of all cause-effect relations.

What sort of context does this account of beauty provide for the relationship between religion and literature? Kant enjoyed literature, but he was not a critic of it. Unlike Aristotle, he did not himself apply his theory of beauty to literary criticism. Like Plato, he was more interested in beauty as it manifested in nature than in the arts. Still, Kant's distinction between purpose and purposiveness can be employed to show how literary criticism differs from scientific experimentation or discovery, and this can free literature from having to answer a demand that might be made of science, that it be "scientific." Science, we might say, aims to situate events in laws of cause and effect and, in doing so, to explain them, while literary criticism aims to articulate the self-suitedness of a novel. In this very process of differentiating criticism from science, and so laying the foundation for a theory of literary criticism, Kant shows himself a friend of literature. Kant's successors built on the foundation, taking it in at least two directions, toward *l'art pour l'art* and toward hermeneutics. The theory of *l'art pour l'art* is suggested by the Kantian notion of self-directed purpose. One feature of a self-purposed object is that it is an end in itself, as Walter Pater would later teach all art objects are. But another feature of it is that its self-purposiveness shows itself not in any universal concepts it illustrates but in the mutual informings of its parts and wholeness, as Hans Georg Gadamer would later teach was the foundation of hermeneutical understanding.[67]

Kant's theory of beauty applies as indirectly to religion as it does to literature. Kant himself does not draw out the implications. For him, religion was a function of ethics. God was a topic that either surpassed the powers of theoretical reason or served as a postulate to practical reason in its registerings of the moral law. Insofar as beauty appears to us in the reflective judgments we make, which are always on sensual representations, and so never on God, it would never occur to Kant to deem God beautiful. And yet there are several suggestive affinities in his account of beauty between beautiful objects and God. The very resistance of God to theoretical reason's concepts is already an affinity for beauty, whose instantiation in either natural or created objects like-wise defies conceptualization. The abundance of associative thought that objects of beauty prompt, but to which they never wholly submit, resembles the stream of words that mystics generate in their attempts to describe what concepts fail to grasp. Both objects judged beautiful and God resist subordination to any ends outside of themselves, nor can they be judged as effects of prior causes. Both beautiful objects and God are unique. Finally, as entities whose purpose is themselves, they both illustrate the idea of self-causation, at least insofar as the purpose of a thing is an effect of it that figures in its cause.

Kant himself was too interested in ethics to elaborate on these hints of religion's affinities for aesthetics. At most, he connects the two indi-rectly through the medium of ethics. Insofar as religion is chiefly an emotional intensification of ethics—a performance of moral duties as if they were divine commands[68]—and beauty is a symbol of morality,[69] through the notions of self-contained purpose, freedom, and universal-ity that characterize both aesthetic judgment and the categorical imperative, religion and beauty are loosely linked. But the connection between them received much fuller and more enthusiastic endorsement at the hands of Kant's romantic and idealist successors. The early German Romantics—Novalis, Schelling, the Schlegels—accepted from Kant that religion found its ground in something outside of itself; they merely switched the foundation from ethics to aesthetics. An ambiguity in Kant's understanding of freedom allowed for that. Apart from the moral freedom that guaranteed ethics, there was the aesthetic freedom that enabled art. The Romantics simply substituted Kant's aesthetic freedom for all freedom and thereby subsumed ethics under art. To be ethical was to create unities, especially between opposites, a function that virtually defines art in the work of the early Schelling. Such expansions of art's import had bearings on nature too. One line of Romantic idealism went something like this: The beauty-constituting purposiveness without a purpose that Kant allowed objects in nature could exhibit to consciousness, could also be exhibited by nature as a whole. Kant himself would not have admitted that because he did not believe nature as a whole was a proper object of consciousness. The first step that idealism took beyond Kant was to allow that nature was indeed an object of divine consciousness, and the second step was the definitive and thought-transforming claim of idealism that nature was a necessary product of acts within divine consciousness. If nature exhibited purposiveness without a purpose, then it was an object of beauty; if it also was a necessary product of acts within divine consciousness, then it reflected that consciousness, but in the most literal way: Nature was the reflection that divine consciousness beheld of itself when it took itself for object, a startling claim that found expression in the early work of Friedrich Schelling in the following way: "The universe is formed in God as an absolute work of art and in eternal beauty."[70] Such a claim extended the suggestive consonance that Kant posited between natural objects and art objects (through their shared exhibition of purposiveness), beyond the limits he set on consciousness, and so constituted a violation of his critical idealism. But romantic idealism counts for an application of Kantian beauty to religion only if it is indeed a religion. On its own terms, it certainly was, as Hegel hinted by titling a chapter of the *Phenomenology of Spirit*, "Religion in the Form of Art."

With the collapse of idealism, the import of the Kantian idea of beauty for religion seemed to have spent itself, except that it reemerged in the twentieth century in an improbable context: the anti-Kantian, theological aesthetics of the Catholic theologian, Hans Urs von Balthasar. Balthasar's theological aim was to reappropriate for Christianity a significance of beauty that in the modern age it had lost. One goal of his massive, multivolume work, *The Glory of the Lord*, was to recapitulate what had been the importance of beauty to Christianity, in its ancient and medieval years, when it lived under the bright, philosophical sun of Plato and to recount the progressive darkening of that sun under medieval, academic scholasticism, and the alienation within the church of its great advocates of beauty, its poets (the theme of our chapter 2). As the story unfolds toward modern times, Kant appears, in the words of one commentator, as the "one who initiated the Fall from authentic unity."[71] The problem of Kant for a revival of Platonic aesthetics, whether within or outside a Christian context, is that within the Kantian framework, beauty has lost both its metaphysical status and its power to disclose knowledge of the highest truths. Where for Balthasar, quoting Dionysus the Areopagite, the spiritual import of beauty is that it moves its beholders beyond themselves, "not allowing them that are touched by it to belong to themselves,"[72] for Kant, beauty is a function of human judgment; however much it arrests the claims of self-interest, beauty remains a product of imaginings that human consciousness must own if aesthetic experience is to occur at all. "We now see the restriction to the human world of the sphere in which aesthetic utterances are possible."[73]

Nonetheless, Kant receives several pages of appreciative attention in volume five of *Glory of the Lord*, which adumbrates the fate of beauty at the hands of postmedieval metaphysics; only the aesthetic category that proves more fruitful for opening up the path to God is, once again, the sublime. Kant acknowledged his own debt to Burke[74] on the significance of the sublime, in contrast to the beautiful, and he advanced the discussion farther. Part of the reason both the beautiful and the sublime come under the rubric of aesthetics for Kant is that they both result from judgments on sensual representations. This was true for Burke as well. But, just as he did for beauty, so for the sublime, Kant freed it from overdependence on subjective emotion by defining it in terms of its relation to concepts. Both the beautiful and the sublime surpassed concepts, but from different directions: beauty, from below, by refusing any overlay of conceptual determination; the sublime, from above, by surpassing the power of concepts to contain it. Kant himself links the sublime's overpowerment of concepts to religion, though in a way determined, predictably, by ethics. The pleasure we have in any judgment of the sublime is in our self-conscious awareness that the power of our concepts to determine sensation is surpassed. By that very awareness, we regain ascendancy over the power we ceded to sensual representations beyond our determinative control. But for Kant, this awareness mirrors in the aesthetic realm what we habitually know in the moral realm through the ascendancy of our determinative practical reason over our recalcitrant sensual life. And so here too the sublime becomes a kind of symbol of ethics and so, by extension, of religion.

There is no escaping that for Kant "sublimity is contained not in any thing in nature, but only in our mind."[75] And yet, by the indirect link to ethics, Balthasar can celebrate in Kant what even critical idealism retains of the direct experience we can have of the sacred, for the ascendancy we gain through our practical reason over sensuality we do so precisely through our freedom. And it is just this freedom which, along with the starry heavens, in all of their sublimity, drew from Kant those feelings of awe he registered in the passage perhaps most often quoted from his works from the conclusion of the *Critique of Practical Reason*. And yet Balthasar uncovered a passage still more redolent of religious feeling from one of Kant's least known works, *Dispute among the University's Schools*. In the passage from that work that Balthasar cites at length, Kant celebrates "our capacity to make the great sacrifice of our sensual nature to morality," by which we demonstrate "the predominance of the supersensual man in us over the sensual man," which is in itself so admirable that "they are to be forgiven who construe this supersensual element in us as on account of its incomprehensibility and its practical nature, to be supernatural."[76] Balthasar senses more than generic religious feeling in these assertions; they retain "a Christian sensorium which, however concealed, still has knowledge of the cross,"[77] high praise indeed from a Christian theologian foraging for links of beauty to God within a philosophical tradition increasingly bereft of them. And now it is as though Balthasar forgives Kant for closing down the access to God beauty formerly supplied, since that beauty still glimmered in the sublimity that Kant reverenced in humanity. Because that sublimity would soon disappear in the monisms of Kant's idealist successors, and with it all sense of the divine transcendence so critical to Christianity, Balthasar's tone toward him is tender. Balthasar holds Kant in what for any Christian theologian can only be that twilight moment within the history of philosophy, just before Christianity disappears into idealism.

Balthasar's recovery of the sublime within Kant points to more than a place within one Christian thinker's theological aesthetics; it reflects what for some critics has become the dominant tone of the modern and postmodern aesthetic sensibility. "In modernity . . . there is no beauty. Instead there is the sublime."[78] It is fitting that this comment, from philosopher John Milbank, comes just a few paragraphs after he has appreciatively cited Balthasar. If the sublime is what over-whelms our conceptual capabilities, rather than what merely playfully and tantalizingly eludes their grasp, then "beauty" in the modern world, seeking to link religion and literature, will show forth most com-pellingly in those literary and religious phenomena that disturb and trouble our reason. Kierkegaard, who opened this chapter by withhold-ing beauty from religion, may, despite himself, now present himself, in his capacity as both novelist and theologian, as "the great forerunner of sublime discourse" in twentieth-century religion and literature.[79] But can the sublimity of stories by such twentieth-century artists as Kafka or Flannery O'Connor have anything to do with the rise of fundamen-talisms, documented so assiduously in a recent five-volume work?[80] We tremble to think so.

Let us close on a happier note that still sounds out to us from ancient Greece: the *Iliad*'s presentation of the god Apollo. Perhaps the Romans were testifying to something definitively Greek about this god when he was allowed, alone among the major gods of the pantheon, to carry his name unchanged into their religion.[81] We already saw how much Poseidon suited Longinus's endeavor to instance the sublime within the *Iliad*. At the same time, Longinus acknowledged that by humanizing the gods, Homer effaced their sublimity.[82] Perhaps Apollo is the only god within the *Iliad* to escape that treatment. In a passage that might well count for sublime, Apollo reproves the Greek, Diomedes, for presuming to strive with a god. Apollo

who strikes from afar cried out to him in the voice of terror:
"Take care, give back, son of Tydeus, and strive no longer
to make yourself like the gods in mind, since never the same is
the breed of gods, who are immortal, and men who walk
groundling."[83]

Apollo insists on the unbridgeable divide between humanity and gods, and the presumption to cross that divide elicits the terror that in this passage evokes the sublime. But the passage is a précis of Apollo's behavior throughout the story. His epithet, "striker from afar," alludes to the arrows he shoots, which indeed brought the plague on which the epic opens, but also connotes the distance he keeps from mortals (within the confines of the *Iliad*), shrouding his acts of deliverance toward them in mists. Apollo is the great respecter of boundaries, both between himself and the mortals, and himself and the other gods. It is just this distance that enables him to image sublimity. It is only fitting that as Homer predicts but does not show, Apollo (through Paris) is the one to finally slay Achilles (22:359), that great violator of sanctioned distance.

But the other face of this god's power to destroy is his ability to heal. Within the larger context of Greek mythology, Apollo is the father of Asclepius, the god of medicine, and this attribute of his opens onto the parts of him that please. He shoots his arrows from a silver bow, as though gray, the color of his half-sister Athena's eyes, must, in association with Apollo, sparkle with the radiance of precious metal. He is the "light-born" god (4:119) "of the unshorn hair" (20:39) who charms the gods with his lyre (1:603). Homer is much more generous than Moses with attributions of beauty to deity. If Apollo is both beautiful and sublime, then it may be a revival of the Apollonian that modernity needs if, from the terrors of the sublime, it seeks a path back to beauty.[84]

Chapter 6

Religious and Aesthetic Experience

We have been considering the analogs in religion to what Kant might have called the three "moments" of art: its creation, completion (in beauty), and appreciation in the experience of spectators, listeners, or readers. In some ways, the religious analog to the last moment presents itself with greater ease and expectation of harmony, if not identity, with its aesthetic counterpart than even creation does. Religious and aesthetic experience reflect so much of themselves in each other that the task can become to differentiate definitively between them. This is especially true for thinkers in the Kantian tradition. The Copernican turn in Kant that imported into our experience of objects such significant contributions from our own determinative concepts opened up a prospect that a naïve empiricism would never have considered, of a different order of experience entirely, defined by its freedom from the operation of concepts. It is within the framework of this alternative order of experience, which for Kant was never itself a focus of serious attention, since no knowledge could occur there, that both religious and aesthetic experience could take up residence.

Kantian aesthetic experience is embedded in the Kantian theory of beauty that we have already considered. A condition of aesthetic judgment is having ceased to apply concepts to representations. The power of conceptualization is engaged, but not its realization. It is as though, in aesthetic judgment, consciousness still works to categorize, only the subsuming category of the judged representation is the representation itself. Insofar as to know a thing is to subsume it under a category larger than itself, subsuming a representation under itself simultaneously invokes and subverts the knowledge-conferring powers of consciousness. But it also opens up consciousness to a new way of seeing. A representation so seen is not an object of knowledge but an appearance of self-contained singularity.

Kant cannot offer an analogous interpretation of religious experience. For, unlike objects of aesthetic judgment, no Kantian God can ever occur in sensual intuition. Nonetheless, around the edges of the concepts that grounded the work of the Kantian Understanding, which Kant wished adequately to equip for knowing and studying the objective world, there were places where the romantically and idealistically inclined might locate a religious experience. One such place was the original synthetic unity of apperception, Kant's term for the action consciousness must perform if it is to cohere as a single stage on which conceptualizable representations may appear at all. The original synthetic unity of apperception is neither a concept nor an idea but rather an indispensable condition of knowledge. In the hands of Kant's idealist successors, it evolved into a philosophical equivalent of God. Kant himself invited that development by the very name he bestowed on this primal act of consciousness. It is *original* because it must precede all other acts of synthesizing in the Understanding. It is a synthetic *unity* because it issues in the representations of *one* consciousness. It occurs at the level of apperception (rather than of apprehension or imagination) because, among the levels of synthesis within consciousness, apperception is the most comprehensive. Kant called it "the highest principle in the whole sphere of human knowledge."[1] In its originality, unity, and subsuming comprehensiveness, the original unity of apperception already takes on traits associated with the divine. Detached as the Kantian consciousness became in the hands of its idealist inheritors from the human mind it assumed a dignity in their thought that assimilated it to the medieval philosophical God of pure action. Part of the idealist program was to demonstrate how the individual human mind could uncover its identity with that purely active consciousness, a process that, as Hegel delineates in the preface to his *Phenomenology of the Spirit*, approaches the mystical. For Hegel, the sheer exercise of thought issues ultimately in a religious experience of identity with a consciousness abstracted from and unconstricted by human finitude.

Another nonconceptual location within the Kantian system opened up the possibility of quite a different kind of religious experience. This was the noumenon. Like the original synthetic unity of apperception, the noumenon was not an object of knowledge but rather a condition of it. Insofar as Kant characterizes the data of consciousness as representations, a connotation is raised of something that is re-presented. This is the noumenon, which defines the limits of sensible intuition. As a condition of the very sensibility in which it can never appear, and so subject itself to conceptualization, the noumenon is a problematic or an indeterminate concept.[2] But it also bears a suggestively inverse relation to the idea of God—one is an idea without an object (God) and the other a sort of object without a determinate idea (the noumenon).[3] A romantically inclined successor to Kant would like to join the two, since each supplies the other's lack.

Rudolf Otto was not, presumably, a Romantic, but rather a scholar of religions. And yet the term he coined for what is known in religious experience, namely, the *numinous*, raises the specter of the old and long since sadly discredited Kantian noumenon. We cannot press the association of these two terms: Otto's *numinous* descends from the Latin *numen*, an ancient Roman term connoting the majesty of the gods. But we certainly can, and shall, press the indebtedness of Otto to Kant into the service of demonstrating the religiously evocative contours of nonconceptual experience. Religiously nonconceptual experience, as Otto understood it, could barely keep itself from spilling over into aesthetic experience. From Otto's own time (1869–1937) a younger contemporary, Clive Bell (1881–1964), whose Kantian inflected theory of aesthetic experience could hardly refrain from taking on religious qualities, rose to reciprocate the compliment. Though Bell was the younger of the two, it was his seminal work on aesthetics, entitled simply *Art*, that appeared first, in 1913, and Otto's, on religious experience (*The Idea of the Holy*), that followed shortly after, in 1917.

It is no accident that a German work on religious experience should be so tantalized by the corresponding phenomenon of aesthetic experience. Ever since Friedrich Schleiermacher championed experience, as over against doctrine or ritual, as the doorway through which enlightened, religiously skeptical Europeans could reenter the realm of religion, religious and aesthetic experience have been conjoined. It is *cultured* despisers of religion whom Schleiermacher addressed in his

seminal work *On Religion,* and in whose homes "the splendid composi-
tions of our poets" had taken the place that might formerly have been
held by Scriptures. But for Schleiermacher, this was not the end of religion but simply a new beginning for it:

> If it is true that there are sudden conversions whereby in men
> . . . the sense of the highest comes forth and surprises them by
> its splendor, I believe that more than anything else the sight of
> a great work of art can accomplish this miracle.[4]

Schleiermacher was the fountainhead for a stream of liberal thinking
about religion that combined a heightened appreciation for its experiential component with a fascination for the bridge to it that the arts
supplied. And this stream of thought also nourished Otto, who cites
Schleiermacher several times in his book. What Otto added to
Schleiermacher, among other things, was a fuller assimilation of religious experience to a Kantian-style theory of knowledge.

When Otto declares early on in his book that "Holiness—'the
holy'—is a category of interpretation and valuation peculiar to the
sphere of religion,"[5] he already speaks Kant's epistemological language.
If holiness is a category of interpretation, then, in Kantian terms, it is a
means by which humans can claim knowledge of something, in this
case, the *numen,* Otto's coinage for the nonrational aspect of what is
known in religious experience. The rational aspect of what is known
there already has a name: goodness. The problem was that, thanks to
Kant, the goodness known in religious experience had completely
usurped the place of what formerly went, in ancient languages, by the
terms *kadosh, hagios,* and *sanctus.* Having claimed all of holiness for
itself, goodness had deprived these ancient terms of any more distinctive reference. And so a new term, besides holiness, was needed to reac-
tivate our awareness that there was more to the experience of holiness
than ethics. And this is what Otto hoped *numen* could be.

With this new term, Otto has drawn our attention to an object of
knowledge within religious experience that is not reducible to goodness, but he has not further elucidated what the numen is. He cannot
further describe it in rational terms, since it is, by definition, nonrational, but he can further indicate it by the emotions it provokes in us.
And here is where the inheritance from Schleiermacher shows.
Schleiermacher had identified religious experience with a feeling of

absolute dependence. Although Otto faults that view for failing fully to specify the unique feelings that constitute religious experience, he does build on it. One of the feelings the numen provokes is an awareness of being, in contrast to it, utterly finite, a self-realization that initially frightens. At its most intense, this response moves from self-deprecia-tion to a sense of self-annihilation. In hopes of eliciting from us some measure of this experience, even while we read his words, Otto borrows from the Latin, and its emotional overtones of ancient and medieval sanctity, to name the aspect of the numen that provokes this response, the *mysterium tremendum*. At the same time, this that appears so fully to constrict us also fascinates and attracts us, leading us on "to the strangest excitements, to intoxicated frenzy, to transport, and to ecstasy."[6] This response is to another aspect of the numen which, from the same motives as before, Otto names with a Latin participle, *fasci-nans*. The link between these two opposite reactions to the one *mys-terium tremendum et fascinans* is not so improbable as first appears. That which shows us our borders in finitude may constrict us, but it also defines us. Finitude and definition are etymological cousins. To be given our definition is to be shown who we are. And, if we are to believe the Delphic Oracle and Freud, to know who we are is the foundation for any real happiness we can have. There remains only to state more directly about the numen what is already implied by its nonrational status, that in the mystery it is to our reason, it draws from us "blank wonder, an astonishment that strikes us dumb," what Otto calls, follow-ing his preference for the religious evocations of Latin, *stupor*.[7]

From the start, Otto notes resemblances between the categories of the holy and the beautiful. Both elude "apprehension in terms of con-cepts."[8] Unsurprisingly, Otto finds more in the sublime than in the restrictedly beautiful that corresponds to the holy: both frighten us by overwhelming our conceptual capabilities, while simultaneously ener-gizing and attracting us. If the similarities were too great, though, reli-gion would risk losing to aesthetics an identity of its own that it had already once lost, under Kant's oversight, to ethics. This was not the fate that Schleiermacher had envisioned for religion, nor is it what Otto hoped for it. To protect the distinctiveness of religious experience, Otto advanced his own "law of the association of feelings." A philo-sophical tradition of predictable association of sensations was at least as old as Hume, who had explained causation, which we never directly beheld, as a constant conjunction of sense impressions. Feelings, too,

that resembled each other could evoke each other. It was only important to distinguish emotional suggestibility from transformability: one
emotion that suggests another can provoke the other into existence
alongside it, or it can cease and give way to it, but not change into it. If
certain emotions exist in such close proximity to each other that each
appears to be the other, then it may be because the objects that provoke
them are themselves bound together by a "true inward affinity and
cohesion."⁹ This is precisely the case with the relationship between the
rational and nonrational elements within the holy: the good and the
numinous. To explain the distinctive affinity between them, Otto borrows the Kantian idea of schematization, the process whereby concepts
are connected to the specific sensations they are most suited to interpret. Schematization is a binary relationship of connection between
elements within two different levels of consciousness by which
together they yield knowledge. By extension, if the moral and the
religious demarcate two different levels of consciousness, then a conjunction between them yielding knowledge of the holy also is a
schematization. But if the numen and goodness are schematized in an
experience of a morally religious holiness, then why should not the
numen and the sublime be schematized in an experience of an aesthetically religious holiness? The schematization allows for religious and
aesthetic experience to partner over a fundamental difference of category, which is never lost, between them. In light of the close resemblances between the religious and the sublime, this distinction of
category between emotions was important for Otto to maintain. For
certain kinds of sublime art—especially, in Otto's view, Asian landscapes depicting vast, empty spaces, or darkness juxtaposed to glim-
mering light in some Western art—so readily evoke, alongside the
feelings of the sublime, the feelings of the numinous, that the two are
easily confounded. As a result of maintaining the distinction, it was
possible for Otto to say, with Schleiermacher, that a distinctly aesthetic
experience can mediate, without desacralizing, a religious one.

Beginning from an analysis of aesthetic experience, Clive Bell
arrives at a similar conclusion, but the philosophical tradition in which
he places himself is English, not German, and therefore not directly
contextualized by Kant's Copernican revolution in thought. Bell
invokes a rendition of British empiricism, just finding voice in his own
day, which defined itself over against German idealism. A leading proponent of this new realism was the Cambridge philosopher G. E.

Moore. It was especially Moore's ethical theory that Bell found so fruitful for aesthetics. Moore did for goodness what Otto did for holiness, namely, to demarcate it as a unique idea irreducible to all others. Bell borrowed that status for his own concept of beauty, which he defined as significant form in visible objects. This coinage of Bell's for beauty, "significant form," like Otto's for holiness, was necessary in order to situate what he intended to refer to in a category of its own, unmistakable for any other. He was not interested, for example, in natural objects deemed beautiful for no other reason than the pleasurable emotions they provoked. Significant form enjoyed with the numinous the rank of an object of knowledge, but unlike the numen, it acquired that rank through being an objective feature of beautiful things situated in an empiricist universe, rather than by being interpreted through an a priori, knowledge-conferring category in a Kantian universe.

But Bell's coinage posed the same difficulty Otto's did: if significant form is irreducible to any other concepts, then by what other concepts can we further define it? Bell's solution resembles Otto's: We look to the distinctive emotion that significant form provokes in us when we behold it. And this emotion is simply aesthetic emotion, a feeling Bell trusts all of us to recognize in ourselves when we feel it. But once again, like Otto, to help us recognize it, he offers a phenomenological analysis of it, though much sketchier than Otto's. Aesthetic emotion exhibits two key features in tandem: ecstasy and detachment. The two features are related, at least to the extent that *ecstasis*, understood as a standing outside, positions whoever feels it apart and in "complete detachment from the concerns of life."[10]

Another way the detachment within aesthetic experience appears is in relation to the object perceived. Like the object of aesthetic judgment in Kant, it shows itself as an end in itself, without exploitable uses toward other goals. On the one hand, significant form begins to sound like another way of describing how representations appear within Kantian aesthetic judgment. It is not the concept a representation might instance that gives it significant form but features discernible within its own self-relationship; in the case of visual objects, their "lines and colours combined in a particular way, certain forms and relations of forms."[11] Bell did not leave his readers to wonder what he meant. An enthusiastic proponent of postimpressionist painting, he cited Cezanne as one of the great artists of significant form, which shows in the attention drawn in his paintings to the abstract relationship between shapes and colors. As one art critic observes, Cezanne wanted "to uncover the permanent qualities beneath the accidents of appearance."[12] If Kant was not so specific about the way in which self-purposed representations showed themselves to our consciousness, then that need not have been because he would have disagreed with Bell but only because he was not, like Bell, an art critic. But Kantian thought shows through Bell in another way too. Significant form is what viewers behold in artworks, but the same form appears under a different name at the point of the artwork's genesis, when the artist is inspired by a vision of objects around him, not in their categorial placement, but in their "pure form."[13] If significant form is just pure form, rendered more obvious in an artwork, then it begins to resemble one of the great desiderata of Kantian epistemology, a reason so detached from content that its pure operations become manifest. It is the same connotation of impurity that hangs over content, as opposed to form, in both Kant and Bell.

In the preface to his book, Bell praises his friend Roger Fry's *Essay in Aesthetics* by calling it "the most helpful contribution to the science that has been made since the days of Kant,"[14] a compliment, too, to the enduring relevance of Kant's own thought. But if a writer's real influence shows in those places where his ideas, while functioning, go uncredited, then we must look elsewhere in Bell for the full import of Kant on his thinking. This occurs, unsurprisingly, in the chapter "The Metaphysical Hypothesis," where Bell advances the provocative claim that what lies behind the significance of significant form is "what philosophers used to call 'the thing in itself.'"[15] Bell need not have been so circumspect; the philosopher who preeminently theorized about the thing in itself was Kant. And the thing in itself was simply the noumenon that we have already encountered, as one of the places within Kant's epistemology where he might have cleared space for nonconceptual, religious experience. Bell does not miss the religious suggestiveness of the noumenon. For the thing in itself, which significant form reveals, is also "ultimate reality," "essential reality," "the God in everything."[16] It is just that, as over against Kant, and in agreement with his idealist successors, Bell allows that this ultimate reality may, through art, come into our experience.

When it does, we respond ecstatically. But is this a religious or an aesthetic ecstasy? Bell is less concerned than Otto was to distinguish between these two kinds of experience. Having already established the integrity of aesthetic experience, Bell's interest in its religious counterpart was more as trapping. On the one hand, he argues, much as Otto did, for a "family alliance" between the two, but on the other, he conflates them, and happily joins the ranks of those Romantic precursors of his who took art for a religion in itself, for "art is a religion," indeed, the only one to "escape the binding weeds of dogma." Otto, who was committed to the singular integrity of religious experience, would take issue with that conflation, but not with the ultimate issue of it, with which he would agree, that art "is a means to states of mind as holy as any that men are capable of experiencing."[17]

And yet, the intimate analogy both Otto and Bell make between religious and aesthetic experience, each from his own side of chief interest, suffers from a major lacuna; there is scant role in either's aesthetic for literature. Both are speaking chiefly of visual art (and to some extent of music). Otto confines to an appendix some reflections on "the numinous in poetry, hymn, and liturgy," but his examples are all from settings explicitly religious from the start: scripture (the Bhagavad Gita), German hymnody, Jewish High Holy Day ritual. It fell to Otto's English book translator, John Harvey, to exemplify the category Otto left empty, of numinous *secular* poetry, with excerpts from, unsurprisingly, the poets Coleridge, Blake, and Wordsworth. The challenge of the numinous for literature is in the medium of words. To the extent that these are signifiers, they impose a distance between what they signify and the reader or listener. And if it is with the signified, rather than the signifier, that the numen resides, then in the very act of indicating it they are simultaneously distancing it. This may be why Otto's own appendix offers so little commentary on the passages he so fully cites from the Bhagavad Gita, as though a reader of interpretive words is distanced still further from what the interpreted words themselves signify. And it is probably for this reason also that immediately after his remarks on the numinous in religious poetry, Otto places an appendix on word sounds that already carry the numinous in them, regardless of what they might signify. This appendix is a small exercise in religious onomatopoeia. The numinosity that such sounds as the Hindu mantra *Om* signify is in their very utterance. But if, to affect us with a maximal impression of the numinous, language must restrict itself to bare syllables, then it is scarcely functioning anymore as literature.

For Bell, the problem of literature is even more explicit. To approach poetry without regard for the impurifying content of its words, and with attention solely to its sounds, must greatly reduce its effect, though it is just this approach that Bell commends to us when he says, "In great poetry it is the formal music that makes the miracle."[18] But insofar as the music of poetry must always pale beside the music of music, literature, within the spectrum of arts, cannot but disappoint, so much so that Bell concedes, "Literature is never pure art."[19] But surely no brother-in-law of Virginia Woolf could long hold to such a claim. And in fact Bell has exceptional praise for two poets, Dante and Milton: Milton, for the service he offers his readers of "getting himself out of one world and into another,"[20] and Dante, for his tribute to the powers of the imagination—"O quick and forgetive power! that sometimes dost so rob us of ourselves, we take no mark."[21] Both poets, Bell implies, had the power of eliciting from their readers that definitive feature of aesthetic emotion: standing outside of themselves, or ecstasy.

Bell is a little like Plato, regretfully banishing literature from an ideal state of the arts. If Otto had his English translator to supply the instances of numinous secular poetry that he omitted from his book, then who might perform for Bell the comparable service of sighting within literature's own domain a wider view of the heights of religio-aesthetic emotion it has provoked? One who might have made good the gap in Bell, had he lived to read *Art*, was Oscar Wilde. Though Wilde's *The Critic As Artist* (first published in 1891) preceded Bell's *Art* by twenty-three years, its formalist tendencies nicely complement the later work. The two books even share a warm appreciation of the postimpressionists.[22] With his pronouncement "Form is everything,"[23] Wilde already allies with Bell. And though he does not mean by form what Bell does—relationships between shapes and colors—what he does mean comes as close to a literary analog for it as language may allow. Form, for Wilde, is language that impresses emotions on its readers (rather than expresses the emotions of its writers). Literary language creates emotion in the very reception of itself. By emotion, Wilde does not mean what Bell means by aesthetic emotion but the broad range of emotions that come to all humans in life. Emotion, in this more common sense, belongs to the content of the words impressing them, but it is a content that logically succeeds, rather than precedes, the utterance of the words. This is the import of Wilde's claim, that language, as form, impresses rather than expresses emotion. The words are prior, not posterior, to their meanings, and in that they sense gain a measure of independence from their content. It is as though Wilde finds in the medium that words are between what they signify and whoever reads them, room for them to behave in a way similar to Bell's significant form: They are themselves sheer abstractions, self-contained detachments from life, but with immense power over life, especially its emotions.[24] Form is everything, in that there is no emotion that language cannot impress on the receptive reader. And because of that, literature too provokes its ecstasies: "It can teach us to escape from experience,"[25] says Wilde, in anticipation of Bell's "Art and religion are two roads by which men escape from circumstance to ecstasy."[26] To the extent that Wilde persuades, he invites back into the kingdom of art a literature that Bell's formalism had worked to exclude from it and so positions literature, along with the other arts, to be the religion Bell wants them all to be. At the same time, if Wilde is right about literary language, then he also provides a way for secular poetry to be more patently numinous than Otto acknowledged it could be. For if Wilde has really cleared literary language of sullying content, then he may have opened up in it a pure space in which the concept-defying numen can reside. The numen need no longer confine itself to religiously onomatopoeic syllables but may directly inhabit the full extent of poems composed by Blake, Coleridge, and Wordsworth.

Having now, thanks to Oscar Wilde, rendered these religio-aesthetic reflections from Otto and Bell relevant to literature, let us explore more deeply the analogs between the emotional responses to the numen, on the one hand, and to significant form, on the other. One of these has just shown itself in the juxtaposed remarks of Wilde and Bell: the response of ecstasy. Otto, for his part, associated this emotional response to the numen with that feature of it that fascinates us: the *mysterium tremendum et fascinans*. For Otto, who also was a scholar of mysticism, ecstasy at its religious heights is mystical rapture, even trance, "a beatitude beyond compare."[27] If by entrancing the mystic, God also enters him, then in the same movement the mystic is expelled outside of himself and made ecstatic. The soul may leave the body, or, more commonly, may cease to receive impressions through the bodily senses but rather through the medium of an inner consciousness fixed directly on the divine, such as Dante himself described in the completion of those verses we only began to quote earlier:

> O quick and forgetive power! that sometimes dost
>   So rob us of ourselves, we take no mark
>   Though round about us thousand trumpets clang;

What moves thee, if the senses stir not? Light
> moves thee from heaven, spontaneous, self-informed.
> or, likelier, gliding down with swift illapse by will divine.[28]

English philosopher John Locke called it "dreaming with our eyes open,"[29] but in its most literal meaning, it is simply "standing elsewhere."[30] Our common expression, to be "beside oneself," captures a shade of this meaning and points to the significance of the location from which we regard ourselves: for when we *under*stand ourselves, we know ourselves; when we stand *beside* ourselves, we are expelled from understanding to a frame of mind that ranges over "bewilderment, insanity, seizure, terror."[31]

As Dante already begins to prove, literature loves to thematize ecstasy. The dramatic potentials of ecstatic states are rich indeed. In chapter 1, we had two examples in the fictional ecstasies of Prince Myshkin and Eustace Cherrington. But what does this quality mean to religion on its own terms? The range of exemplars of ecstasy within the frameworks of Judaism, Christianity, and Platonism is so wide that we have but to choose one among them to enter more deeply into this side of the numinous experience. Socrates himself exhibits something akin to ecstasy when he stops someplace "in a fit of abstraction . . . losing himself without any reason"[32] and remaining there unresponsive to his friends. But the full-throttled language of ecstasy belongs for Plato more to the poet's world than the philosopher's; only in some of his Neoplatonic descendants, such as Philo, do we find an approved philosophico-religious experience described in openly ecstatic terms.[33] But since Plato does allow to the Greek prophet, who foretells the future, "an inspired madness,"[34] let us follow that hint in another direction, toward that treasure trove of prophecy we have in the Bible. Otto, too, points us there, when, as evidence of religious experience in the lives of the Old Testament writers, he cites the ecstasies of the prophet Ezekiel.

Biblical prophecy provides a hospitable home for ecstatic experience, for the premise of the great written prophets is that, while functioning as mouthpieces for God, they are exiled from their own identities. This comes most to the fore at their callings, for few could happily accept the office that fell to the biblical prophets, of critiquing their counterparts in the political realm, the kings. This is so true that one of them, Amos, declares, "I am no prophet, nor a prophet's son, but I am a herdsman," whom God took from his accustomed place and commanded to prophesy (Amos 7:14–15). If Amos prophesies, it is from a place outside of his own identity. As one scholar explains about the prophetic experience of calling, it "appears to have been marked by a degree of ecstatic rapture not subsequently repeated. . . . The significant thing is that this original experience introduces the prophet into a new, standing relationship to his God."[35] The mention of "standing" speaks directly to the meaning of ecstasy. Part of what the prophet experiences in his new place of standing is a melding of what the senses usually quite clearly distinguish between, such as sights and sounds. Prophets typically hear the words they are given to speak, but sometimes they also see them (Isa. 2:1), or else the words come to them in a vision without explicit pictures (Isa. 1:1).

One of the most striking instances of visionary ecstasis within the prophets is Ezekiel, who opens his book with this dramatic announcement: "In the thirtieth year, in the fourth month, on the fifth day of the month . . . the heavens were opened and I saw visions of God" (Ez. 1:1), a rarity within Hebrew scripture. The vision presented in the first chapter of Ezekiel provoked centuries of fascinated reflection within Judaism, which built upon it a tradition of pictorial mysticism. The vision occurs not just within chapter 1 of the text but later on, twice, within transports that underscore, as if this were not already clear, that Ezekiel practiced ecstasy in its most literal sense: "The Spirit lifted me up between heaven and earth and brought me in visions of God to Jerusalem" (Ez. 8:3), first to behold the idolatrous corruptions of the contemporaneous Temple cult and later to the vision of a purified future cult.

It is notoriously difficult to summarize the vision. This in itself points to its numinous quality, which reduces language speakers to silence and stupor. Ezekiel does of course attempt a description, but in highly qualified ways. What he sees are appearances of likenesses to such ordinary things as wheels, faces, and fire. Otto himself faults the vision for its "excessive fantasy and imagination,"[36] which corrupts the purity of the sensed numen. But the profusion of images also can be interpreted more according to their form than their content, as emphatic similes. The whole of the vision is an "appearance of the likeness of the glory of the Lord" (Ez. 1:29), which, if the glory of the Lord is itself an appearance, positions the experience at a point at least three stages removed from the actuality of God. Ecstatic prophetic visions are intermediaries that hover at some distance from what they signify and therefore invite interpretation. Ezekiel's vision proved most fruitful in that regard, since a lasting inheritance from it was, besides Jewish mysticism, the fourfold typology of man-ox-lion-eagle that would later find application in the iconography of the Christian evangelists.

Ezekiel's immediate reaction to the vision is to fall on his face before it (Ez. 1:28). This suggests a response more to the *tremendum* within the numen than the *fascinans*. But it also points to an important feature of prophetic ecstasy, that it is not necessarily joyful. On the contrary, insofar as the prophet's message is a judgment, it is painful to deliver. Ezekiel's own transport takes him "in bitterness" to the Israelites in exile (Ez. 3:14). And from a purely psychological standpoint, the fits of paralysis and convulsion (Ez. 3:15.25, 12:18) that Ezekiel undergoes in his ecstasies are hardly pleasant. But then ecstasy is not an end in itself for the prophets but rather a means of clearing a path through them for the divine message to flow.

It is not just Jewish mysticism that built on a prophetic vision; according to some analyses, mysticism is the natural successor and interiorization of prophecy. How does the presentation of ecstasy change over the course of that succession? We owe to art what is perhaps the best-known image of mystical ecstasy, Bernini's sculpture of St. Teresa, in the chapel of St. Maria della Vittoria in Rome. The sculpture is based on a passage from Teresa's autobiography in which she describes a vision that she repeatedly has of "an angel in bodily form," who held "a long golden spear," with which "he seemed to pierce my heart."[37] The image of the ecstasy comes from the depth of the piercing, "so that it penetrated to my entrails. When he drew it out, I thought he was drawing them out with it and he left me completely afire with a great love of God."[38] (In a less graphic image from the same book, she describes the divinely enraptured soul as "not in itself at all, but on the roof of its own house."[39])

One way Teresa's ecstasy is more internally rich than Ezekiel's is in its emotional content: it involves the element of attraction toward (love for) the numen that Otto associated with the *mysterium fascinans* and a "sweetness" "so excessive . . . that one can never wish to lose it."[40] Another way is that, within the larger corpus of Teresa's writing, it is contextualized by a subtle, psychologically sophisticated distinction between the intellect and the imagination. Teresa did not just experience ecstasies, she analyzed them so that she could teach about them to her spiritual charges. One of the distinctions she makes is between imaginary and intellectual visions. In both, the immediate stimulant is God, but in the one case it is pictures of things we perceive and in the other intensified ideas we have. It was the medieval, Neoplatonic tradition that underlay the notion that an intensification of ideas could constitute a *vision*. (The Platonic perception of the Good was an intellectual vision, experienced with the eye of the soul.) Where the data the prophets conflated in their visions were sensory—the seen and the heard—what Teresa conflated in her visions were inner operations of mind.

The vision of the angel can illustrate. It proceeds from imaginary pictures to thoughts. What Teresa first beholds is the angel. He is a simple picture of the imagination—"not tall, but short, and very beautiful," and in his hand "I saw a long, golden spear." But suddenly the spear tip loses its immediate presentation to consciousness, for there "I *seemed* to see a point of fire."[41] The piercing, too, is a *seeming*, and by the time the spear is withdrawn, the extraction of the entrails is *thought*. In the progression within the vision from sensory data to a seeming of data to thought, Teresa traces a movement within consciousness from imagination to intellect. The sculpture cannot show that passage, but the later poem by Richard Crashaw, *Hymn to the Name and Honor of the Admirable Saint Teresa*, can indicate it. What, the poet asks, does Teresa experience in her deathlike ecstasy? "O what? Ask not the tongues of men. Angels cannot tell."[42] In the felt union with God, images fail, and we are returned to the stupor that comes in response to the *mysterium tremendum*.

But Teresa joins the prophets in the evaluation of these ecstasies that they imply and that she explicitly states, that they have no point but to further "the birth of good works, good works." To think of the ecstasies as "for the sake of giving delight to these souls" who receive them would be "serious error." Of themselves, the ecstatic states could even be a nuisance for the interruptions they made in Teresa's demanding work, administering a string of Carmelite convents. Ecstasies should come unsought, "while the soul is heedless of any thought about such a favor being granted it." Ones that present themselves as ends in themselves are more devilish than divine. Here are the marks of a divine rapture: a heightened sense of God's majesty and of one's own lowliness. That is, from Teresa's perspective, interpreted through Otto, the response in ecstatic attraction to the numen must be balanced by the response in dread.[43]

It is just here that aesthetic ecstasy, as interpreted by Bell and Wilde, departs from its religious counterpart, for otherwise the two have much in common. Aesthetic ecstasy also is founded on a perception of reality at its depths, where significant form resides, bordering, as we saw, on the Kantian noumenon. To perceive a thing as it is in itself arouses "a profounder and more thrilling emotion than ever we felt for [things] as means." It *moves* us, not only emotionally but epistemologically, to a place outside our customary way of viewing things. The experience is "unearthly," "a little out of this world," and, in an echo of Teresa's own remark about the rooftop, "outside and above life." "The appreciation of art is certainly a means to ecstasy," he summarily pronounces.[44] Unlike the prophets and St. Teresa, Bell need not invoke imaginary or intellectual visions for his ecstasies, because the objects of his aesthetic ecstasies are already visual realities. Perception within aesthetic ecstasy resembles vision within religious ecstasy in that what is experienced belongs to a different order of perception or vision than we ordinarily have. But just here we confront the beginning of significant difference between the two types of ecstasies, for visionary ecstasy within religion involves a conflation of ordinarily distinguished data, a confusion across orders of experience or consciousness. The vision is several stages removed from the reality it signifies. In contrast, the ecstasy within aesthetic experience, as Bell describes it, results from a direct knowledge of what is signified, namely, significant form. The perception of this is a clarification of sensation, not a conflation between sensory orders, all of which culminates in the fork in the road of ecstasy that confronts us here, as Teresa diminishes the importance of these experiences, and Bell rhapsodically commends them. He knows the religious critique and rejects it. The aesthetic experience may not inspire good works, but

> He who can withdraw into the world of ecstasy will know what to think of circumstance. He who goes daily into the world of aesthetic emotion returns to the world of human affairs equipped to face it courageously and even a little contemptuously. . . . He need not on that account become unsympathetic or even inhuman. . . . He may learn in another world to doubt the extreme importance of this. . . . What he loses in philanthropy he may gain in magnanimity.[45]

It is an irony perhaps to find this otherworldly art critic in disagreement with the ultimately this-worldly nun on the import of ecstasy, for
both Wilde and Bell want to claim the mystics for their friends.[46] Perhaps it is a matter of perspective. Ecstasy is not the only feature
common to religious and aesthetic experience. Teresa's caution on
ecstasy was that it had to be linked to humility. But Bell would agree.
"Those who achieve ecstasy are those who have freed themselves from
the arrogance of humanity. He who would feel the significance of art
must make himself humble before it."[47] Otto would take both comments as evidence for the kind of emotion the *tremendum* provokes.
Self-depreciation, he told us, was an emotional register of the numen's
presence, intensifying, as the religious experience does, toward a sense
of self-annihilation. It is not so much the self as such that is annihilated
but its self-referential interests. With that reformulation of the meaning of humility, religion excites in aesthetics a sympathetic tremor, for
from deep within its own history, aesthetics, too, values this quality,
which it names "disinterest."

Disinterest is a species of detachment such as we have already
encountered in Bell. It is detachment from self-interested desire. Like
ecstasy, it too receives thematizations in literature. Tolstoy's Varenka
(cited in chapter 1) illustrates the quality and perhaps Ralph Touchett
from Henry James's *Portrait of a Lady*. As a trait of fictional characters,
disinterest will return to us in the final chapter on saintliness, but the
appreciation of literature as such already invokes a long tradition of
envalued disinterest. Though the concept figures as early in the history
of modern aesthetics as the philosophy of Lord Shaftesbury, it was
Kant who provided, by his transcendental philosophy, an optimal context for explicating it. Insofar as anything whose existence pleases us
becomes something we desire, a space opens up for desireless pleasure
in a thing whose success or failure at existing escapes our notice. But
this is just what happens when, in our aesthetic judgments, we suspend
the operation of conceptual categories, of which existence is one. An
object experienced as beautiful sheds its objective status and occupies a
space outside the distinction between existence and nonexistence. In
Kantian terms, it is sheer representation, not in the sense of mediating
a noumenal object to us but in the sense of re-presenting itself to us
outside the context of objective reality. So situated, whatever pleasure it
excites in us is now divorced from its existence and so, by extension,

from desire, which cannot hook onto an object of attention that it cannot wish to exist. Kant, with characteristic attention to presuppositions, opens up a space in which self-interested desire does not merely fail to exist but, from want of nourishment, necessarily cannot exist. Purity, a concept with which Kant was virtually obsessed, now receives an aesthetic counterpart to the theoretical and moral expressions it attains in the other critiques. If theoretical reason is pure in its operations apart from contingent representations, and practical reason is pure in its freedom from natural impulses toward pleasure and pain, then aesthetic judgment is pure in its indifference to desire. Since Kant's day, disinterest has become a nearly textbook condition of what is sometimes called the "aesthetic attitude."[48]

Suppose now from this location in our aesthetic framework we cast an anchor back toward the religious one and see where it most naturally lands. If our anchor implants in the ancient religious world, then it probably will not be in the Bible. The Bible is too passionately concerned about our salvation or redemption to accommodate disinterest as Kant presents it. And it too much locates that salvation in a system of reward and punishment to be able to commend an attitude that is so wholly blind to issues of cause and effect. What the Bible does recommend is laying aside self-interest for the sake of God's commands. And it tells stories and excites actions that do model very dramatic self-disregard. An example is from 2 Maccabees, which narrates a paradigmatic case of martyrdom. Seven brothers and their mother fall prey, successively, to the cruel torments of the Seleucid king, for "we are ready to die rather than transgress the laws of our fathers" (2 Macc. 7:2). But the disregard here is less for themselves than for their this-worldly fate, for, "the King of the universe will raise us up to an everlasting renewal of life, because we have died for his laws" (2 Macc. 7:9). Christ, too, enjoins a radical detachment from our self-interest in this world, represented by wealth, in the story of the rich man seeking eternal life (Matt. 19). But here, too, "everyone who has left houses or brothers or sisters . . . for my name's sake, will receive a hundredfold" in the next life (Matt. 19:29). Perhaps Bell had this story in mind when, in *Art*, he defended the religiosity of starving artists who allow their wives and children to starve too.

But just as Teresa obliged us with an account of religious ecstasy, so another mystic, this time Meister Eckhart, takes up the cause of disinterest. One of his sermons is devoted to this very topic. In Eckhart's hands, the self-disregard that disinterest implies becomes absolute. This he expresses most dramatically by allowing that the disinterested can accept "all the pain of hell, purgatory and the world," if God so will.[49] But a subtler account builds on the Magnificat of Mary. Eckhart wonders why Mary calls attention in her famous song to her humility rather than to the disinterest she also must have had, and he explains that the logic of disinterest blocks any self-reference to it, for it evaporates under the gaze of self-consciousness in a way that humility need not. That mystical disinterest resists self-consciousness is already an affinity with aesthetic disinterest, but there are others. Both kinds of disinterest draw to themselves the vocabulary of purity, in Eckhart's case because of the divine presence that fills the void left by detachment from objects. Both create sanctuaries of objectlessness within the world of empirical objects. The disregard for existence within Kantian disinterest finds its echo in Eckhart's interpretation of Christ's ascension, after his resurrection, that it was necessary to break the disciples' attachment to his enworlded presence.[50] Some interpreters feel that there is enough similarity between mystical disinterest in Eckhart and aesthetic disinterest in Kant to locate them along a religio-aesthetic continuum in the history of ideas.[51]

Still, Eckhart's mysticism dramatically and paradoxically reformulates the context of disinterest, for now disinterest, which from an aesthetic point of view inhibits all concern with exterior ends, itself becomes directed toward an end, namely, union with God. This really is the point of it. God, who is himself disinterested, moves to fill those spaces of disinterest that humans create within themselves. Eckhart says of disinterest what Kant would never say, that it quickens desire— desire for God. And now we are back in Otto's domain. We recognize in Eckhart what Otto told us results from the experience of the tremendum, namely, self-diminishment, which shows here in Eckhart's claim for disinterest that it "comes so near to zero that nothing may intervene," or that "pure disinterest is empty nothingness."[52] It is just this personal nothingness that creates an opening for divine presence, but aesthetic experience does not move to unite with whatever has excited it. Insofar as our aesthetic attention is directed toward a sublime object, distance is absolutely necessary.

At just this juncture, we may begin to feel morally troubled by both kinds of disinterest, for a condition of the mystic's desired union with God is distance from God's creatures. Eckhart's first definition of

disinterest is detachment from creatures, because it ranks higher in
Eckhart's scale of values than humility. "The less one pays attention to
the creature things, the more the Creator pursues him."[53] We seem
back in that troubling domain of Abraham and Isaac, as interpreted by
Kierkegaard. Not simply the religious and aesthetic but the religious
and ethical are opposed. Maximal relation with God entails diminished
relations with humans.

Eckhart understands our moral distress and is ready with an answer
to it: We are in fact two people—"a person is not one, but two"—an
"outward man" and an "inner man."[54] The one is sensual and the other
spiritual. The five senses are the "agents" that the outward person uses
to communicate with the sensual world. The inner one only wants to
unite with God. Moral commandments do indeed address us, but only
our outward person, while the inner one remains disinterested and
detached. In especially intense mystical states, Eckhart believes that the
outward senses shut down completely, as Dante suggested they do in
flights of fantasy. But even in such a state we maintain the impressions
of the outside world we need to behave altruistically, because God
implants them directly on our mind.

This religious defense of disinterest against a perceived moral critique of it may not sufficiently credit the role of inward intentions in
outward acts, but it does invite from aesthetics an unexpected support
in the idea of allegory. On Eckhart's analysis we become dual in our
being, like a story read allegorically, with both material and spiritual
meanings. Aestheticians in Bell's camp fare even worse under the moral
critique, for there is no pretense that the aesthetic experience, in its
ecstatic detachment from worldly matters, allows for any remainder of
attention, however shallow or merely outward, to extend toward our
neighbor's need. Instead, it is the regrettable transience of aesthetic
experience that opens up a space for moral acts to occur, as though in its
afterglow, for even the memory of the encounter with beauty is powerful enough to so inhibit our bad tempers that we become generous in
our dealings with others. But on either analysis of disinterest, Eckhart's
or Bell's, the moral act takes second place to an inwardly experienced
height, whether mystical or aesthetic, which may move us to ask: Is that
where ethics belongs in its relation to religion and literature?

Chapter 7

Ethics

The locus classicus for the debate between religion and ethics, over which is more fundamental, is Plato's dialogue *Euthyphro*. Here Plato speaks to us less as the founder of a religious sensibility than as a philosopher. We assume that God loves the good. But does he love it because it is good, or is it good because he loves it? If the first, then God is limited by goodness; if the second, then the seeming self-sufficiency of our moral sense is false and, by consequence, such moral objections to divine behavior as have been raised (by Abraham, by Job) become senseless.

At the opening of the dialogue, Socrates and Euthyphro meet by chance at the steps of the chief archon, who oversaw public sacrifice and judicial cases involving the state religion. Socrates, charged with impiety, is there to submit to a preliminary inquiry. He explains that the charge has three parts: that he invents new gods, denies old gods, and corrupts youth. The ethical nature of the last charge points out how broadly inclusive the charge of impiety was. The scope of piety broadens still further in light of Euthyphro's reason for visiting the archon, to make his case against a seeming murderer. Murder, which we would judge a moral offense, was an impiety in the sense that the blood of the murdered religiously polluted the whole city. What complicates the case and introduces a competing value within piety is that the person Euthyphro is charging is his own father. These conflicts within the

157

value of piety set the stage for the reigning question of this dialogue: What is piety?

The question never receives an answer. But in the process of pursuing one, the dialogue indirectly accomplishes another aim, of teasing out a distinction between the hitherto conflated values of religion and ethics. Socrates hopes that if he can find out what piety truly is, then he will have a means of judging between conflicting standards of it. But that probing, openly investigative stance toward piety is already itself an affirmation of moral values distinct from religious ones, for the questioning stance is motivated by human reason, not piety. As Socrates says in the *Apology*, such wisdom as he claims is what "may perhaps be attained by man" rather than "a superhuman wisdom."[1] But a humanly attained wisdom about how we should behave already indicates the philosophical subdiscipline of ethics. Within the framework of this dialogue, Plato founds ethics as the province in which it is possible to question, in hopes of refining, the overly broad ancient Greek concept of piety. Ancient Greek piety that becomes self-conscious and self-questioning gives birth to philosophical ethics.

But Plato would not have Socrates found that subdiscipline on his own authority. As Euthyphro notes, Socrates is blocked from certain actions by an inner voice that sounds when he is about to perform them. Presumably, the voice only has occasion to sound when Socrates' reason has not already given warning, which implies that a higher arbiter than human reason is needed to discern the viability of certain acts. Socrates identifies it as a god's. Since the voice has not blocked his open questioning of state piety, Socrates has divine sanction for that activity. In the *Apology*, his philosophical activity receives an even more positive divine endorsement: "To philosophize has been commanded of me . . . by god through oracles and through dreams and by every other means in which a divinity has commanded anyone to do anything."[2] And now it is not only a case of religion giving birth to ethics but, in the process, of allowing itself to be undermined by what it spawns. The old myths Euthyphro tells of the children of gods undermining and superseding their parent gods foretell Plato's own use of that idea—a new ethical activity undermines an old religious one.

And yet Socrates' inner voice, which sanctions his activity, comes not from a new god but from an old and a widely accepted one. The voice is traceable to the Delphic oracle of Apollo. Socrates explains in the *Apology* that a friend of his, Chaerephon, on inquiring of the oracle, learned that no one was wiser than Socrates. Socrates, knowing that his only real skill was in questioning, had to conclude that this was the wisdom the oracle was commending in him. It is interesting that Plato should have chosen this god as the medium through which to introduce the assertion of a new ethics against an old religion. For early Christianity, too, may have found appeal in Apollo, to the extent that he served as one of the pagan bases of the iconography for Christ.[3] And yet if Apollo was a just god by ancient Greek standards, then he was not always a kind one. The other side of the healing he could bring was sickness and plague. Euthyphro indirectly indicates for us how un-Socratic the imposition of pain is when he says of Socrates that he cannot "believe that [he is] the prosecutor of another."[4] This accords with the ethic that Socrates represents in other dialogues, that it is better to suffer harm oneself than to inflict it on others.[5] In the *Republic*, Plato extends half of this view—that it is never good to cause harm—onto divinity, where he says that God does not cause everything in the world but only the good things.[6] In that case, Apollo, reconfigured by Socrates' ethic, could not have caused the plague that opens the *Iliad*. Perhaps the charge against Socrates should have been that he reinvented old gods.

Moral standards *are* independent of the gods and constrain them as much as us. If piety in ancient Athens included both ritual and moral behavior, then part of what Socrates wishes to show in *Euthyphro* is that any attempt to define ethics in terms of what pleases the gods must fail. But the question of piety begins in any case to lose its force, for the transformation Socrates began to effect in the gods, by holding them to moral standards beyond them, Plato completed when he raised the idea of the Good to the highest value in his new religion of ideas. God and gods fall by the wayside as much in this new philosophical religion as they had already begun to do in the philosophical science of the earlier generations of Greek philosophers.

In the contrasting world of the Bible, there is no more a clear distinction than there was in ancient Greece between religion and ethics. Neither of these words occur in biblical Hebrew, but this is because the Bible is so steeped in them that it lacks the distance to articulate them as distinct concepts. The reigning concept of Hebrew scripture is commandment, which subsumes both ritual and ethical injunctions, as in the Ten Commandments. When Jesus offers a précis of the law, he gathers together one moral and one religious command without so labeling them (Matt. 22:37–40). When he characterizes the second "moral" command (to love your neighbor as yourself) as "like" the religious command (to love God with all heart, mind, and soul), he implies that there could never be conflict between them.

On the issue of potential tensions between religion and ethics, the Bible offers no abstract speculations of the sort that Socrates does. Instead, it presents narratives in which the conflict is implicit. Perhaps the most famous of these is the commandment that God gives to Abraham to sacrifice his son Isaac. But there are other instances: the story of Jephthah's daughter (Judg. 11); of Elisha and the taunting boys (2 Kings 2:24); of Jesus' rejection of his parents and siblings (Mark 3:31–35); and of the withered fig tree (Matt. 21:18–19). One of the most affecting of these stories, and the only one to create a sense of tragedy, is that of Saul.

Saul fills the requirements for tragic heroism as defined by Aristotle. He is an exceptional character who errs in judgment. His exceptionality comes, in part, by way of his beauty (1 Sam. 9:2) and susceptibility to ecstasy (1 Sam. 9:2). He also gives evidence of high moral character because of what appears to be his humility—that he is chosen to be king takes him completely by surprise (9:21, 15:17)—and his foresightful good will—he takes care to spare an innocent people, the Kenites, who might otherwise have suffered, when he attacks, at God's command, an enemy, the Amalekites, who live nearby them.

But no sooner has he been declared king than he commits his first error. The ancient Israelites, as newcomers to the land, were besieged by various enemies, among them the Philistines, famous for supplying David's imposing opponent, Goliath. Poised for attack, Saul awaits the prophet Samuel to offer up a sacrifice to God. But Samuel is late, the troops begin to disperse, and, worried over the outcome of battle if he delays longer, Saul offers up the sacrifice himself. At that point Samuel appears and denounces him for taking that priestly function into his own hands. In punishment, Saul's descendants will not inherit the kingship. (The Bible does not explain why Samuel was late, nor does it explain why the judgment on Saul was so harsh, especially inasmuch as the later kings, David and Solomon, performed ritual acts with impunity.)

This theme is recapitulated in the story of the Amalekites Saul is commanded to utterly destroy them, but instead he spares the best of the livestock and the king. And now not only his progeny but he himself will lose the kingship. The spirit that had come upon him in his ecstatic moments departs (16:14), replaced by an evil spirit that God has sent. Desperate for guidance, and in defiance of his own prohibitions on witchcraft, he invokes the witch of Endor to raise Samuel from the dead. But the ghost of Samuel simply reiterates for Saul that he is lost. Shortly thereafter, Saul, wounded by the Philistines, takes his own life.

Critical to our theme are verses 15:22–23, where Saul tries to excuse his disobedience by claiming that the livestock he took was for sacrifice. But Samuel responds that obedience is better than sacrifice. Samuel anticipates the sin of witchcraft to come when he likens Saul's disobedience to divination. But the accusation also prefigures what will become the later prophetic critique of ritual sacrifice, except that instead of obedience, it is social justice that the later prophets prefer to it. But then suppose Saul's acts of clemency are indeed just. If God rejects them, then ethics is implicitly subordinated to religion. Or, more forcefully, if we think Saul has behaved ethically, then we are mistaken, for, pace Plato, it is God's commands that supply our moral understanding in the first place.

Between them, Plato and the Bible supply the opposing extremes of response to the question of which of the two, religion or ethics, is derived from the other. Each position has its modern defenders. Once again and unsurprisingly, Kant continues in the Platonic tradition. Part of what defines moral behavior for Kant is its freely willed conformity to laws that our own practical reason determines, in which case it cannot be God who determines them. Indeed, heteronomous behavior cannot count for ethical. "Morality does not need religion at all."[7] Insofar as Kant concedes to religion a domain of our life to govern, it collapses back into ethics. Religious behavior is simply moral behavior that is additionally (and unnecessarily) understood as divinely commanded. Kant brings full circle the movement Plato began. Plato, having extracted a separate domain of ethics out of ancient Greek religion, granted religion its separate purview, but subordinate to ethics. Now Kant takes that movement to its final conclusion. Religion is not simply subordinate to ethics; it ceases to be distinct from ethics at all. Religion is collapsed back into ethics so that, as in pre-Platonic times, it is not possible to distinguish them anymore.

The opposing view, of the Bible, that ethics falls indistinguishably under the broad range of behaviors commanded by God, found theological champions throughout history, including, preeminently, Duns Scotus and William of Ockham. In modern times, a spokesman for this view is the Swiss Reformed theologian Karl Barth (1886–1968). "The good in human conduct is the determining by the divine commanding."[8] Writing against a liberal tradition within theology, informed in part by Kant, Barth sought to define a context for ethics utterly opposite to Kant's. What makes an act ethical is that it is performed in response to a command received from God in faith. That command claims a response from us in complete independence of any universal standards of moral valuation we may think we have reached by reason or experience, and that would render us "judges and masters"[9] of God, our judge. "Ethics is understanding of the good not as it is known to us as a general and theoretical truth, but insofar as it reveals itself to us in our doing it or not."[10] What makes an act ethical for Kant, that we determine it for ourselves, is precisely what blocks it from evincing any moral character, for Barth. We have barely any claim to possess goodness at all, except as a conduit or reflection of its only true subject, God. It does not follow that God can or will command us anything. The divine commands have a context in covenants of love that God has already established with human beings, preeminently through Christ. Christianity, grounded in Judaism, supplies Barth with a ready tradition of divine covenants, lending some predictability to the kind of commands we can expect to hear from God. But the commands each of us hears, from moment to moment, are addressed to each of us in our unique individuality and situation within the world. It is this feature that provides a Barthian way to evaluate the tragedy of Saul. The divine command to Saul, to destroy the Amalekites, was contextualized by the responsibility Saul had for the well-being of the Israelites, which, as long as the Amalekites existed, was always under threat. Within the context of the covenant God had with the Israelites, Saul's clemency toward the Amalekite king was a failure in goodness.

An analogous debate with ethics arises for literature, but a Barthian position toward literature, founded on analogy with his defense of religion's primacy over ethics, is difficult to find, except in the modern age. Certainly Plato denied literature any autonomy over against ethics. Ancient Greek literature, which for Plato was enmeshed with ancient

Greek religion, stood with religion under the same moral critique. Ethics, having gained its independence from religion, was not about to acknowledge in literature a limit to its scope. The Platonic attitude toward literature carries through to modern times, where we hear it voiced in Samuel Johnson: "It is always a writer's task to make the world better."[11] Kant may have conferred on the art object an independence of external aims, but even this independence falls finally under subordination to the ethics that is always paramount in Kant. Whatever seriousness aesthetic freedom could claim derived from the symbol it could be of moral freedom.[12]

It was Nietzsche who reframed within the context of literature the old Platonic question of ethics' ultimacy, and in such a way as to open the option of not only literature's independence of ethics but of ethics' derivation from literature. Nietzsche inherited the tradition of ethics' subordination to religion. And so his extrication of literature from the judgments of ethics begins with his radical deconstruction of Christianity, "the one great curse, the one great intrinsic depravity, . . . the one immortal blemish of mankind."[13] Ethics, for Nietzsche, is largely Christian ethics, especially such biblically based ethics that valorize humility and pity. According to Nietzsche's famous critique of Christian morality, it is a mendacious cover for weakness. In our ethical thought, we are "accustomed to lying."[14] The lie we tell ourselves about our ethics is that it has a basis in anything other than our own needs or preferences. For this reason Nietzsche bids us to turn away from the pretensions of moral philosophy to a typology of morals. Moral systems, compared, establish how much each is relative to a particular society, history, and, to use Nietzsche's own preferred term, *genealogy*.

But Nietzsche's ethics is not a simple relativism. A consistent moral relativism withholds from commending any one morality above another. Nietzsche shows too strong a preference among possible moralities to be a relativist. As the title of his book, *Genealogy of Morals*, implies, espousing a morality is like belonging to a family, and it takes as much effort to free oneself of an inherited morality as to divorce oneself from a birth family. This accounts for the virulence of Nietzsche's critique of Christianity, the worldview that supplies his inherited perspective on ethics. It is precisely literature that Nietzsche would substitute for Christianity to supply his perspective on ethics. If we want a model for who we should be, then we should look to the memorable characters of literary art, for if they are indeed memorable, it is because of the integrated wholeness they exhibit as characters within the context of the works they inhabit.

If Kant collapsed religion into ethics, then Nietzsche in his turn collapses ethics into aesthetics. If our lives are to be analogous to novels, and novels are works of creative artists, then our lives become the novels of which we are the authors. "We want to be the poets of our life."[15] But if these novel lives are to be genuine works of art, then they must be unique. This accounts for Nietzsche's disdain for all conformist moralities. Of course, by his own perspectivism, he cannot claim objective merit for his aesthetic ethics, but he can recommend it with all of the literary style and dynamism at his command, and with all of the honesty that requires him to admit that his persuasiveness extends only as far as his performance, which, far from extending into objective reality, concludes at the end of his book.

But a lingering doubt remains. Will any memorable character from literature do for our moral inspiration? If the noble but falsely deceived Othello might do, will Iago? Alexander Nehamas comments, "There are many cases in which we feel absolutely free to admire characters who are dreadful people: we do so constantly in the case of literature. In their case we freely place our moral scruples in the background. What concerns us about them is the overall manner of their behavior, the very structure of their minds, and not primarily the content of their actions."[16] This comment suggests that we can admire Iago insofar as we realize he is a character in a play. But for Nietzsche, who reduces ethics to aesthetics, and who, according to the same critic, "always depended on literary and artistic models for understanding the world,"[17] there appears to be no difference between admiring Iago as a character in a play and as a person in real life. Having recommended an aesthetic ideal of unity as his criterion for evaluating character, Nietzsche seems forced to allow that characters such as Iago are admirable, whether fictional or real. Perhaps he would say that the only way Iago can be aesthetically satisfying is in Shakespeare's play, in which his speech and acts are so carefully honed in relation with the other characters' that they cannot be extracted from it and survive in their aesthetically satisfying unity. Life is always too messy. All the same, suppose someone *could* fashion his life so that the aesthetic unity in it was as great as Iago's?

Two opposing responses to Nietzsche come from Oscar Wilde and Leo Tolstoy. Wilde already echoes Nietzsche when he titles one of his books on literary criticism *The Decay of Lying*. In a gesture that minorities and minority views sometimes make in both self-defense and self-affirmation, Wilde adopts for the badge of literary art the very feature of it that Platonic and Christian religion had, for centuries, critiqued in it: its falseness. If Wilde characterizes literary artistry as a rebuke of the conventional morality of truth telling, then he has precedent in Nietzsche, whose more sardonic point was that by the creative self-deceptions implict in most moralities, "one is much more of an artist than one knows."[18] It is not truth that judges the value of literature, but literature that judges the value of truth. As Wilde puts it, "Those who do not love beauty more than truth will never know the inmost shrine of art."[19] And just to assure us that he has not only the morality of truth telling but all morality in mind when he asks us to abandon truth at the portals of art, he tells us in a famous quote from the preface to *The Picture of Dorian Gray*, "There is no such thing as a moral or immoral book. Books are well written or badly written. That is all."[20]

But this claim already shows a departure from Nietzsche. For Nietzsche, by the collapse of ethics into aesthetics that he promoted, could have characterized the well-written book as precisely the moral book. Wilde still concedes a separate realm of morality apart from literature. He insists that there is an "impenetrable barrier of beautiful style" between art and reality,[21] which Nietzsche had moved radically and subversively to erase. This may account for the different types of energy that inform the tones of their respective works. Nietzsche preaches a social revolution, a new morality beyond the old for all society, whereas the contrasting poignancy of Wilde's work and life owes in part to the untoward intrusion into his life of a social reality that he largely dismissed. His critique of the ill effects of life on art—that it "gets the upper hand and drives art out into wildnerness. This is the true decadence and it is from this that we are now suffering"[22]—applies as well to his own life, understood as he himself wished it to be, as an artwork. Wilde, who holds back from following Nietzsche's ideas to their radical conclusion, admits the very morality he excludes from judging literature back into his own stories, for the central conceit of *The Picture of Dorian Gray* is both biblical and Puritan: that moral wrong begets physical punishment (biblical), and that inner evil must show on some outward surface (Puritan), even if that surface is only the painting in an attic. This suggests that Wilde does indeed follow the lead of one of his own characters, as Nietzsche would advise, but against Nietzsche's own morality: Lord Henry, who is accused of being "much better than you pretend to be."[23]

If Wilde shows secret affinities for conventional morality, howsoever much it is to be excluded from aesthetic judgment, then Tolstoy openly proclaims that morality is the touchstone of good art. Whereas for Wilde our common human nature was a "most depressing and humiliating" reality[24] from which art protected us, and Nietzsche disdained all commonality, the late Tolstoy, in his seminal essay *What Is Art?*, celebrated artworks precisely for their capacity to heighten communicative bonds between humans. Tolstoy's philosophy of art was expressive in the same sense that Collingwood's would be: Artists express feelings in their art that they hope thereby to awaken in audiences. "In this freeing of our personality from its separation and isolation, in this uniting of it with others, lies the chief characteristic and the great attractive force of art."[25] Wilde's philosophy of art was, in contrast, *im*pressive. Whatever an artist fashions enjoys independence from her feelings, which in any case will relate to the artwork only through a kind of lie. The artwork bears its own potential for feelings, which it realizes in its audience, not through awakening emotions already latent there but by imposing them there itself de novo. The Wildean artwork occasions no emotional communication between the artist, who remains mysterious, and the audience.

In the spirit of Plato and Kant, Tolstoy enlarges the scope of ethics by subsuming religion under it. He defines the religious perception of a society as "the highest good at which that society aims."[26] The highest good of his own time "lies in the growth of brotherhood among all men."[27] Literature finds in this theme the perfect content for itself, for it harmonizes so perfectly with its form to effect emotional communication. It is as though, in a kind of Hegelian synthesis, the form of literature has for the first time found in Tolstoy's own time a content with which it can unreservedly identify. All good art serves the cause of brotherhood. Literature so moralized holds up poorly to Wildean critique. Wilde might well say that life had banished art from Tolstoy's late work, a cutting criticism of a writer whose great, epic novels are renowned for the life their art created, and that "this is the true decadence." But, as much as Wilde undermines his own critique of ethics by embodying classic moral themes in his stories, so Tolstoy, having written the novels he did, calls into question the so imperious ethics of his late years. Why, we may wonder, did he not rewrite *Anna Karenina* with Varenka the heroine? Perhaps because he knew that a vivified literature was not her medium, and that nothing less than life itself could properly hold her.

Tolstoy's is an extreme case of literature judged morally. It mitigates the extremity of it to read it in the context of his conversion to Christianity. His late theory of literature can be read as a self-castigating judgment on his own earlier literary achievements, in the spirit of Emily Gosse. Still, the idea that literature has moral import probably plays a larger role in our lives than many of us would guess. Literary critic Wayne Booth suggests that the literature we read influences us morally in the same way our friends do, indirectly through their actions and speech.[28] Choosing books to read is similar to choosing friends. An author such as D. H. Lawrence communicates a view on how people should behave: with openness to their natural sexual drives and willingness to build human relationships around the expression of them. It was precisely his critique of Christianity that it inhibited that. Not all authors communicate their moral views so forcefully, and it can become the task of ethical literary criticism not so much to recommend or critique moral views embedded in literature as to discern their presence there in the first place so that we know what is influencing us. Literature so critiqued might become fuel for Nietzsche's typology of morals and so for the freedom from morals that Wilde preached without practicing.

But Tolstoy would not relish such a reconciliation of his own theories with Nietzsche's or Wilde's. Tolstoy, who outlived both Nietzsche and Wilde, regretted their influence on his times.[29] "People of the upper classes, more and more frequently encountering contradictions between beauty and goodness, put the ideal of beauty first, thus freeing themselves from the demands of morality."[30] If we allow the contradictions between beauty and goodness to stand, in the persons of Nietzsche and Wilde, on the one hand, and Tolstoy on the other, then suggestive alliances form between them and their counterparts in the dialogue of contradictions between goodness and religion. Tolstoy takes his place with Plato and Kant among the promoters of ethics over all contenders with it, Nietzsche and Wilde with Barth and the Bible, among those for whom ethics meets its limits, or indeed uncovers its very foundations, in either literature or religion. Plato, Kant, and

Tolstoy are a natural grouping. It is the pairing of Nietzsche with the Bible, Wilde with Barth, that occasions surprise. And yet Nietzsche found in Hebrew scripture just the kind of morally challenging stories he relished. He only regretted the interpretation they found in the New Testament.[31] But he must have had the story of Saul and the Amalekites in mind, too, if only unconsciously, when he wrote of Roman ethics that, for it, "an act of pity was not considered either good or bad . . . and even when it was praised, such praise was perfectly compatible with a disgruntled disdain as soon as it was juxtaposed with an action that served the welfare of the whole, of the *res publica*."[32] And Wilde and Barth also exhibit unexpected affinities. The Christian story of redemptive suffering finds as good a retelling in fairy-tale form as it can hope to find in Wilde's "The Selfish Giant." And Barth, for his part, acknowledged the importance of what turns out to be, perhaps without his knowledge, gay playwrights, when he lingered with such appreciative attention over a word that occurs recurringly in Tennessee Williams's *Night of the Iguana* but might have appeared too in *The Picture of Dorian Gray:* "fantastic."[33]

Part 3

Short Religio-Literary Readings
of Six Perennial Themes

Chapter 8

Love

Both religion and literature speak the language of love so naturally and authoritatively that any incompatibilities between what they say may take us by surprise. It was Anders Nygren, in his book *Agape and Eros*, who laid out most markedly the contrast between two Greek understandings of love, one from Plato, the other from the New Testament. The two "have originally nothing whatever to do with one another" and define "two different general attitudes of mind."[1] Drawing from the classic passages on divine love in the New Testament (1 Cor. 13, 1 John 4:7–5:3), and from Plato's *Symposium*, Nygren defines erotic love as an effortful, egocentric desire to possess a recognized good, while agapeic love is gracious, selfless giving toward whomever is open to receive it, regardless of merit or virtue. Insofar as Plato is a religious voice, the contrast Nygren identifies is intrareligious. It is by way of the *Symposium* that this intrareligious squabble between Platonic and Christian religion over the meaning of love acquires bearing on literature, for what motivates that dialogue is an observation from one of the characters that "whereas other gods have poems and hymns made in their honor, the great and glorious god, Love, has no encomiast among the poets."[2] The dialogue comprises literary tributes to love which, according to one of the speakers, Agathon, is itself both "a good poet" and "the source of poetry in others."[3] If so, a contrast between eros and agape regarding literature already sounds, for no analogous claim is made for agape in the New Testament.

171

Of course, Socrates does not agree with Agathon. He doubts that Love is a god in the first place. If the gods are happily self-contained, then eros, insofar as it is desire, cannot be divine, for desire is an unmistakable sign of dependence and lack. Love's relation to beauty is to want it, but since whatever it wants it lacks, it cannot itself author beauty or inspire it in others, as Agathon claims. On the contrary, eros is the very picture of want, a quality that Socrates dramatizes, according to the pattern of divine genealogy, by understanding its parents to be Prosperity and Poverty. What uniquely defines eros is a poverty that the goods of the world provision by attracting it to themselves, without ever wholly giving themselves to it to possess. (The image foretells what would become Aristotle's understanding of the unmoved mover's impact on the world.) Eros so understood draws to itself characterizations—"rough and squalid," "plotting against the fair and good . . . a mighty hunter, always weaving some intrigue . . . an enchanter, sorcerer"[4]—that contrast most strikingly with the features of agape that Paul famously itemizes in 1 Cor. 13. But if Socratic eros is unfit for St. Paul, then it finds a ready home in Shakespeare's plays. And so whether on Agathon's or Socrates' understanding, eros still allies with literature.

Socrates' characterization provides a further link to literature. His eros is an ambiguous figure, strung between the poles of poverty and prosperity. It is no surprise, then, that Socrates assigns eros not to the rank of the gods but to that of the *daimons*, those spirits that inhabit an ill-defined liminal space between the divine and human.[5] To the extent that literature thrives on ambiguity, as Hawthorne taught us, then eros is its natural theme. Agape, in contrast, has a single parent, God, and an unerring self-expression toward the good of others. How does literature capture it?

If eros is a sorcerer, then it can assume other shapes, even that of its opposite, agape. It already moves in that direction when it sets its desiring sights on wisdom, and so it becomes a philosopher, loving wisdom;[6] and more so by the image of homelessness that it sports, assimilating it to Jesus, who had "no where to lay his head" (Matt. 8:20, RSV). It is by eros' ability to don aspects of agape that literature finds enough play of ambiguity in agape to thematize it. Among many examples, let us consider a triad of poems that over the course of an unchronological sequence they suggest gradually frees agape from the bondage to eros it seems to need for its literary expression: Alexander Pope's *Eloisa to Abelard*, John Donne's *Batter My Heart*, and George Herbert's *Love*.[7]

The famous medieval love affair between Abelard and his gifted student Heloise provides a historical ground for exploring tensions between eros and agape. Having been discovered in an illicit love affair, the two entered religious orders and maintained a correspondence, which became famous for several years thereafter. Pope's poem, which draws on the correspondence, opens with a statement of the conflict within Heloise over her love for Abelard and for God. The loves do not simply conflict but transform into each other by an alchemy of disguise, a theme Heloise already voices when she pleads on behalf of Abelard's name, "Hide it, my heart, within that close disguise, Where mixed with God's, his loved Idea lies" (v. 11–12). That her own heart, rather than God, is the addressee of this plea already binds her to the eros from which she simultaneously and painfully tries to free herself, as she continues, "O write it not my hand—the name appears Already written—wash it out, my tears" (v. 13–14). Soon after, Heloise, in justification of her love for Abelard, quotes one of her first lessons from him, that "twas no sin to love," (v. 68) a dictum whose persuasive force in this case derives in part from its ambiguity—it is never a sin to love agapaically but surely sometimes is one to love erotically. It is only by masquerading as agape that eros can claim of itself to never be sinful. Only so gross a conflation can allow Heloise to sing the praises, as she does, of extramarital sexual love. What aids the persuasive power of the disguise is the implicitly cited authority of Plato, whose own religion of eros hovers between Heloise's love for God and for Abelard, who already early on transforms into a "loved Idea" (v. 12). Soon the God of whose jealously Heloise must beware is not the Bible's but that very eros that Plato fêted in the *Symposium*. In a relation as intellectually charged as Abelard's and Heloise's, Plato can convert what seems an illicit sexual love into a sanctioned love of ideas. Both loves are erotic.

But Heloise is never quite persuaded by the disguise that her own sexual love for Abelard assumes, whether as biblical agape or Platonic eros. Positioning herself with St. Paul, who famously said of himself, "I can will what is right but I cannot do it" (Rom. 7:18), Heloise laments, "I ought to grieve [over her forbidden love], but cannot what I ought" (v. 183). In that realization, coupled with her resignation to life without Abelard, she longs for death. But through the lens of that longing, a genuine note of agape does finally sound: Heloise envisions a divine love that "absolves our frailties" (v. 316). This plea for a pure agape, unencumbered by eros' simulations, does not go unanswered. At the very end of the poem, Heloise hopes for "some future bard" (v. 359) to tell her story, for "the well-sung woes will soothe my pensive ghost" (v. 365). Pope himself is that bard, and it is in his generous act toward her that Heloise, in her final anticipatory gesture, invites the reader to contemplate a picture of genuine agape.

So elusive a presentation of agape, following so prolonged a postponement in eros, may have been mandated by a poem so long. Agape fares better in the fewer, more concentrated verses of a sonnet. In John Donne's poem *Batter My Heart, Three-Personed God*, agape does not so much play against eros as allow itself to be borne it. Donne capitalizes on a feature of biblical agape often overlooked, that the Greek words that Paul uses to characterize it are verbs not adjectives.[8] It is less that love is patient and kind, in the RSV translation of 1 Cor. 13, than that it waits patiently and shows kindness. Accordingly, Donne's plea that God "knock, breathe, shine" his way into his heart extends what is already the active nature of divine love. The verbs match themselves to the several persons of the Trinity: breathing, to the Holy Spirit; shining, to the Son, the light of the world; and knocking, the most forceful of the three verbs, to the Father. These three acts intensify to a second triad of verbs—"break, blow, burn"—that now carries erotic overtones, almost to the point of rape, as though to suggest, as Heloise did, that the human heart is too weak to invite the divine love into itself but must be stormed. A rape by God renders the recipient uniquely chaste. This is a dialectic, rather than an alternation, from eros to agape. It may be that Donne's bondage to God is also his freedom, as he claims, but agape has not yet freed itself from dependence on eros for its literary expression.

It comes closer to that freedom in George Herbert's poem *Love*. Though the opening words—"Love bade me welcome"—invite the picture of a "seductive woman encouraging her shy lover,"[9] they equally suggest the original meaning of *agape* in Greek, of honored welcome. That interpretation finds an echo at the end of the poem, in the meal indicated there, which early Christians enjoyed under the name of a lovefeast or, once again, *agape* (Jude 12). It is no wonder the whole poem has been read through the lens of the Eucharist: the communicant is naturally shy of approaching the divine altar and must be assured that love makes that numinous place safe before he dares to "sit and eat." The behavior of Love in this poem conforms more closely than in Donne's to the kind of acts that Paul ascribed to agape, and to the characteristics that Nygren identified in it: Herbert's Love bears the blame of the inadequacy the speaker feels, as though to create in him the value he perceptibly lacks. The operative verbs do not suggest rape but service. And lest we think that agape, so freed of dependence on eros for its literary expression, fails to communicate in poetic form, we may hear Simone Weil's assessment of this work, that it is "the most beautiful poem in the world."[10]

There is a third word in ancient Greek for love, *philia*, which in the New Testament refers to either love for a friend or a fellow in the faith. In its second meaning it shades into agape, as indicated by the New Testament, when it characterizes the love between Jesus and his disciples as, alternatively, agape or philia. In its first meaning, it shows features of eros, but perhaps it is Latin that ties the closest knot between love and friendship when it derives its words for both from the same root: *amor* and *amicitia*. In the ancient world, friendship drew the particular attention of philosophers, perhaps because of all human ties it seemed the most reasoned. And of those philosophers, it is Cicero who left what would become one of the most enduring treatises on the topic. Cicero more clearly locates for us the place of friendship somewhere between eros and agape. He pointedly distinguishes it from Platonic eros when he denies it to be the "daughter of poverty and want."[11] Instead, it descends from wisdom and virtue (30). This inflection toward agape intensifies in that it does not calculate or seek gain (58) but instead strives for accord (20). For the good of his friend, a person will even sacrifice his life (24). On the other hand, like eros, it recognizes value in its object rather than creates it there. Cicero advises a testing period for new friends (85). Its origins are naturally human (32) and not divine. Like eros, it draws those who feel it for each other into a particularly close, exclusive intimacy, so much so that two friends feel as one (80–81). But then, unlike either agape or eros, it is based on mutual equality and likeness (50, 69).

By its location between and apart from agape and eros, friendship invites the attentions of both religious and literary texts. It would be difficult to decide which of the two ancient friendships, the "religious" one between David and Jonathan or the "literary" one between Achilles and Patroklos, more fully illustrates Cicero's criteria of the relationship. Part of what justifies their claims to paradigmatic status among friendships is their exclusive intensity. The force of that intensity is one of the critical causes moving David and Achilles into their appointed destinies. Intense friendships are a natural theme for literature, and not just for fiction. If friendship involves a period of trial, as Cicero claimed, then the literary form that most perfectly matches it is the essay, by definition itself a test or trial. The writer, Montaigne, who was credited with founding that form, also wrote what has become a classic essay on friendship. The friendship Montaigne celebrated in that essay, between himself and Etienne de la Boetie, had the Ciceronian intensity: "so perfect a union that the seam which has joined [us] is effaced and disappears."[12] It is just this intensity, bordering on the erotic, that proves troubling to some religious sensibilities, so much so that his essays appeared on the Index of Prohibited Books.

For its part, the Church embraced a structure that seems a fertile ground for friendship, the religious order. "In the Middle Ages . . . it is not an accident that the great theoreticians and practitioners of friendship were then cenobitic monks."[13] But the inclinations of friendship toward exclusive intimacy troubled the monastic world, in part because of the overtones of eros they carried. An erotic note sounds in the monastic writer, Walafrid Strabo (809–849), who wrote of his friends, "Wherever you are . . . you will be mine,"[14] and encouraged friends to exchange love poems. A need arose to discern the line between spiritual and erotic friendship, which monastic theorists found in the concept of particular friendship. Such a friendship, marked by exclusiveness, jealousy, absorption of mind, and sentiment, was "detrimental to the universal charity due to all"[15] and marked the bound on feeling appropriate between monks or nuns. And yet insofar as friendship provided an emotional space for two to feel as one, could it help but be exclusive?

Happily for monasticism, a theorist arose within it to address this issue, Cistercian monk Aelred of Rievaulx (1110–1167). In his book, *Spiritual Friendship*, Aelred takes his bearings on friendship from Cicero, whom he credits with clearing a path for him in the protean world of human emotion. At the very start he concedes the erotic component in friendly love, which "seeks something for itself with desire and strives to enjoy the object of its desire."[16] The only limit that Cicero had placed on the love friends show each other was a political one, that it not be seditious. For this limit, Aelred substituted sin, which provided a check on any violations of chastity that friendship might incite. But what more positively tamed the exclusive intimacy of friendship was the context that Christianity provided for it. Aelred's treatise, which is in the form of a dialogue, opens with these words, addressed to

Aelred's interlocutor, Ivo: "Here we are, you and I, and I hope that Christ makes a third with us."[17] The presence of God in friendly love is so patent to the speakers that they can wonder whether what John really meant by "love" in his paradigmatic "God is love" (1 Jn. 4:7) was friendship. Aelred's response to the problem of exclusivity in spiritual friendship is that by God's presence in it, it is not really exclusive in the first place. Does this open a space for a third human being to join the threesome that two friends make with God?

When Aelred quotes Cicero, that friendship makes "one from many,"[18] he seems to allow a friendship to expand from two to three or more. But he shows more debt to biblical thought than to Roman when he incorporates into the narrative of his dialogue a challenge to this thesis. The dialogue opens with a sharp contrast between the intimacy of two that Aelred and Ivo make, and the community of monks—the "many"—that chatters in the background. Aelred and Ivo withdraw from the community so that "no one's voice or noise will break in upon the pleasant solitude of ours."[19] But later, while Aelred is in private dialogue with another monk, Walter, a third does break in upon the privacy. It is by introducing this third, Gratian, that Aelred illustrates the problem of friendship's exclusivity. Walter greets Gratian as one who is "excessively eager for friendship," to which Gratian replies that had he been invited into the conversation from the start, he would not have had to be excessively eager for it.[20] Under the guise of pleasantries, both Gratian and Walter are piqued, apparently from jealousy of their friendships with Aelred. When Gratian is further invited into the conversation on grounds that it will help him distinguish "friendship according to the flesh from one that is spiritual,"[21] the implication of imperfection in Gratian's part in friendships casts an additional pall over this intrusive third, but ironically so, since it is just Gratian, by being the third, who takes up the part of that ever-present third in spiritual friendships, Christ himself. Soon the tangle of three takes back place to a wonder raised over Aelred's friendship with a fourth, unnamed monk, especially prone to a quality that Aelred has said impedes friendship, namely, anger. The wonder is that, according to Gratian, Aelred prefers this monk "to all of us."[22] Aelred does not deny it and simply responds, "Since I have received him in friendship, it will never be possible for me not to love him."[23] This unlikely friendship provides the occasion for a lesson in forbearance, but it also tilts the scale of Aelred's love so far toward agape that both the interlocutors and the reader must wonder what makes that relationship a friendship and not simply an expression of the "charity due to all."

Aelred's service in the cause of spiritual friendships was to provide a doctrine that sanctifies them—Christ as the ever-present third—and a narrative that helpfully but inconclusively problematizes their exclusivity. The Cistercian order was uncomfortable enough with the narrative that, not long after Aelred died, his work fell from favor.[24] That a noted historian, John Boswell, could say that "there can be little question that Aelred was gay"[25] must force consideration of whether Aelred was more a theorist of Christian *philia* or of Platonic *eros*. If the second, then he works less to resolve for Christianity the problem of exclusivity in friendship than to express the attraction that Platonic religion, whose chief love is erotic, has always had for philosophically inclined Christians.

Chapter 9

Death

Whereas love divided in two, lending itself as agape to religion and as eros to literature, death is one and uniform. In its simplicity, it unites religious and literary texts around it, the way a funeral does distant family members. The divisions over death relate to its significance, but they occur within the religious texts themselves. Between the voices of Hebrew scripture, the New Testament, and Plato, death is understood, respectively, as a shadowy end, a prelude to resurrection, and a portal to immortality. In addition, a religious voice consistent with all of them enjoins us to ponder our deaths while we live. This will both enhance our life and ease our death when it finally comes. For each of these religious views of death, it is easy to find novels or poems that give them literary expression.

In the foundational texts of Western religious and literary history—the Bible, Homer, and Hesiod—there is remarkable agreement about death. For both Genesis and Hesiod death is troubling enough to require explanation; for Genesis, death is punishment for a moral failing in humans, namely, sin; for Hesiod, it is a natural phenomenon to which primordial Night gives birth. In Job and Homer we find intersecting families of metaphor for human mortality: "Man, that is born of a woman, is of few days and full of trouble. He comes forth like a flower and withers; he flees like a shadow" (Job 14:1–2); "insignificant mortals . . . are as leaves are, and now flourish and grow

179

warm with life, and feed on what the ground gives, but then fade away and are dead."[1] Leaves and flowers are kindred images of transience, but it is the metaphor of shadow that emerges most prominently to bridge the biblical and Homeric views. Like a flickering shadow cast by the sun on an intermittently cloudy day, Sheol, the biblical place of death, is indeterminate in its very meaning. It could be related to either the Hebrew verb for asking, or for being hollow, suggesting in the first case a question mark and in the second a hollow within the earth.[2] Doubts surround the place. It sometimes seems a habitation for the whole of a once-living person (Ps. 139:8) and other times only for her soul, or *nephesh,* which animates the body. The inhabitants of Sheol may or may not be aware of their position. Sometimes they are aware of God (Ps. 139:8). Though their existence there is neither reward nor punishment, the Bible sometimes makes a point of consigning the wicked to its regions (Ps. 9:18).

The picture of afterlife in the *Iliad,* which fills the role of our literary representative in comparison to the Bible, is remarkably similar. The place of Greek death, Hades, is also underground. The Homeric notion of the soul, which translates as the Greek *psyche,* is close to the Hebrew *nephesh.* Both connote the breath imparted to persons while they live and the insubstantial shadow of them that remains after they have died. The breath of afterlife is itself a shadow of the real thing, or so Achilles implies in reference to the ghost of his friend, Patroklos, who lacked "real heart of life."[3] Homer describes the soul "flying" to Hades at death, a picture in sync with Job's of our withering life, which "flees" like a shadow. Indeed, when Pope translated the *Iliad* into English, he rendered *psyche* as shade, so shadowy is this idea, and "disembodied spirit" remains a dictionary definition of shade.[4]

Ghosts are a vehicle for both Homer and the Bible to accentuate the bounds between the living and the dead. Both Samuel's ghost, which Saul raises from the dead, and Patroklos' ghost, which comes unbidden to Achilles in a dream, are recognizably continuous with their former living selves, but neither should have had occasion to rise from the dead. In accordance with Torah teachings (Lev. 19:31), Saul himself had forbidden necromancy, but neither was there any need for Samuel to rise, as he had no comfort for the stricken Saul, now rejected by God, and no knowledge for him that was either new to him (that God had abandoned him) or helpful (that he would die the next day). Patroklos for his part would not have risen had Achilles fulfilled his responsibility toward his deceased friend and buried him. Passage to Hades is guarded by other shades, who do not admit newcomers until their earthly remains have been cremated and buried. Patroklos's ghost has been hovering, uncomfortably, between the realms of life and death. Again, the ghost has nothing to impart that the living do not already know (that they must bury their dead), and it appears on earth only through the blamable fault of survivors.

Mortality is not an accidental feature of human being according to the Homeric and scriptural worldviews but a defining mark of it. The divide that they both maintain between the living and the dead works to support the still starker separation that they uphold between the human and the divine. A human that could die and subsequently live calls into question not only the distance between the living and the dead but the finitude of humanity that for both Homer and Hebrew scripture works, in contrast, to indicate the infinity of the sacred. Of course, it is precisely the teaching of Christianity that Jesus of Nazareth does just that. Within Christianity, the doctrines of Resurrection and Incarnation are twinned departures from Homer and Hebrew scripture, and both are equally essential to the faith. When Paul comments, "If Christ has not been raised, then ... your faith is in vain" (1 Cor. 15:14), he locates Resurrection doctrine at the center of Christian belief.

But death as prelude to resurrection takes on a different hue from death as shadowy end. The death that both Hebrew scripture and Homer lamented was an inevitable sadness of life. Both texts carry the sentiment that any kind of life is better than death. But Irene Sourvinou-Inwood, in writing of Homer's attitude toward death, speaks also for the Hebrew Bible's when she says of it that it was "a hateful, but familiar, not frightening event."[5] The New Testament inverts that assessment of death. The death that interests the Gospel writers, which is Jesus's, is not hateful in the Homeric sense, because it holds a place in a larger and loving divine scheme. But it is far from familiar or unfrightening. Death by crucifixion was both an agony and an ignominy, qualifying for what Simone Weil would call "affliction." According to Matthew, the immediate impact of Jesus' death was terrifying: the daylight ceased, "the earth shook, and the rocks were split; the tombs also were opened" (Matt. 27:51–52). If the New Testament works so hard to present Jesus' death as a terror, then it is in part so that its cancellation or opposite, his Resurrection, can appear to be all the more remarkable.

But the terrors of death are not, for Paul, confined to Jesus. He does not even draw attention to that death. Death for Paul is a cosmic, moral problem, not simply the pervasive punishment of human beings. "The whole creation has been groaning in travail together until now" on account of its "bondage to decay" (Rom. 8:22). In the wake of Adam's disobedience, death did not simply exist, it "reigned" (Rom. 5:14). For Paul, death was "the signature of the world."[6] It carries a sting. The Greek term *kentron* connotes the sting of a venomous scorpion. It is the "last enemy to be destroyed" (1 Cor. 15:26), not simply in order of time but in grade of ultimacy. As Karl Barth puts it, "Death is the peak of all that is contrary to God in the world, the last enemy."[7]

So dramatic a statement of death's dreadfulness surpasses the Homeric and Hebrew scriptural views. It is the foundation for the glory claimed for the miracle of Resurrection. Up to a point, death in the guise of horror functions in the Western literary tradition as a prop in a plot that scripts a triumphant part for Resurrection. There is no more memorable instance of that than personified Death in *Paradise Lost*. Death, unlike the much more rounded character of Satan, is an allegorical figure in the poem, designed to waken sheer horror. He is a product of incest, the union of Satan and his daughter, Sin, who sprung spontaneously from his head. Death both destroys Sin's beauty, at his birth, then rapes her, conceiving within her a brood of vicious dogs that continuously torment her. Though there is precedent for his indeterminate shape in Hebrew scripture, alternatively substance and shadow (P.L. 2:667–669), Milton leaves no doubt that, beyond what Hebrew scripture would say, Death is, according to Milton's various characterizations, "fierce, horrible, monstrous, execrable, grisly, deformed, and foul." Lest we miss the Pauline inspiration for this figure, he sports a "dreadful dart" and wields a "whip of scorpions" (P.L. 2:701). Milton heightens the drama of Death's entrance by withholding his identity until Sin reveals it. Death is first named in a cry from Sin that peals through hell, which trembles "at the hideous name" (P.L. 2:788). Sin does not bestow the name but recognizes her son as the bearer of it, as though he were the fulfillment of a prophecy, rather like the Antichrist. That would indeed make him, much more than Satan, "the last enemy."

And now the stage is set for Resurrection, itself named only once in the whole poem, toward the end of the last book (P.L. 12:436), where it appears in Raphael's speech foretelling the coming of Christ. If, as Adam suggests, the resurrected life he now anticipates surpasses the immortal life he might have known in Eden, had he never sinned, then death is a necessary catapult to the highest life. For all that Milton advanced the independence of literature from religion, here he remained a faithful child of the Church.

Our third religious take on death, from Plato, communicates still a different tone. There is no urgency in Plato to extract a sting from death. Immortality is too assured for death to ever develop a sting in the first place. Unlike Resurrection, immortality carries no mystery, for it is susceptible to proof by reason. Plato introduces a distinction between body and soul that the Bible does not concede. The distinction is so marked that the good and evil of each belong to different categories. The soul, as the seat of moral decision, can only be affected by moral evils, not bodily ones. And as moral evils fail to destroy it, it must be indestructible. Paul could never accept such an argument. If there is no Resurrection, then there is no end to sin and death, and we might as well enjoy life while we have it, whether morally or immorally. If Resurrection enables ethics, and the body is what is resurrected, then the body conditions ethics. But the Platonic soul, feeding on ideas, enjoys a sanctuary of immortality utterly immune to the ills of the body, which, as Socrates demonstrates, need barely be noticed when its life finally and thankfully fails.

Transposed to literature, a death preceding immortality must be serene. And there must be a barely noticeable change in landscape over the transition from life to death. A poem that captures these features of a death allied with immortality is Emily Dickinson's much quoted *I Could Not Stop for Death.*" Here the personification of death is precisely opposite to Milton's: a courtly gentleman who accompanies the speaker on her funereal carriage ride. Immortality is in the carriage, too, and is presumably the presence that enables the speaker to see that the "Horses' Heads were toward Eternity." The houselike habitation of the tomb diminishes the difference between the look of life and death, as immortality would have us believe. Unlike Resurrection, which occupies a moment in salvation history, immortality, allied with eternity, asks for a place outside of time. It was Boethius who first defined eternity as "the complete, simultaneous and perfect possession of everlasting life."[8] And the final stanza, which locates the speaker in a place where centuries occupy less than a day's worth of consciousness, could be a figure for Boethian eternity. It is just the precise middle of the poem, in the passage from the third to fourth stanza ("We passed the

Setting Sun, Or rather—he passed us"), that, by the seeming reversal of motion communicated there, undermines the serenity. Dickinson evokes that unsettling change of perspective, informing relativity theory, that comes to a passenger on a stalled train when she realizes the effect of motion she is experiencing is actually produced by another train passing outside her window, which makes us wonder whether eternity is an optical or a tactual illusion,[9] far from the perfection Boethius claimed for it. In that case death, too, for all his courtliness, takes on a sinister air that allies him with his Miltonian forbear. Perhaps Dickinson really means to parody immortality,[10] unlike Milton, who affirms the Resurrection he presents, in which case, we must await another to take up Plato's cause.

What all three religious views of death share is a sense that the anticipatory thought of it can be salutary. As Paul puts it, "To die is gain [for] . . . my desire is to depart and be with Christ" (Phil. 1:21–23). The Platonic philosopher, for his part, is "always occupied in the practice of dying."[11] Milton is more Platonic than Christian when he commends to Adam, having sinned, death for "his final remedy" (*Paradise Lost* 11:61–62). Even Hebrew scripture, in the voice of Ecclesiastes, invites an improving, if admonitory, contemplation of death (Ecc. 12). These strands of thought are combined in the medieval devotional tradition of *ars moriendi*, a genre of guidebooks to the final days of life. The idea was to internalize the teachings in life so as to be sustained by them in death. "If we make death present to us, our own death . . . if anything will quench . . . the greedy, passionate affections of this world, this must do it. . . . Frequent use of this meditation [on our own death] by curing our present inordinations will make death safe and friendly."[12] But the idea is also very contemporary and finds expression in modern prayer books.[13]

Though poetry offers a ready medium to express so potentially lyric an idea, the greater challenge is to find extended, narrative treatments of *ars moriendi*. How does a novelist sustain dramatic interest in the prolonged, salutary contemplation of death? A tempting place to look is Tolstoy's late story, "The Death of Ivan Ilych," which has been called "the most comprehensive literary treatment of death available."[14] But Tolstoy's account of his own anticipatory thoughts of death, in his *Confession*, does not inspire confidence—far from enhancing his own life, the anticipation of his own death drove him to thoughts of suicide.[15] Ivan Ilych illustrates the opposite of *ars moriendi*, even refutes it, for

Ivan lives badly, in vain and irritable pursuit of his own desires, with scarcely any thought of death. In his illness, it is rather his past life he contemplates; until suddenly, through no effort of thought, he finds the death that is now so imminent for him converted into a kind of light, in the glow of which his accustomed nastiness converts to compassionate concern for his family members. The implication is that a good death can happen unexpectedly to the least attractive of the mortally ill. A closer approximation to *ars moriendi* appears in Dostoevsky's *The Idiot*. Prince Myshkin is suggesting as a theme for a painting the impending execution of a criminal he once witnessed.[16] The criminal, like Ivan Ilych, has lived badly, and in his convulsive kissing of the cross held out to him, there is no "religious feeling." What there is, however, is a heightened sense in the criminal's face that in the seconds before his death he "knows and remembers everything." This condensation of everything into the look on a face reads as yet another figure of Boethian eternity. It was painful for Myshkin to watch the actual face of the criminal, since he was instantly thereafter to die. But a *picture* of that face "would do good," for it would freeze the face in a benign stasis from which it could communicate to all its viewers its salutary awareness of "everything." The viewers of the picture, if not the criminal himself, reap the benefits of *ars moriendi*.

But the most sustained representation of *ars moriendi* in modern literature may be Willa Cather's *Death Comes for the Archbishop*. As Father Latour's life drew to a close, he realized that "he was soon to have done with calendared time, and it had already ceased to count for him. He sat in the middle of his own consciousness; none of his former states of mind were lost or outgrown. They were all within reach of his hand, and all comprehensible."[17] The bishop has entered Boethian eternity already before his death, as the art of dying would have us do. Cather has so contrived to tell his story that all that came before can be read as preparation for those few sentences. Her sustained use of the past tense creates an effect precisely opposite to that of the historical present, a common rhetorical trick for heightening the interest of the past (presumed to be inherently boring) by pretending it is present. Joseph Wood Krutch, reviewing the novel in 1927, observed that what Cather had achieved over the course of her 300-page novel was elegy. "When things are recalled in the mood of elegy there is no suspense and they do not take place one after the other because all things being merely past, there is no time but one."[18] Rather than depict such a frame of mind in her character, she has, in the way she narrates his story, created the mood of it for her readers. By the time the bishop's death comes, the reader is prepared. Insofar as the bishop invites the reader's identification with him, the death he anticipates is also the reader's own. Cather has given us a modern, literary exercise in *ars moriendi*.

Chapter 10

Evil

In terms of the response it draws from our illustrative texts, evil synthesizes features of love and death. For, like death, evil provokes a range of analyses from the Scriptural and Platonic traditions, all of which easily find literary analogs. But like love, evil shows a different face of itself to the religious and literary texts. To religion, evil is a problem, so much of one that within monotheistic theology it shapes a subdiscipline of its own: theodicy. But for literature, evil awakens a fascination that glamorizes it. Perhaps there is no more striking acknowledgment of this than the Roman Catholic baptismal ritual. In the rite for the "Christian Initiation of Adults," approved by the National Council of Catholic Bishops, one of the charges to the candidate is to "reject the glamour of evil." Alternatively, she can "reject Satan, father of sin and prince of darkness."[1] If, by the conjunction of these two admonitions, Satan is identified with glamour, then we have, in part, the literary tradition of his presentation to thank for that.

Philosophers in the monotheistic traditions distinguish between two kinds of evil: natural and moral. Natural evils are the sufferings that fall to us from nature; moral evil is a function of deliberate human will to harm. According to Scripture, the two are related: Natural evils are divinely ordained punishments for moral evils. Death, for example, is a punishment for sin. The two biblical testaments differ on how they understand moral evil to manifest. In Hebrew scripture, evil shows primarily in the human free choice, always available, to disobey God. A

187

striking illustration of this view appears in a juxtaposition of verses from the beginning and end of the Torah, Gen. 3:7, in which Adam and Eve eat from the Garden of Eden's forbidden tree and thereby acquire knowledge of the difference between good and evil, and Deut. 15–20, in which the choice between good and evil, already guaranteed in the Genesis verse, is reaffirmed. If the Bible is, as rabbinical tradition claims, never redundant, then one reason for this repetition may be to teach that the human decision between good and evil is never definitively made. At no point does the decision for one or the other close off the possibility of deciding differently at a later time. We live constantly under the necessity to decide, or, as Barth might say, in crisis.

In the New Testament, evil takes on the aspect of supernatural menace, independent of human choice and perilous to it. Though the book of Job had personified temptation in the minor person of a *satan*, meaning adversary, this figure is magnified in the New Testament book of Revelations into a monstrous, seven-headed dragon. The sin that was a function of human choice in Hebrew scripture becomes, under the influence of the Greek *daimones*, a "prince of the power of the air," in Ephesians 2:2, a malevolent spirit that possesses us. For Paul, sin is a volitional agent that infects and enslaves us. The infection spreads beyond humans who fall prey to it to nature itself. This view can be read as an elaboration on the Hebrew scriptural view. If the paradisical state was as happy as it seemed to be, then why would Adam and Eve jeopardize it by willfully choosing wrongly? The serpent offers motive for that choice, through the temptation he supplies. But this account of wrong choice falls away by the time of Deuteronomy, which simply presupposes that evil is as capable as good is of wooing human choice. It fell to the New Testament to identify the Edenic role of tempter with evil, and to personify it as the Devil, who is Christ's seductive adversary, or *diabolos*, in the wilderness.

The Platonic position distinguishes itself from both Scriptural views at the foundation by failing to acknowledge any significant difference between natural and moral evil. All evil is characterizable in natural terms, as a disordering of parts. The suffering that accrues to evil persons is part of the disorder that evil is rather than a consequence willfully imposed by a divine judge. Plato's famous argument rests on his identification of moral evil with disorder in the soul; since the disordering is also an unhappiness, and no one desires to suffer, then it is impossible for anyone to deliberately choose evil. If anyone does so, it

must be out of ignorance or confusion. It is in the intimacy of that correspondence, between ignorance and evil, that Plato's radical revisioning of human nature shows itself. From a monotheistic standpoint,
Plato renders us radically split and self-divided beings. Who we are is a
function of the objects of our attention. Where Hebrew scripture
locates good and evil inclinations within one human soul, Plato fashions one unit from the alliance of the good in us with its counterpart in
the eternal world of ideas and another unit from the alliance of the bad
in us with an ignorance of those ideas. The human soul in its goodness
is a unification of its knowledge of good with the good it knows. The
human soul in its evil is a union of its ignorance with the absences of
good that ignorance registers. A Platonic tree of the knowledge of good
and evil is impossible, because evil, itself a confusion, cannot be an
object of knowledge but only of ignorance and confusion.

Of these theories, it is especially the Scriptural ones that receive in
literature some stunningly glamorous personifications. Especially
where evil manifests as tempter, it lends itself to glamour, which supplies the seductive lure. Even Platonic evil can be beautiful when it
holds us to confused physicality rather than turning translucent before
the eternal form it properly mediates. Our illustration of the Scriptural
view of evil, as deliberate, wrong choice is Shakespeare's Iago; of the
New Testament view of evil as personified menace is Milton's Satan;
and of the Platonic view of evil as confusion is Hannah Crean-Smith,
in Iris Murdoch's novel *The Unicorn*.

Shakespeare's *Othello* makes a natural alliance with Genesis 2–3.
They are both stories of innocence succumbing to temptation. It is an
innocent, unknowing love that binds Adam to Eve and Othello to Desdemona. Iago plays the role of serpent, but he is much more overtly evil
by Hebrew scriptural standards than the serpent, for he violates several
of the commandments, not to hate (Lev. 19:17), not to covet anything
of thy neighbor's (Ex. 20:17), not to take vengeance (Lev. 19:18), and
not to murder (Ex. 20:13). It is an interesting feature of Pentateuchal
law that it does not forbid hypocrisy. It is perhaps too subtle a vice for
legal prescription and may positively serve the cause of Scriptural law,
which implicitly believes that right action will eventually bring right
motive in its wake. But the prophets do condemn it (Isa. 29:13), and it
is mostly under their condemnation that Iago falls, since seeming to be
what he is not is the vice he most artfully cultivates. This appears most
dramatically very early on when Iago declares, in a blatant parody of

God's self-naming (Ex. 3:14), that "I am not what I am" (1:1:64), an achievement that works its way into Othello, too, as Desdemona signals when she despairs, in dismay over her husband's false accusations, "My lord is not my lord" (3:4:125).

Iago retains throughout the play a self-conscious awareness of his willing role in the harm he promotes. This too mirrors the Garden of Eden story, which implies that the goodness of Adam and Eve remains to them only insofar as they are unaware of it in themselves. The story subtly implies that self-consciousness corrupts. In accordance with Hebrew scripture's view, Iago pictures his inner life as a garden of different growths, any one of which he can freely choose to nurture (1:3:320–327). But his self-consciousness is also the beginning of his appeal to the reader or audience. From the start, the audience is his confidant. In his soliloquies, Iago both displays his self-awareness and invites the viewer to hold the privileged place of witness to his schemes. The flattered viewer may persuade himself that the criminal who confesses repents and reforms. It is just the withdrawal of that confidence that so shocks the viewer with a sense of betrayal when at the end of the story Iago speaks for his last words not only to the other characters but also to the audience: "From this time forth I never will speak word" (5:1:301). Iago also attracts the audience with his sense of humor.[2] It is the humor of diabolic parody, inverting not only God's words to Moses but Christ's to the people (cf. Matt. 5:5 with *Othello* 2:1:118–160). But it perfectly fits his cultivated arts of dissimulation. A third attractive feature is his capacity, unique among the characters, to read the other personalities correctly. He knows, what Desdemona denies (3:4:30), that Othello can be made jealous. It is just this feature that allows him to parody the Aristotelian idea of the tragic flaw, for his own superior insights fail him in the least likely case of his own wife, Emilia, whom he never imagines could betray him. Finally, Iago attracts by the artistry of his schemes. It was not his original intention that Desdemona die. He merely wanted compensation for the double hurt he believed he suffered, first for the adulterous relation he suspected Othello of having with Emilia, and second for the promotion Cassio won over him from Othello. He would cause Othello to suspect his favorite, Cassio, of adultery with Desdemona, and so "plume up my will in double knavery" (1:3:392–393). Iago's skill at machination may so win the viewer's admiration that he declares, "Villainy is Iago's vocation, and it is no sin for a man to labor in his vocation. He is the villain as artist, who, deeply considered, has nothing to do with evil."[3]

Never has the glamour of artistry worked more forgivingly on an evil character's behalf as Laurence Olivier must have demonstrated when he played Iago.[4] This is so true that some critics doubt the humanity of Iago's evil. The given motives for his malice do not support the audacity of his acts and leave him shrouded in what Coleridge famously called "motiveless malignity." No wonder, by the play's end, Othello could expect to see hoofs for Iago's feet. Coleridge's observation recalls Thessalonians: "The mystery of malignity is already at work" (2 Thess. 2:7) and begins to move us out of the Hebrew scriptural view of evil toward the New Testament's.

Milton follows the New Testament in shifting the explanation for human wrong choice to a personification of evil, namely, Satan. Why did God create such a being? Milton's answer, which contributes to the glamorization of evil, is that Satan was first Lucifer, the light bearer, whose radiance surpassed that of all the other angels in heaven. It was from his own self-conceived pride and envy, over God's begetting of the Son, that Lucifer fell and became Satan, adversary to God and humankind. This mythic account of Satan was centuries old by Milton's time. Milton's innovation is to emphasize the free will in Lucifer by which he fell in the first place. Lucifer was, in a phrase that summarizes Milton's theodicy, "just and right, sufficient to have stood, though free to fall" (P.L. 3:98). Satan is aware of his freedom. Like Iago, he displays that awareness in soliloquies that invite the reader's sympathy. But unlike Iago, he can admit that it was his own pride and ambition that "threw me down" (P.L. 4:40), that it was foolish to rebel, that the bold face he assumes for the benefit of the other devils is false since they do not suspect "under what torments I inwardly groan" (P.L. 4:88). In a moment of high pathos, he exclaims, "Me miserable! What way shall I fly infinite wrath and infinite despair? Which way I fly is hell; myself am hell" (P.L. 4:73–75).

Satan's relations to beauty further glamorize him. There is negative witness to this in the disgust he feels over the ugliness of Death. But later, on approaching Eden, he cannot but admire God's new creation, and especially Eve, before whom, as we know, he stood "stupidly good." Milton, the Puritan, owes outward approval to the simple speeches he gives to God, but Blake cannot have been the first to suspect that in the "baroque" and "serpentine"[5] language of Satan, Milton finds a higher outlet for his poetic gifts. The complexity of Satan's language mirrors the ambivalences of his character. If he opposes God and humanity, then he also shows "loyalty in leadership, fortitude in adversity, unflinching courage, and splendid recklessness."[6] If, "in Satan, we recognize our own divided wills,"[7] then Satan works as much to exemplify human failings as the purportedly human Iago does to represent Satan's. Both Satan and Iago are motivated by a sense of "injured merit." And each schemes, by revenge, to wreak havoc on a peaceful union. But if it is Satan rather than Iago who invites our identification, then Milton surpasses Shakespeare in the glamorization of evil.

The Platonic view of evil, that it is a function of ignorance, finds more opportunity of expression in social psychology and criminology than in literature. As David Tracy notes, "There is something both strange and courageous about Iris Murdoch's decision to develop a form of Platonism in the late 20th century."[8] *The Unicorn* is the seventh of Murdoch's some twenty-five novels. The title is itself already ironic in its reference to a beast of mythic Christianity who atones for others in its death. The Platonism of the novel aims to dispel the delusive mists of that myth that deceptively veil the character, Hannah Crean-Smith, who turns the plot. Hannah is a beautiful and mysterious woman who lives reclusively in a house on the coast of West Ireland, surrounded by a small host of attendants. She projects a mood that ambiguously combines elements of dreaminess, seduction, and suffering resignation. Years ago she had nearly murdered her unfaithful husband, who now lives estranged from her. She confines herself to their house, but whether at her own or her husband's bidding is unclear. All of the characters are fascinated by her and react to her with varying degrees of comprehension. The story turns on the unfolding of her character, which the reader only gradually comes to see truly, through the eyes of her attendants.

It is perhaps too obvious a ploy, in this early Murdoch novel, that the foil to the mistily glamorous Hannah is himself a scholar of Plato named Max. It is he who warns another character about Hannah, that it is important to "see her as real."[9] The Platonic trope of seeing courses through the novel in italic letters. Evil begins through not *seeing* clearly. Hannah's problem was that she cultivated airs of ambiguity to block true visions of herself. By making ignorance in others an object of her desire, she forfeited the chance to develop an actual identity of her own. The other characters who wonder over her identity eventually receive the implicit answer that she had none. She had become the confusion she cultivated in others about herself. As Max puts it, judging her by the Platonic standard of unreality and evil, "she loved what wasn't there" (294). Hannah herself confesses, toward the end, in a moment of self-understanding, "Do you know what I have been really? Nothing, a legend . . . I have lived on my audience, on my worshippers . . . and we have deceived each other. You all attributed your own feelings to me. But I had not feelings, I was empty" (248–49). Her death by suicide, a parody of Socrates,' was simply the outward, bodily manifestation of an inward chaos. Murdoch at this early stage is not above exploiting the pathetic fallacy to drive home her Platonic points. The house sits by a beach whose waters are peaceful only from a distance; close up, the waves are treacherous and conceal a violent, lethal undertow in which visitors have drowned.

Plato had suggested that suffering could be salutary by restoring the order of the soul. And in Max's former student of Platonism, Effington, Murdoch illustrates that alternative outcome to the chaos that claims Hannah's life. Another natural feature of the surroundings of the house are bogs that behave like quicksand if improperly navigated. One evening, Effington loses his way in this natural symbol of chaos. Like the romance of a Hawthorne story, the fairy fire that plays over them lends itself to explanations either supernatural and satanic, or chemical and scientific. Confused, Effington feels in the fairy fire "something coming up from below, . . . a great dark positive force" (184), which moves him to wish for a crucifix. But Murdoch awakens this glamorized Christian view of personified evil only for the foil it provides to the Platonic view that she will now positively dramatize. For as Effington sinks into the bog, by sheer attention to his predicament, he experiences an epiphany: "He looked and knew, with a clarity which was one with the increasing light, that with the death of the self the world becomes quite automatically the object of a perfect love" (188). The light Effington experiences is an inner one by which he now correctly sees the world around him. And in that light, he faces serenely his own death, as Socrates did. At this point, a rescuer appears, and he is led off the bogs to safety.

It was Murdoch who offered a philosophical defense of Plato's suspicions of artistic beauty. One way she reconciled her artistry with her suspicions of art was by vilifying fantasy in her novels. Fantasy was the trope for any distortion of reality through mental imaging. But the imagination also could shape a fiction that was continuous with reality, as Tolstoy had the reputation for doing. The glamorous characters who personified evil for all three of our writers all came to unhappy ends. In that way, the writers ultimately allied themselves with the religious worldviews they dramatized. But the outcome may be opposite to their intentions. Insofar as characters such as Iago, the Miltonic Satan, and Hannah Crean-Smith people our imagination, long after we have left the works that realized them, they enliven that fascination with evil the baptismal liturgy asks us to renounce. Our well-intentioned writers thereby prolong the tension between the problem evil is for religion and the glamorization it has found in literature.

Chapter 11

Suffering

Suffering, as part of the problem of evil, for religion, and the glamorization of evil, for literature, draws our illustrative texts into configurations very similar to the ones that evil catalyzed. The Scriptural traditions generate a range of responses to suffering, all of which find literary analogs. Temptations to glamorize suffering within literature are so great that we find ourselves cautioned "against the glorification of suffering."[1] Suffering differs from evil in the response it draws from literature, in that in the face of its reality, literature may lose its voice. If writing about evil works in some way to define and tame it, this is not the effect sought in writing about actual suffering. The literary problem for those who transform real suffering into art is not to tame it but to extend its reality into the psyche of the audience to awaken compassion. But "compassion is empty if I haven't made the other's suffering my own."[2] The writer must erase the barrier between sufferer and reader. This was Holocaust writer Elie Wiesel's challenge when he wrote his novel *Night*. The inconclusive ending of that story opens up a space for the suffering it depicts to continue into the life of the reader. The outbreak of the AIDS epidemic in the early 1980s posed a similar challenge to gay writers. In an essay, "Reading and Writing," gay writer Andrew Holleran confessed a fictional writer's block in the face of AIDS. "How could one write at all, in fact, when the only work that mattered was that of the men organizing social services, taking care of friends, trying to

195

find a microbiological solution to a microbiological horror in laboratories one could not see?"[3] By now the force of the virus has lightened enough in the gay community that lines such as these can appear in novels: "Jules had once said to me at a time when he didn't believe we were infected, that AIDS was a marvelous disease. And it's true that I was discovering something sleek and dazzling in its hideousness."[4]

Suffering is a problem for religion only to the extent that it cannot be explained. But some suffering is indeed explicable as either punishment for, or expression of, evil. These two alternative explanations ally themselves, respectively, with biblical and Platonic religion. The biblical book of Deuteronomy and the historical books that follow it in Hebrew scripture—Joshua, Judges, Samuel, Kings—provide both the theory of divinely ordained punishment and illustrations of its narrative expression. The biblical view is grounded in a still more fundamental theory of covenant. God has supplied a bond or yoke to himself through the revealed law. If the Israelites obey the law, then they enjoy potential rewards, including abundant crops, economic success, and fertility. But disobedience renders them prey to a host of potential sufferings. Both the rewards and sufferings receive extensive elaboration in the Prophets, where they are detailed in ingenious ways. Disobedient acts result in consequences that alternatively mirror, fulfill, or frustrate the acts themselves. For example, God says, "Since you have forgotten the law of your God, I also will forget your children" (Hos. 4:6), or, again, the punishment for idolatry is more idolatry but practiced in foreign lands to which Israelite idolators are exiled (Deut. 28:64). Alternatively, under a wrathful divine watch, the ordinary schema of promise and fulfillment that infuses much biblical teaching runs awry: "They shall eat, but not be satisfied" (Hos. 4:10); much worse, what parents will eat in times of famine will be their own children (Deut. 28:53). If, seeking food, they return to Egypt to sell themselves as slaves, "no man will buy you" (Deut. 28:68).

The Bible distinguishes natural from moral evils and assigns the first as punishment for the second. But for Plato, since moral evil is itself a type of natural evil—a misordering of nature's parts—suffering is already given in that misordering. Evil is so much its own unhappiness that it needs no additional suffering to punish it. Plato obtains by this view results very similar to Deuteronomy's, minus the divine, retributive agent and colorful expression. Those who harm others are themselves, in the process, harmed.

In literary illustration of this view, Plato would not direct us to the writings of his compatriots, for they, in contrast, were mesmerized by the phenomenon of unjust, irrational suffering, or *pathos*. As is typical of Plato and the Greek poets, they disagreed on which ideas should properly manifest in art. Plato feared that dramatic expressions of unjust suffering on stage would mislead viewers into misidentifying the source of their own life sufferings in agents outside of themselves, when in fact they had only their own internal disorders to thank. But we cannot blame the poets. Unjust suffering depicted on stage holds viewers in suspense, like a note toward the end of melody, awaiting resolution, that has not yet returned to the tonic. Merited suffering makes a fitting ending but only with difficulty sustains an unfolding story line. One for whom it did, however, successfully structure a plot was Dante. Dante obtains movement for this theme in the *Inferno* by arranging ever-intensifying illustrations of it in a sequence that follows the dramatic descent of his poet pilgrim into Hell. He heightens the impression of movement by the accompaniments he sets to the downward dropping topography, sometimes precipitous, the pilgrim must negotiate, for example, the decreasing willingness of the sinners to proclaim their identities and the lessening of compassion the poet pilgrim has for them.[5] The sins that are punished may follow a typology more classical than biblical, but the form of the punishments is Deuteronomic. The punishments are the sins themselves, intensified and ingeniously frustrated. Dante cues us to this already at the gates of Hell, where the poet pilgrim learns that what moves the condemned sinners to their punishment is their own desire for it. The hypocrites of the eighth circle illustrate—beneath the bright colors of their outward cloaks, the internal linings of heavy lead, which weigh them down, are visible. That the hypocrites eye Dante askance and confer with each other before addressing him suggests devious natures. These they show themselves to have when they address the poet pilgrim with a courtesy that fails to conceal, from either Dante or the reader, their resentment at his exemption from their punishment. Their punishment is persistence in their sin but without the concealment of inner motive essential to success in their sin.

In one important respect, Dante departs from Hebrew scripture. The dramatic finality of the inscription over the gate of Hell, "All hope abandon, ye who enter here"(Inferno 3:9), is foreign to the biblical-prophetic understanding of punishment, for the sufferings that punish also atone. Biblical prophecies of punishment are balanced by prophecies of redemption. The Talmud stipulates that suffering atones for all of the capital sins of the Bible except the profanation of God's name, which is forgiven only in death.[6] More than divine forgiveness, the atonement involves a change in the nature of the sinner, who no longer wishes to sin. Just as the punishment for idolatry is more idolatry, the forgiveness of it is in the desire the sinner develops to renounce idols and return to the one true God.

Suffering that simultaneously punishes and atones for sin makes a richer theme for literature than merely punishing pain, since it allows for development of character. *The Scarlet Letter* illustrates. Like the rabbis of old, the Massachusetts magistrates within the novel judge that though the Bible would condemn the adulterous Hester to death, suffering will suffice to atone for her sin. Hawthorne underscores the intensity of Hester's suffering not only in the public "procession and spectacle that have been described, where she was made the common infamy" but also "in her first unattended footsteps from the threshold of the prison" into the succession of days to follow, each of which "would bring its own trial with it."[7] But hardly had her daily routine of estrangement from the community begun than her means of reintegration with it presents itself. The letter "A" she wears, as the mark of her sin, which she had embroidered herself, so effectively advertises her needlework skills that the townsfolk commission many additional feats of her artistry. In just the way the biblical prophets describe, the punishment becomes the transformative conduit for the atonement. This is so true in Hester's case that, apart from the ruffs, bands, gloves, funeral clothes, and baby linens she produces for the townsfolk, she herself becomes a sustaining presence in their lives, assisting them in their impoverishments, illnesses, and deaths. "Into the household that was darkened by trouble . . . there glimmered the embroidered letter, with comfort in its unearthly ray" (160). In the end, the letter has come to stand in the minds of the people not for Adultery but for Able.

But Hawthorne complicates this transformation, for it is never clear that Hester actually repents of her adulterous affair with Arthur or judges it to have been wrong. The narrator himself suggests that "her sin, her ignominy" had the effect of a "new birth" for her (79). It is just her love for Arthur, which she secretly indulges (rather than renounces), that keeps her rooted to her place of public disgrace. In that case, the suffering she endures does not effect atonement and raises the

possibility that not only from Hester's standpoint but from the narrator's (and, by projection, the reader's) Hester illustrates a different type
of beneficial suffering. The character within the novel who by inwardly
repenting attains forgiveness for what the reader is expected to judge a
genuine sin, namely, hypocrisy, is not Hester but Arthur. But, as in
Hester's case, the suffering that Arthur endures over this sin becomes
the conduit of his redemption, for it is just out of his suffering that he
delivers the climactic sermon of his life, which communicates a gener-
ality of "suffering humanity, that touched a sensibility in every bosom!"
(242). The sermon, in whose tones of pathos the congregants hear a
plea for forgiveness, but for a sin they never suspect, prepares the way
for Arthur's public confession, which ends his hypocrisy. The sermon
generates a power that not only moves the listeners but carries Arthur
through to that final, self-disclosing act of his life, by which, the reader
is assured, he obtains God's forgiveness too.

   If Hester, for her part, is unjustly punished, then she illustrates a
different religious explanation for suffering. The notion that suffering
positively transforms those who have sinned finds extension to innocent sufferers. An innocent who suffers may be enduring a test by God
that establishes him more firmly in his goodness. This is one way of
interpreting what Abraham must have suffered in the test God made of
his willingness to sacrifice what was dearest to him, his son Isaac. The
story of Job can be read this way, and even the life of Jesus, insofar as
through his sufferings he advances in self-understanding. If the stories
of Isaac, Job, and Jesus are all temptation stories, then it is easy to see
why a plea within the Lord's Prayer is to be spared divinely sanctioned
temptations. For Plato, who denies that the just ever suffer, this explanation of suffering is impossible. It is Greek drama that gives this idea
its fullest expression, as Aeschylus suggests with his much quoted verse:
"Wisdom comes alone through suffering."[8] But it is not clear whether
Hester herself illustrates it, for Hawthorne does not establish that her
inward life changes substantially from the beginning to the end of the
novel. At the same time, Hawthorne leaves no doubt that others benefit from her outward solicitudes. This assimilates Hester to another
figure from the Bible on which Judaism and Christianity, if not Plato or
any of the Greeks, based a major theodicy: the Suffering Servant.

   The Second Isaiah, who prophesied during the Babylonian exile of
the ancient Israelites, conceived a radically new understanding of
human suffering—that, experienced by an innocent, it could atone for

others' sins. The idea was not entirely new. Guiltless animals had long been sacrificed as part of priestly rituals of atonement. The idea was extended to humans through the notion of corporate guilt—later generations of a family line could suffer the punishments due earlier ones. In that case, though, the punishment was still understood as just, falling as it did on the corporate individual that subsumed the children under the moral category of the parents. The Second Isaiah signals the radicality of his teaching by introducing it with these words: "Who has believed what we have heard?" (Isa. 53:1). The teaching must have comforted a people who had never experienced so draconian a punishment as the Babylonians brought to them: destruction of their principal means of worship (the Temple) and exile. Later rabbinic teachings made explicit for the Jewish people what the Second Isaiah only implied—that they were, themselves, the Suffering Servant in corporate form. But Judaism, in time, largely ceded the concept to Christianity, which built its theology upon it. In the cycles of prescribed Torah readings, Jews stop a verse short of reading publicly about the Suffering Servant, presumably from distaste over the Christian associations that the concept came to have for the rabbis who designed the Jewish liturgy.

Those associations have now so thoroughly triumphed that expressions of this explanation for suffering in literature take the form of Christ figures. Hester does not qualify, because she lacks the requisite innocence. By her complicity with Arthur's hypocrisy, she shares in it, as the narrator signals to us when he corrects his first impression, that Hester had become a "self-ordained Sister of Mercy" (166). It was more that "the world's heavy hand had so ordained her, when neither the world nor she looked forward to this result" (166). But Dostoevsky's Prince Myshkin does approach a literary translation of the Suffering Servant. He is an innocent who suffers over the suffering of others. The plot is partially driven by Myshkin's reaction to Nastasya Filoppovna, in whose face he sees "something that always tortured him."[9] Her suffering commands his active solicitude for her, which he takes to the point of proposing marriage, not from love in any erotic sense but for the care he feels he can provide. Like the Suffering Servant, who "poured himself out to death," (Isa. 53:12), Myshkin, the narrator tells us, "seemed really to look on his marriage as some insignificant formality, he held his own future so cheap" (573).

The problem is that for all that Myshkin identifies with Nastasya's suffering, he does not ultimately ease it. Nastasya finally rejects his offer, marries Rogozhin, and dies at his hand. It is not obvious how others are "made whole" (Isa. 53:5) by Myshkin, an effect the Suffering Servant, according to Isaiah, is supposed to have. Myshkin had a complex origin in Dostoevsky's imagination. The problem was how to show a Christ figure in a genre of literature, the novel, which presumes a world "abandoned by God." Dostoesvky found a partial model for such a figure in Don Quixote, whose underlay of Myshkin actually surfaces in one of the scenes. Pushkin had written a poem in tribute to Don Quixote, which implicitly refashioned his chivalrous ideal around the figure of the Virgin Mary. So blasphemous a gesture caused the poem to be censored,[10] even as it revealed a potential of the don to be interpreted in Christian terms, howsoever distorted. The character, Aglaia Epanchin, who is drawn to Myshkin but frustrated over his self-sacrificing zeal for Nastasya, has occasion to read the poem to a gathering of family and friends, but in her reading, she substitutes for the reference to Mary a clear indication of Nastasya. In so doing, she both identifies Myshkin with the don and seemingly mocks his love for Nastasya. But as her recital proceeds, her tone becomes respectful, even solemn, so that by the end the hero of the poem has won her heart. Dostoevsky implies that this transformation comes about through the identification Aglaia makes in her mind between that hero and Myshkin, so that Myshkin does effect a momentary wholeness in Aglaia, insofar as, over the course of the reading, she moves from ironic mocking of the words she speaks to wholehearted affirmation of them. Pushkin's poem more accurately foretell's Myshkin's fate than Don Quixote's. The hero of his poem dies insane. Don Quixote returns to sanity at the end of Cervantes' novel; it is Myshkin who lapses back into insanity. This is not necessarily a failure in the Suffering Servant but a natural consequence of his appearance in a world the Bible never imagined could exist: a God-abandoned world.

This notion effectively introduces our last biblical theodicy, that of Job. The book of Job is the Bible's cornucopia of theodicies. The friends do not simply repeat the Deuteronomic theodicy, they refine it through their suggestion that all of us, on account of our inevitable imperfections, stand guilty before God. The frame story of the satanic trial, which most scholars judge a later addition, elaborates on the theodicy of testing that the story of Isaac's binding introduced. But the original contribution of the book of Job is that suffering also can be interpreted as rationally inexplicable. For many moderns, this is the only acceptable understanding of suffering. Like Tertullian, who believed because it was absurd our reason finds the end of its searchings in the nonrational. In protest of his suffering, Job requests a trial before God, by which, he is sure, he would "be acquitted for ever by my judge" (Job 23:7). He never receives his trial. Instead, he is given a divine self-disclosure that underscores what he already knows, moved now to a deeper, affective level, that God is the omnipotent creator of all. This does not answer his questions over suffering but does silence his impulse to ask them. The implication is that had God not appeared the questions would stand and continue to gnaw.

And so they do, in a writer who many critics take for the modern literary counterpart to Job, namely, Kafka. Though Kafka himself never cites the book of Job in any of his fiction, his novel *The Trial* invites comparisons with it. In both, the central character is an innocent who stands under arbitrary judgment. Both characters seek a fair trial that neither receives. Both suffer acutely, and even if, of the two, only Job is morally improved by his pains, the question remains whether such extreme deprivations were needed to extract from him the improvements they do. The famous parable of the law, at the end of the novel, works as a précis of it. The Law which condemns also beckons. It emits an attracting glow that the man who is forbidden access to it can see through the many gates that separate him from it. These images recall associations that Hawthorne made with the scarlet letter. It, too, is a function of a condemnatory law that at the same time during Hester's public humiliation bore her up. It also defies clear interpretation, hovering ambivalently between Adultery, Able, and, we might add, Atonement. Like Kafka's Law, it also glows in the dark. Both symbols, of the law and the letter, occasion a suffering that appears to redeem. In analogy to Hawthorne's world, the Law is merely ambiguous. Contextualized by the Bible, Kafka's parable reveals what Margaret Susman called its "icy chill."[11] The paradox of the man's relation to the law, which shows a path to itself uniquely his own from which he is simultaneously blocked, resembles a biblical punishment: the promise of a much desired or needed thing is given only for the sake of dramatically frustrating its fulfillment. Kafka has imported the form of biblical punishment into his story, without the covenantal context that explains it. So decontextualized, that form becomes an image of inexplicable suffering—precisely the image that Job, at his most original, holds up for us.

Chapter 12

Forgiveness

Within the Scriptural traditions, suffering that atones for evil issues finally in forgiveness. Forgiveness is akin to love in its opposition to anger and hatred. Forgiveness entails "wiping out an offense from memory"[1] and all negative emotion it entailed, whether resentment in the wronged or guilt in the wrongdoer. In the response it draws from religion and literature, forgiveness resembles love in that it divides between biblical and Platonic understandings of it. For Judaism and Christianity, forgiveness is an emotion-transforming act of high moral value. But it is largely an irrelevance within the Platonic scale of goodness. The good soul within Platonism is immune to harm and so never has the opportunity to forgive. Outside Plato, within the Greco-Roman tradition, forgiveness occupies a place of dubious moral value because of what Seneca called its consequence in "the remission of deserved punishment."[2] If Seneca acknowledged anything analogous in his own culture's scale of values to Judeo-Christian forgiveness it was clemency or mercy. But this was a largely juridical or even political virtue that he enjoined upon emperors; its value was not intrinsically moral or indicative of any emotional transformation in the emperor but politically instrumental because of the devotion to him it nurtured in the populace.[3] Such a politicized forgiveness held less interest for Judaism or Christianity. They were more concerned about the conditions within personal moral life for the emotional transformation forgiveness involved. Both religions recognize two types of forgiveness,

203

one that is conditioned by repentance in the wrongdoer and one that, like agape, is unconditioned. Such conditioned forgiveness enjoys all of the potential for dramatic display that atoning suffering does. But unconditional forgiveness, like agape, translates with greater difficulty into engaging literary form.

For all of its dependence on evil and resemblance to love, forgiveness also bears an unexpected relation to death. In the previous chapter, we noted the teaching within Jewish tradition that suffering atones for all evils but one—blaspheming God's name, which is only finally forgiven in death. The second creation story of Genesis taught that death punishes sin; it would fall to later Jewish tradition to extract the implications of that teaching for what would become its belief in afterlife, that death is also a passage through forgiveness of even the worst sins to a happier existence in the next world. For biblical evidence, we must turn to a book of the Apocrypha, canonical only for Catholics, the "Wisdom of Solomon." Chapter three of that book, which begins with the verse "The souls of the righteous are in the hand of God," offers so much hope to mourners on behalf of their recently deceased beloved that the Episcopal Book of Common Prayer recommends its reading at funerals. The key verse is, "God tested them and found them worthy of himself" (Wis. 3:5). What qualifies the deceased soul to count for righteous is that it has passed God's test. Part of what accounts for the comfort this verse is to mourners is the implication that the deceased has passed the test that admits him or her to the ranks of the righteous. But what test is there that the liturgy can presume to know whoever has just died passed? An ambiguity in the meaning of the verb "to pass" suggests an answer. Passing is what we do when we receive an acceptable grade on an examination; it is also what we do when we die. The test that all who have just died have passed is precisely that of dying. Analogizing dying to sitting for an examination makes a certain sense. Both are anxiety-provoking situations. If the mark of having passed the test of dying is death itself, then here is a test, unlike all others, that we are all guaranteed eventually to pass.

L. P. Hartley's novel *Eustace and Hilda* provides an illustration. The closing, death scene of the novel has been called "the quietest, most subtle and therefore most shocking death in contemporary English fiction."[4] Eustace Cherrington, whom we encountered earlier as the impressionable child who projects himself into a stained glass window, has, by the end of the novel, much need of forgiveness, chiefly from his sister, whom he has accidentally almost killed. He also has a serious heart condition. In the novel's penultimate scene, he dreams that he is taking an examination. The single question on the exam is, "What do you know about the souls of the righteous?" While everyone around him in the examination room writes speedily and confidently, he, alone it seems, cannot answer the question. At last, within minutes of the examination period's end, he writes on his paper the verses from chapter three of the "Wisdom of Solomon." And yet he knows that no sheer Bible verses can possibly be the correct answer, until from behind him he hears his sister's voice, assuring him he has answered correctly. And "suddenly there was a shout, 'Eustace has passed. Three cheers for Eustace,' and the ancient rafters rang with acclamations."[5] As we often do in our dreams, he has transposed the reality of what he is then experiencing, his own death, into a mental vision. He has chosen the perfect metaphor for his death, an examination. By the end of the dream, he has passed, and received, not only his sister's but the ultimate forgiveness, by which he himself becomes one of the souls of the righteous.

Within Judaism, death is a condition of God's final forgiveness of all sins, but the fact that we all die and so satisfy the condition guarantees the divine forgiveness and so renders it, in effect, unconditioned. The issue of whether forgiveness is conditioned or unconditioned by repentance weaves throughout Jewish and Christian thinking on the subject. The division within Jewish thought on this issue mirrors another there, on whether the covenants God makes with Israel are permanent or revocable. Both Judaism and Christianity capture the logic of this sequential triad—sin, repentance, forgiveness—in their liturgy. On the paramount day of forgiveness within Judaism, Yom Kippur, the confessional prayers find their resolution in the climactic words from God, "I have pardoned in response to your plea."[6] Within the liturgy of the Christian Eucharist, confession too precedes the forgiveness implicit in the climactic act of that rite, communion. If words of forgiveness are instated in the liturgy, there to be repeated at each performance of the rite, then they too, like death, carry a guarantee of divine forgiveness, howsoever much they follow and are predicated on prescribed words of confession. On the other hand, if the words draw the psychological response they intend, then the worshiper who has just emerged from confession receives the forgiveness as an unexpected grace on which he has no claim. By the emotional logic of the rite, repentance conditions forgiveness.

That is already implicit in the biblical-prophetic view of atonement, according to which the measure of forgiveness for the wrongdoer is in the outcome of his repentance: a newfound wish no longer to sin. But the rabbinical tradition, commenting on the Bible, also communicates an ideal of divine forgiveness unconditioned by repentance or by anything at all. In the prescriptions the book of Exodus gives for construction of the portable tabernacle, provision is made for an ark to hold the tablets of the law. Above the ark sits the *kapporet*, or mercy seat. *Kapporet*, from the Hebrew root meaning "cover," connotes the place where sins are covered over, or forgiven. One purpose of the tabernacle is to supply the sacred place where repentant Israelites offer up the animal and vegetable sacrifices that condition the divine forgiveness of sins. Forgiveness is assured at the conclusion of the prescribed rites of sacrifice just as, for later Judaism, the conclusion of Yom Kippur and, more ultimately, of life, assures forgiveness.

Chapters 25–40 of Exodus reveal the most striking instance in Torah of Israelite obedience and disobedience dramatically juxtaposed. Chapters 25–31 supply the instructions for building the tabernacle, which chapters 35–40 show punctiliously executed. The later verses are largely repetitions of the earlier verses, transposed from the imperative voice to the indicative. But interrupting this model display of obedience to divine command is what, for Judaism, has remained the paradigmatic story of disobedience, that of the golden calf. The rabbinical tradition implied an ingenious explanation for this interruption: it demonstrated that God anticipated the sin of the golden calf and commanded the tabernacle in advance of it, as a sign he would forgive it: "My sanctuary in their midst will be a testimony to the forgiveness of their sins."[7] His assurance of forgiveness precedes not only Israelite repentance for sinning but the very committal of the sin itself. It is as though a savings account of forgiveness is set up before any debt is incurred. Such an unconditional promise of forgiveness invites a punning misspelling of the word, which the rabbis would have exploited had an equivalent presented itself in Hebrew: "foregiveness," to connote the unconditioned priority of the pardon granted.

But the tradition does not hold humans to the same high standard. Rather, Torah presumes that forgiveness is difficult for human beings. This is part of the import of Deut. 15:1–11, which commands a general amnesty for debt every seven years. The law suspects that wealthy Israelites will refuse to lend to needy brethren in the sixth year, for fear of not being repaid. It demands that the lending occur, and unbe-grudgingly, even in the face of the pending, obligatory forgiveness. The rabbinical tradition even allows for wronged parties to withhold forgiveness, though it expects them to grant it after it has been asked of them three times. The rabbis expected wrongdoers who harmed their fellows to repent and discouraged the wronged from granting forgiveness too easily for fear of enabling wicked behavior. A wrong-doer might be forgiven the same offense up to three times, but not thereafter. The unconditionality of divine forgiveness was not the model for human beings.

Christianity opened up a path for inverting that disparity between divine and human forgiveness. The Lord's Prayer implies that God's forgiveness is not unconditional but depends on the wrongdoer having first forgiven "those who trespassed against" him. Matt. 6:14–15 makes explicit that those who do not forgive others will not receive divine for-giveness themselves. Judaism has no public, liturgical prayer that imposes this condition on divine forgiveness.[8] On the other hand, Matt. 18:21–22 pushes human forgiveness toward unconditionality: far from withholding forgiveness from the wrongdoer who commits the same sin for the fourth time, the wronged person should forgive "sev-enty-seven times." This Christian asymmetry between divine and human forgiveness is logical. If Matthew makes God's forgiveness of us conditional on our forgiving others, then to maximally assure God's forgiveness, we must ourselves maximally forgive.

Martha Nussbaum suggests that fiction is inherently forgiving by virtue of the circumstances it details behind even evil characters' acts.[9] The condition of forgiveness in this case is not repentance in the fic-tional wrongdoer but the extenuating circumstances shaping his life that the all-seeing novelist discloses. It is easy for literature to portray conditioned forgiveness. The challenge is to dramatize unconditional forgiveness in ways that hold interest and avoid sentimentality. One way of doing that is to introduce the idea of unconditional forgiveness as a foil to a major plot line of conditioned forgiveness. Shakespeare achieves this in the *The Tempest*, which has been called a "comedy of forgiveness."[10] The forgiver in this case is Prospero, who has been wronged by a triad of plotters, including his own brother, Antonio, and Alonso, the king of Naples. Because Prospero enjoys the power of sor-cery, he can manipulate the wrongdoers into their punishment and prospect of repentance. In the banquet scene of Act 3, Scene 3, he reminds Antonio and Alonso of their joint sin against him through a device reminiscent of the Bible: by his magic, he raises before them the promise of a feast, which he summarily withdraws. In the confusion that follows, he supernaturally communicates to them the memory of their crime against him. From here, two tracks of forgiveness open up, one that proceeds through Alonso, who repents, and the other, through Antonio, who does not. The memorable song that Ariel sings to Alonso's son, Ferdinand, which falsely tells of death by drowning—"full fathom five thy father lies; Of his bones are coral made; Those are pearls that were his eyes; Nothing of him that doth fade But doth suffer a sea change into something rich and strange" (I:ii:397–400)—indirectly foretells the transformation that Alonso will undergo by repenting and receiving Prospero's forgiveness. Alonso begins to change already at the banquet scene. He is the only one to feel the impact of the crime recalled to him. When he finally meets Prospero again, he is ready to "entreat Thou pardon me my wrongs" (V:i:118–119). Prospero does forgive, not so much in words as in deeds—he uncovers an idyllic chess game between his own daughter, Miranda, and Ferdinand, which both reunites the separated father and son and offers happy prospects that the two families will soon be joined by marriage.

Against this plot line, which unfolds according to the biblical model of sin, repentance, and forgiveness, Shakespeare sets another, but more deeply puzzling. Antonio's response to the supernatural communications sent during the banquet scene is to challenge the spirits (actually Ariel) who beset him. Far from repenting, he sinks deeper into wrong by planning to assassinate Alonso. And yet he is the only one Prospero directly pardons, in explicit words of forgiveness, and not once but twice (V:i:78 and V:i:131). Lest we think it is the extenuating circumstance of the sibling tie between them that conditions this forgiveness, we hear Prospero virtually disown Antonio, for "to call [him] brother would even infect my mouth" (V:i:131). This is a hard forgiveness that retains the anger of the wronged; it comes down on Antonio almost as a punishment, the way Myshkin's generous acts of forgiveness are sometimes received by the other characters in *The Idiot*. But it does come unconditioned by repentance.

The two-track plot of forgiveness multiplies into several intertwining stories of forgiveness within Tolstoy's *Anna Karenina*, of which it has been said that "the word 'forgive' or one of its cognates appears every few pages."[11] The note of vengeance, which Tolstoy sounds in the epigraph for the novel, taken from Romans—"Vengeance is mine; I will repay, says the Lord"—sets off, in contrast, the theme of forgiveness all the more strikingly. One of the climactic scenes of the novel dramatically foregrounds a conditional forgiveness against the background of its unconditioned counterpart. Anna and her brother Stiva are both adulterous. This puts the two spouses, Dolly and Alexei Karenin, in sympathy with each other. At one point, Dolly tries unsuccessfully to dissuade Karenin from divorcing Anna, citing as a model her own multiple forgivings of Stiva. But Karenin, consumed by the "wrong she has done me," judges Anna "corrupt and depraved."[12] What begins to move Karenin from this state is a telegram he receives with startling news that Anna is ill, perhaps terminally. The image of her death effects a conversion of emotion in him that culminates at her bedside. What was "emotional upset" is suddenly "bliss" (419) in the power he finds in himself to forgive. It is not clear what Anna's own demonstrations of repentance play in this. For one, she is delirious. But her self-distancings of her adulterous side from her faithfully conjugal side feed so easily into self-exoneration—the adulterous Anna was not herself but someone possessed—that we cannot be sure Karenin is moved by them. But he is clearly moved by what appears to be her impending death. The impact of it on him outlasts her recovery and actually becomes an irritation to Anna while she recuperates: "I hate him for his generosity" (432). But this problem with forgiveness, that it can be humiliating to receive, does not detract from the power Tolstoy shows death has to evoke it. It is as though as death enters body and soul, they enact in response a genuine repentance, inherently and transparently sincere, howsoever expressed, or unexpressed, in words.

But we might already suspect that from the religions, at least insofar as dying is, for them, the final exam we all pass. Can Tolstoy show us the harder thing, to forgive without the dramatic stimulant of impending death and without the overt or even covert suggestion of sincere repentance? The famous opening sentence of the novel, "Each unhappy family is unhappy in its own way" (17), alludes to the marriage of Dolly and Stiva. Stiva commits adultery repeatedly. And in an earlier mirror-image scene of the one in which Dolly comforts a disconsolate Karenin over Anna's adultery, Anna consoles Dolly over Stiva's most recent indiscretion. Stiva invariably begs forgiveness, but his many repetitions of the same offense put him beyond the pale of conditioned forgiveness. Under Anna's counsel, Dolly perceives the depth of her own love for Stiva, which enables her to forgive even the multiple transgressions. If she does so it is on the grounds of the New Testament model of forgiving, "seventy-seven times," which is to say, she forgives unconditionally, and "just as if nothing had ever happened at all" (85). According to John Garrard, she is thereby "the female character who embodies the highest ideals of the novel's value system."[13] In accordance with Jewish teachings, Tolstoy shows the emotional effort involved for Dolly in forgiving her philandering and profligate husband. Toward the end of the novel, Stiva beseeches Dolly to sell her estate and with the proceeds to pay off the alarming amount of debt that he has accumulated. Dolly "was in despair, hated her husband, was thinking of asking for a divorce, but she ended by consenting to sell part of her estate" (776). Dolly's emotional turmoils over the forgiveness she invariably bestows enrich her character with the realism that is Tolstoy's hallmark. But they have two other effects besides: They deprive her of the grace in forgiving implicit in the New Testament model, so much so that it becomes doubtful whether she does indeed image the novel's highest ideals, and whether that honor should not rather fall to the much more minor character, Varenka, whose forgivings of the petulant Kitty are spontaneous and without dramatic effect; and, they raise the question of whether they do not in fact point to an equally and perhaps even more viable course for her to withhold forgiveness from her husband, whose behavior might have needed to stand under harsher judgment. In any case, Dolly, for all the sympathy she draws from the reader, does not leave the deepest mark in memory, a distinction that must always be Anna's. And so we are still left wondering whether literature ever offers up a memorable picture of unconditional forgiveness that matches the highest ideals of Judaism and Christianity. In other words, does literature at its most expressive ever successfully portray a saint?

Chapter 13

Saintliness

According to a surprising consensus of critical opinion, literature cannot portray saints.[1] W. H. Auden gives one of the most interesting reasons for this: "The gospel defines a good deed as one done in secret. . . . This means that art, which by its nature can only deal with what can and should be manifested, cannot portray a saint."[2] But Auden has conflated goodness with saintliness. It was Rudolf Otto who taught us that the holy, or sanctified, was, while intimately related to goodness, still distinguishable from it. The genealogy of the concept of sanctity, back through the Latin *sanctus*, Greek *hagios*, and Hebrew *kadosh*, bears him out. For the root meaning of *kadosh* is simply "separate." The earliest glimmers of sanctity in the Hebrew scripture will show not in the first attainments of consummate goodness but in those figures whom the Torah most sharply distinguishes from everyone else. And though several kinds of persons in Torah carry divinely sanctioned distinctions, including the Israelites themselves, one figure especially stands out in this role: the Nazirite.[3] These individuals, described in chapter six of Numbers, voluntarily vowed themselves to an ascetic lifestyle either in thankfulness for or in hopes of receiving a particular blessing from God. The vow was not for life but for a set period of time, which later rabbinic tradition set at thirty days. But the signs of Nazirite status were visible: uncut hair, abstention from wine, and absence at funerals. That these self-denials were significant within ancient Israelite culture shows in the scope of the sacrificial rites that marked the completion of a period devoted to this ascetical practice: one each of a burnt, sin, peace, and wave offering, representing between them major categories of sacrifice prescribed for tabernacle worship.

The Nazirite dropped from view in Jewish tradition. In time, intentional acts of separation from the community, however nobly motivated, came to be viewed with suspicion. Christianity, however, made ample room for separated individuals who exhibited higher degrees of goodness than most others. But even here, the distinction of saints from others preceded their goodness. The earliest Christian saints were the martyrs who suffered under Roman persecution. These exceptional figures were judged to be able to endure their extraordinary trials only by virtue of a special closeness to God that they must have enjoyed. With the end of the persecutions, self-willed asceticism replaced martyrdom as the distinguishing mark of the Christian saint. But neither of these kinds of figures could serve as models for ordinary Christians in a rapidly growing church. And so it was, finally, that moral goodness, a broadly imitable quality, came to be attached to the figures officially venerated in the church as saints.[4]

If saints were merely good, then they might be harder to import into novels, but the element of separateness in their lives should enhance their aesthetic appeal for fiction. These two features of the saint—separateness from others, goodness toward others—are already inherently so paradoxical that the challenge they pose is not simply to literature but to reality as such. For at the same time their radical distinctiveness pulls them away from the world, their goodness pulls them toward it. This lends saints an element of uncanniness. The trouble with saintly uncanniness is that it invites psychological explanation, in terms of, say, schizophrenia, or passive-aggressive syndrome, or any illness that turns on radical self-division. Visionaries have been interpreted as victims of hysteria and mystics of adult infantilism. A novelist who successfully portrays a saint convinces the reader that the uncanniness of the character lies not in neurosis or psychosis but in a feature of saintliness that has been claimed for it since its Nazirite beginnings, in exceptional closeness to God. This is no mean feat for writers in a genre that has been abandoned by God. Simone Weil suggests that the literary portrayal of saintliness requires extraordinary genius.[5] It does at least demand a kind of talent for awakening religious experience, for insofar as the writer persuades us that one of his characters is motivated by an unseen and uncharacterized divine presence, which, by virtue of its absence from the novel itself, must occupy the reality outside it, she has, in effect, provoked in us something like a religious experience. All of the complexities of the approach-avoidance relationship between religion and literature converge on the figure of the saint. Perhaps the problem of saintliness for literature is not that the novelist cannot image the saint but that, once imaged, the saint transposes the words that created him into revelation. Literature that succeeds in portraying the saint ceases to be literature and becomes something akin to Scripture. In this case, the writer drawn to saints but true to his calling must either failingly depict saints or successfully show saints that fail in their calling. Let us consider three different literary negotiations of this puzzle: *The Idiot* (once again), George Eliot's *Middlemarch*, and Dreiser's *The Bulwark*.

Prince Myshkin's separateness from the other characters in the novel already shows in his epithet, the Idiot, descending from the Greek *idiotes*, connoting one who is fully private. Myshkin's idiocy is most literally the disease from which he suffers, epilepsy, which at its worst cuts off all ties of communication. But he also provokes incomprehension, to the point of resentment, in the other characters. Perhaps the most dramatic statement of resentment toward him comes from the tubercular and histrionic Ippolit, who, at the close of one of the gatherings of the characters turns to Myshkin with these words, "I hate you more than everyone and everything in the world! I don't want your benevolence, I won't take anything."[6] Ippolit implies that Myshkin's generosity toward him undermines his character and subtly indebts him. Myshkin does indeed take onto himself the blame for Ippolit's outburst, which had embarrassed all present. But much later Ippolit reconciles with Myshkin in a way typical of Myshkin's relations with all of the characters, through facial communications of transparent trust and affirmation. Before a suicide attempt that will fail, Ippolit embraces Myshkin so as to look him in the eyes and thereby "say good-bye to man" (406). It is telling that Ippolit should choose Myshkin to receive this face-to-face parting gesture, for throughout the novel, Myshkin shows an acute sensitivity to faces, in which he reads the whole of lives. We have already seen this in his response to Nastasya's face, and to that of the man about to be executed. In an extended study of the role of faces in *The Idiot*, Leslie Johnson calls them "emblems of exteriority."[7] They are the portals through which the souls of the characters show. All of the characters want to be read through their faces, but only one,

Myshkin, acts and speaks consistently to that need in others, howsoever much they fail to reciprocate. "People act differently when they come face-to-face with the prince. His regard alters the space between them, renders it more intersubjective and conducive to communication—a space where they feel safe enough to reveal themselves."[8] This is Myshkin's goodness, which stands throughout the novel, despite the confusion he occasions, through his own indecisions, in the lives of the other characters, especially Nastasya and Aglaia.

The paradox of Myshkin's simultaneous estrangement from and intimacy with the other characters is part of his uncanniness. But a theme of uncanniness also inflects his conversations, for example, one with Rogozhin in chapter four, part two, of the novel. Myshkin is parting from Rogozhin after a visit. In a conversation already colored by strange turns, unexpected gestures, uncertainty, and surprise, Rogozhin suddenly asks whether Myshkin believes in God. Myshkin does not respond directly but by narratives that recount recent experiences he has had of: an atheist whose disbelief seemed unrelated to denial of the actual God; a murderer who prayed to God for forgiveness in the very act of slaying his friend in order to steal his silver watch; a drunken soldier who overcharged for a tin cross he was selling; and a mother who crossed herself at the sight of her infant's first smile, exclaiming that God had as much pleasure in a sinner's prayers as a mother does in "the first smile on her baby's face" (213). The stories are improbable responses to Rogozhin's question. Part of their import is that responses to questions about faith do not conform to expectations of faith held from outside it, that what is meant by faith in the first place can only be understood from inside it. Faith is literally beyond our ken, or uncanny. This is why the atheist's denials struck Myshkin as being besides the point. The next two stories demonstrate that however faith may be characterized from a stance outside it, it is not as reasoned ethics. Only the last story is overtly edifying. For Myshkin, the mother's remark captured "all the essence of Christianity." Contextualized by the novel's theme of faces, this story assimilates Myshkin's innate ability to read faces to the divine fount of forgiveness.

But Myshkin's stories assimilate him to the New Testament Jesus as well. His narratives are like the Gospel parables that Jesus tells in response to questions put to him. Like Jesus, Myshkin tells stories set in ordinary life that by confounding expectation of what should happen there provide a window onto an alternative, sacred dimension. But Jesus is merely an underlay for Myshkin, not his puppeteer. If Myshkin is to be, for literature, a successful portrayal of a saint, then he must remain wed to the novel that gives him life, and not translated out of there into the New Testament. Dostoevsky discourages any such translation by the distance he sets between Jesus' parables and Myshkin's stories: the first are artfully constructed teaching tools, while the second are simple recountings from Myshkin's own life experience. Here is a test of whether Dostoevsky persuades the reader that Myshkin's uncanniness is divinely grounded: Does the reader herself find in Myshkin an astute interpreter of her own face, so that she anticipates with pleasure and even relief his appearances in the novel? If the fourth story Myshkin tells Rogozhin succeeds as it should, to imply that face reading is God's work, then, without having made a character of God within the novel, or otherwise presupposed his existence, Dostoevsky will have provoked in readers especially receptive to Myshkin a sense that behind this fictional character stands a real, divine presence.

Though George Eliot did not share Dostoevsky's Christian beliefs, she was fascinated by that paradox of strangeness and goodness that characterizes the saint. In her late novel, *Daniel Deronda*, she explored this phenomenon in a Jewish context. But her most memorable attempt to draw such a figure in fiction is Dorothea Brooke of *Middlemarch*. Dorothea is not conventionally Christian. When she articulates her religion as "desiring what is perfectly good,"[9] she sounds more like a Platonist.[10] But differences in doctrinal backdrop to literary saints do not necessarily affect their genesis. Eliot's techniques for producing her version of a saint are very similar to Dostoevsky's. Like Myshkin, Dorothea is an oddity in her social setting, a "cygnet . . . reared uneasily among ducklings" (viii). Her estrangement from the other characters derives from the mismatch of "the intensity of her religious disposition" (30), yearning after "some lofty conception of the world" (10), with the conditions of provincial life in which she is fated to live. Like Myshkin, she endures harsh judgments passed on her for what are deemed, alternatively, extravagance or lapse (viii). "Those who had not seen anything of Dorothea usually observed that she could not have been 'a nice woman'" (811). But again, like Myshkin, despite these misalignments, she is "endowed with an innate ability to provide spiritual direction and hope to others."[11] Dorothea differs from Myshkin in that she is a saint in the making. If Myshkin enters his novel fully formed, then Dorothea only gradually and painfully grows into her saintliness. At the start, she is a poor reader of faces. She completely misreads the face of Mr. Casaubon. "He is remarkably like the portrait of Locke," Eliot has Dorothea say of Mr. Casaubon, in words that provoke amusement not only in her sister Celia but in the reader, and "everything I see in him corresponds to his pamphlet on Biblical cosmology" (22). It is only after her unhappy marriage to Mr. Casaubon, and his death, that Dorothea progresses into the figure we see by the end of the novel, whom another character likens to the Virgin Mary: "She evidently thinks nothing of her own future . . . as if she wanted nothing for herself but a chair to sit in from which she can look down with those clear eyes at the poor mortals who pray to her" (746). This attribution to her of indifference to her own future is another commonality with Myshkin. By the clarity in her eyes, she shows herself to have become an astute reader of faces.

But the Virgin Mary is not the underlay for Dorothea, as Jesus is for Myshkin, that helps readers receive her as a bearer of divine presence. That role falls from the beginning to St. Teresa of Avila. A saint so conjointly active and mystical suits Dorothea. The statement of the likeness is not restricted to the novel's famous prelude. Traveling in Rome with her husband, she is spied, momentarily distracted, in a pose that recalls the famous Bernini statue of Teresa: "Her long cloak, fastened at the neck, was thrown backward from her arms, and one beautiful ungloved hand pillowed her cheek, pushing somewhat backward the white beaver bonnet which made a sort of halo to her face. . . . Her eyes were fixed dreamily on a streak of sunlight which fell across the floor" (186). Even the building projects she envisioned for Casaubon's estate recall the convent reforms that Teresa instituted. But the test of Dorothea's success as a literary saint is the same as that for Myshkin: Does the "spiritual direction and hope" she has for her co-characters in the novel extend outward, across the boundary between fiction and reality, into the heart of the reader, so much so that her appearances in the novel are anticipated with pleasure and relief? And is it a divine hand the reader is led to suppose underlies that feat? Eliot herself might refuse any such suggestion. But it is a striking fact of modern prayer book publishing that the concluding lines of Eliot's novel, which link the constricted goodness of Dorothea's life to our own well-being now, and so erase the distinction between fiction and reality, appear in the Reform Jewish *Gates of Prayer* as a suggested reading in prelude to the *kaddish*, or prayer for the dead.[12] Those memorable lines about the "growing good of the world" and its dependence on those who "lived faithfully a hidden life and rest in unvisited tombs" (811) would not have been transposed from a novel by a non-Jew (howsoever philo-Semitic) into a Jewish liturgical text unless the figure they described, namely, Dorothea, was judged, consciously or unconsciously, a credible conduit of divine presence.

Dreiser's *The Bulwark* takes an entirely different approach to the challenge of the literary saint. Instead of fashioning one out of his imagination, Dreiser integrates into his novel, as part of the plot and character development, words quoted verbatim and at surprising length from the journal of a historic Quaker saint, John Woolman. Apart from Dreiser's own reference to "the figure of this early American saint,"[13] and from the room that William James, that great analyst of religious experience, makes for Woolman's *Journal* in his chapter on saints in *The Varieties of Religious Experience*, students of this eighteenth-century abolitionist, pacifist, and advocate for the poor will recognize in him the by-now familiar marks of saintliness: the uncanny coincidence of movements, grounded in a sense of the sacred, toward and away from others. Distinctively ascetic even by Quaker standards, Woolman extended his consideration for others even to slaveholders, whose exploitative practice he abominated, but whose feelings he considered in his efforts to persuade them to free their slaves. In Dreiser's novel, tracing three generations of life within a Quaker family, Woolman is occasionally cited as an author dear to some of the characters. But it is only at the end as the central character, Solon Barnes, nears his death that his daughter, Etta, whose wisdom, we remember, "was related to beauty only," offers to comfort her father by reading aloud from the *Journal*. What one critic calls this "grand display"[14] of the *Journal* within the novel takes the reader by surprise. The author willingly suspends his own voice for another's over the course of several paragraphs. It is as though Dreiser transposes onto this excerpt from Woolman's *Journal* a feature of its author's own saintliness, namely, its separation from its surroundings, for the passage is recognizably distinct from Dreiser's own words, which the double quotes around it, owing to the oral reading of it that Etta performs, underscore. But the passage also works like a saint in the good it brings to at least two of the characters, Solon and Etta. Upon hearing Woolman's words, Solon, for all of his weakness, "appeared to capture an unusual degree of vitality" from them (330); Etta, for her part, is moved to newly appreciate "something beyond human passion and its selfish desires and ambitions, the love

and peace involved in the consideration for others" (331). The implication is that as Solon dies, Etta begins to experience what he knew, but
she had not until then: "an intimate relation to the very heart of being"
(331). For at least one reader, Quaker scholar Rufus Jones, this concluding scene between Solon and Etta is the high point of the novel,[15]
which is to say Dreiser's incorporation of Woolman's *Journal*—itself a
work of artistic merit—into *The Bulwark* succeeds for Jones both as literature and as the evocation of a saint.

     If our three attempts at literary sainthood succeed, then their suc-
cess is highly conditioned by reader responses that are inevitably varied
and unpredictable. But this conditionality speaks to both Auden's
remark and to the paradoxical need for literary saints to fail. Insofar as
their life as saints depends on the reception they receive in reader consciousness, as catalysts of religious experience there, Myshkin,
Dorothea, and the Woolman passage will fail many times over. That
assures the hiddenness that, according to Auden, their goodness
requires, but they also will occasionally succeed, insofar as even a few
readers are moved by them to religious experience. As portraits of saintliness, they are discontinuous, intermittent, and evanescing. That is the
faltering extent to which a muse can fashion a saint.

Notes

Preface

1. Jean Leclercq, *The Love of Learning and the Desire for God: A Study of Monastic Culture*, 3rd ed., trans. Catharine Misrahi (New York: Fordham University Press, 1982).

2. See, for example, *Derrida and Religion: Other Testaments*, ed. Yvonne Sherwood and Kevin Hart (New York: Routledge, 2004).

3. Here I am thinking of the several references to the friend the Church has in "true art," or "the noblest forms" of art, and to the need of art to be motivated by "genuine inspiration." The characterizations "true," "noblest," and "genuine" are difficult to read except as implicit, ecclesiastical restrictions on (or, indeed, censorings of) what artists themselves may proffer as works of art. See Pope John Paul II, *Letter to Artists* (Chicago: Liturgy Training Publications, 1999), also widely available online, for example, through the Vatican Web site, http://www.vatican.va.

Chapter 1: Introduction

1. For the muses as agents of memory, see Robert Sardello, "Urania," in *The Muses*, ed. Gail Thomas (Dallas, TX: Dallas Institute of Humanities and Culture, 1994), 11. For the muses as agents of forgetfulness, see Penelope Murray, "Plato's Muses: The Goddesses that Endure," in *Cultivating the Muses: Struggle for Power and Inspiration in Classical Literature*, ed. Efrossini Spentzou and Don Fowler (New York: Oxford University Press, 2002), 39.

2. Charles Kegley offers several definitions of literature, including one he takes from T. S. Eliot: "any work of the imagination." See Charles Kegley, "Literature and Religion: A Study of Three Types of Relation," in *Proceedings of the 6th International Congress on Aesthetics*, ed. Rudolf Zeitler. Uppsala Series in the History of Art, nova ser., 10 (Uppsala, Sweden: Universitet, 1972).

3. Plato, *Republic* 607, in *The Dialogues of Plato*, trans. B. Jowett (New York: Random House, 1920).

4. Plato, *Laws* in *The Dialogues of Plato*, 719.

5. Michael Morgan, "Plato and Greek Religion," in *The Cambridge Companion to Plato*, ed. Richard Kraut (New York: Cambridge University Press, 1992), 232.

6. George Lukacs, *Theory of the Novel* (Cambridge: MIT Press, 1973), 88.

7. Antiquity had novels, but they were not considered serious literature, even by the ancient world itself. Drama was serious. Novels were fantastic adventure stories that held roughly the same status in the ancient mind that the mysteries, romances, and westerns sold in pharmacies hold for us today. The East preceded the West in the production of serious novels. The first Eastern novel is often taken to be *The Tale of Genji*.

8. See, for example, Eric Ziolkowski, *The Sanctification of Don Quixote: From Hidalgo to Priest* (University Park: Pennsylvania State University Press, 1991). The reading cited here is especially Kierkegaard's.

9. Giles Gunn, *The Interpretation of Otherness* (New York: Oxford University Press, 1979), 78.

10. R. W. B. Lewis, "Hold on Hard to the Huckleberry Bushes," in *Religion and Modern Literature: Essays in Theory and Criticism*, ed. G. B. Tennyson and Edward E. Ericson (Grand Rapids, MI: Eerdmans, 1975), 63.

11. Max Weber, *The Protestant Ethic and the Spirit of Capitalism*, trans. Talcott Parsons (New York: Charles Scribner's Sons, 1930).

12. Among the Reformers, Calvin may have had the most developed social ethics. If he did not go so far as to picture an individual's private sin manifesting outwardly in physical deformity, he did believe, in accordance with Old Testament teachings, that individual sin polluted the whole society: "When crime is left unpunished, it pollutes the whole country." See John Calvin, *Commentary on Genesis*, quoted in William Bouwsma, *John Calvin: A Sixteenth Century Portrait* (New York: Oxford University Press, 1988), 49.

13. And hypocrisy. The weight of evil that idolatry and adultery carried in the biblical world hypocrisy and cruelty carried in the classical world. Hawthorne's scale of values is the Enlightenment one based on Greek and Roman ethics, not the Puritan one based on the Bible. Although it is an "A" that appears on Arthur's chest, it is not adultery that drove it there but hypocrisy. But then, from a distance, an "H" might look like an "A."

14. Nathaniel Hawthorne, *The Scarlet Letter* (Boston: Houghton Mifflin, 1960), 67.

15. See, for example, A. Whigham Price, "D. H. Lawrence and Congregationalism," *The Congregational Quarterly* 34 (July 1956): 242–252; Dean Peerman, "D. H. Lawrence: Devout Heretic," *The Christian Century* (February 22, 1961): 237–241.

16. D. H. Lawrence, "Hymns in a Man's Life," in *The Later D. H. Lawrence*, ed. William York Tindall (New York: Knopf, 1952), 383.

17. D. H. Lawrence, *Sons and Lovers* (New York: Viking, 1958), 251.

18. Ibid., 153, 251.

19. Lawrence Hussman, *Dreiser and His Fiction: A 20th-Century Quest* (Philadelphia: University of Pennsylvania Press, 1983), 169.

20. Quoted in Conrad Eugene Ostwalt, *After Eden: The Secularization of American Space in the Fiction of Willa Cather and Theodore Dreiser* (Lewisburg, PA: Bucknell University Press, 1990), 101.

21. Theodore Dreiser, *The Bulwark* (New York: Doubleday, 1946), 129–30.

22. Edward Jones, *L. P. Hartley* (Boston: Twayne, 1978), 15.

23. L. P. Hartley, *Eustace and Hilda* (New York: Putnam, 1958), 150–51.

24. *Scarlet Letter Handbook*, ed. Seymour Lee Gross (San Francisco: Wadsworth, 1960), 33.

25. *Russian Orthodoxy under the Old Regime*, ed. Robert Nichols and Theofanis George Stavrou (Minneapolis: University of Minnesota Press, 1978), 21.

26. Donald Treadgold, "Russian Orthodoxy and Society," in *Russian Orthdoxy under the Old Regime*, ed. R. Nichols (Minneapolis: University of Minnesota Press, 1978), 31.

27. Leo Tolstoy, quoted in Ernest Simmons, *Tolstoy* (London: Routledge, Kegan Paul, 1973), 120.

28. Wayne Booth, *The Company We Keep* (Berkeley, CA: University of California Press, 1988), 339.

29. Leo Tolstoy, *Anna Karenina*, trans. David Magarshack (New York: New American Library, 1961), 230.

30. Ibid.

31. Ibid., 225.

32. Isaiah Berlin, "Tolstoy and the Enlightenment," in *Leo Tolstoy*, ed. H. Bloom (New York: Chelsea House, 1986), 93.

33. This is D. H. Lawrence's interpretation of Tolstoy too. "As a true artist, he worshipped every manifestation of pure, spontaneous, passionate life kindled to vividness." Lawrence, quoted in T. G. S. Cain, *Tolstoy* (New York: Harper & Row, 1977), 84.

34. Quoted in Kenneth Lantz, *The Dostoevsky Encyclopedia* (Westport, CT: Greenwood Press, 2004), 195.

35. Robin Feuer Miller, "The Notebooks for *The Idiot*," in *Dostoevsky's* The Idiot: *A Critical Companion*, ed. Liza Knapp (Evanston, IL: Northwestern University Press, 1998), 76.

36. Fyodor Dostoevsky, *The Idiot*, trans. Constance Garnett (New York: Bantam, 1971), 218–9.

CHAPTER 2: A RELIGIOUS CRITIQUE OF LITERATURE: THE PLATONIC LINE

1. Martin Buber, *Eclipse of God: Studies in the Relation between Religion and Philosophy*, trans. Maurice Friedman et al. (New York: Harper, 1957), 38.

2. Jeremy Bernstein, "Dr. Donne and Sir Edmund Gosse," *The New Criterion* 16:7 (March 1998): 16–24.

3. Edmund Gosse, *Father and Son* (New York: Scribner's, 1913), 254.

4. Ibid., 179.

5. Ibid., 23–24.

6. John McNeill, *History and Character of Calvinism* (New York: Oxford University Press, 1954), 103.

7. William Bouwsma, *John Calvin: A Sixteenth-Century Portrait* (New York: Oxford University Press, 1988), 114.

8. Calvin, *The Institutes of Christian Religion*, trans. Ford Lewis Battles (Philadelphia, PA: Westminster Press, 1960), 83.

9. Margaret Deanesly, *The History of the Medieval Church, 590–1500* (London: Methuen, 1972), 245.

10. Augustine, *Confessions*, trans. Albert Outler (London: SCM Press, 1955), 1:17.

11. Ibid., 1:13.

12. Augustine, *City of God*, trans. Marcus Dods (New York: Modern Library, 1950), 54.

13. Ibid.

14. Calvin, for all his appreciation of classical literature, did also detest the theater: "Theaters resound with lying fictions." Calvin, quoted in Bouwsma, *John Calvin*, 179.

15. Georges Bataille, *Literature and Evil*, trans. A. Hamilton (New York: Marion Boyars, 1997), 79.

16. Augustine, *Confessions* (trans. Albert Outler) 3:5

17. See Robert J. Forman, *Augustine and the Making of a Christian Literature: Classical Tradition and Augustinian Aesthetics* (Lewiston, NY: Edwin Mellen, 1995).

18. Walter Burckert, *Greek Religion*, trans. John Raffan (Cambridge, MA: Harvard University Press, 1985), 120.

19. Christopher Janaway, *Images of Excellence: Plato's Critique of the Arts* (New York: Clarendon, 1995), 5.

20. Maimonides, *The Book of Knowledge from the Mishneh Torah*, trans. H. M. Russell and J. Weinberg (New York: Ktav, 1983), 31.

21. Homer, *Iliad*, trans. Richard Lattimore(Chicago, IL: The University of Chicago Press), 16:94, and many other places.

22. Ibid., 15:247.

23. See, for example, Simone Weil, *The Iliad, or The Poem of Force*, trans. Mary McCarthy (Wallingford, PA: Pendle Hill, 1956).

24. This account is taken from books 6 and 7 of Plato's *Republic*.

25. Plato, *Republic* (trans. Jowett), 387. Subsequent references are cited parenthetically in the text.

CHAPTER 3: A LITERARY CRITIQUE OF RELIGION: THE DANTEAN LINE

1. Friedrich Schelling, *The Philosophy of Art*, trans. David Simpson (Minneapolis: University of Minnesota Press, 1989), 45.

2. Northrup Frye, *The Great Code: The Bible and Literature* (New York: Harcourt Brace Jovanivich, 1982), 218.

3. Ibid., xiv. Cf. Richard Chase, *Quest for Myth* (Baton Rouge: Louisiana State University Press, 1949), where we read that "the central premise of this book is that *myth is literature,*" vi.

4. David Bidney, "Myth, Symbolism, and Truth," in *Myth and Literature: Contemporary Theory and Practice,* ed. John Vickery (Lincoln: University of Nebraska Press, 1966), 7.

5. For a somewhat cynical itemization of definitions of myth within the framework of literary criticism, see William Righter, *Myth and Literature* (London: Routledge and Kegan Paul, 1975), 5–6.

6. Frye, *The Great Code,* 51.

7. See Gregory Nagy, "Ancient Greek Poetry, Prophecy, and Concepts of Theory," in *Poetry and Prophecy: The Beginnings of a Literary Tradition,* ed. James L. Kugel (Ithaca, NY: Cornell University Press, 1990), 56, 61.

8. Though these rites, if not the myths underlying them, could become the target of a dramatist's critique. See Mark McPherran, *The Religion of Socrates* (University Park: Pennsylvania State University Press, 1996), 26.

9. Richmond Lattimore, Introduction to *Oresteia* (Chicago: University of Chicago Press, 1953), 5.

10. John Milton, *Paradise Regained,* in *The Portable Milton,* ed. Douglas Bush (New York: Viking, 1999), 4:295.

11. Robert Alter, *Canon and Creativity: Modern Writing and the Authority of Scripture* (New Haven, CT: Yale University Press, 2000), 50.

12. Dan Pagis, "Poet as Prophet in Medieval Hebrew Literature," in *Poetry and Prophecy,* ed. James L. Kugel, 147.

13. Alter, *Canon and Creativity*, 145.

14. Ibid., 121, 146.

15. Bialik is not the only modern Hebrew poet for whom this claim is made. We also read, "Tschernichowsky may be justly called the only myth-making poet in the history of Hebrew literature." See Eisig Silberschlag, *Saul Tschernichowsky: Poet of Revolt* (Ithaca, NY: Cornell University Press, 1968), 39. Alter observes that Bialik, like some of his medieval predecessors, saw his role "as Hebrew poet in light of the vocation of the biblical prophet" (Alter, *Canon and Creativity*, 53).

16. Harry Slochower, *Mythopoesis: Mythic Patterns in the Literary Classics* (Detroit, MI: Wayne State University Press, 1970), 19.

17. In any discussion of one of these poets, references to one or more of the other three are not uncommon. Some examples from the secondary literature follow: "In the originality, comprehensiveness, and sheer energy of his analysis of the religious dimensions of human experience, William Blake's artistic achievement is matched in Western literature only by that of Dante and Milton." See Robert Ryan, "Blake and Religion," in *The Cambridge Companion to William Blake*, ed. Morris Eaves (New York: Cambridge University Press, 2003), 150; "In the use of tradition, Blake exceeded Milton and was second, if to anyone, only to Dante." See M. O. Percival, *William Blake's Circle of Destiny* (New York: Columbia University Press, 1938), 1; "The interrelationships, often noted, between the Book of Revelation and other prophecy (especially Daniel's) are archetypal for those that exist between Milton's epics and those of Blake, and between Blake's epics and the lyric-epic vision of Yeats." See Joseph Anthony Wittreich, *Milton and the Line of Vision* (Madison: University of Wisconson Press, 1975), xv. Each of the three successive pairs that the four poets make, when listed in chronological order, has inspired monographs of comparative literary criticism.

18. Dante, *The Banquet*, trans. and with an introduction and notes by Christopher Ryan (Saratoga, CA: Anma Libri, 1989), 66.

19. See Amilcare Iannucci, "Dante's Theological Canon in the *Commedia*," *Italian Quarterly* 37 (Winter–Fall 2000): 143–46.

20. Charles Singleton, *Dante Studies 2: Journey to Beatrice* (Cambridge, MA: Harvard University Press, 1958), 7.

21. Erich Auerbach, *Mimesis*, trans. Willard R. Trask (Princeton: Princeton University Press, 1953), 202.

22. Ernest Fortin, *Dissent and Philosophy in the Middle Ages: Dante and His Precursors*, trans. Marc A. LePain (Lanham, MD: Lexington Books, 2002), 130.

23. See, for example, Joan Ferrante, "A Poetics of Chaos and Harmony," in *Cambridge Companion to Dante*, ed. Rachel Jacoff (New York: Cambridge University Press, 1993), 153–171. See also Peter Hawkins's wonderful story of the moment of epiphany among a group of Dante scholars, when it seemed as though they had discovered the precise numeric center of the poem in the thematically key word: "amor," which, spelled backwards, indicated its key complementary theme: Rome. See Peter Hawkins, *Dante's Testaments: Essays in Scriptural Imagination* (Stanford, CA: Stanford University Press, 1999), 9.

24. Dante Alighieri, *Paradise* 17:69, *The Divine Comedy*, trans. Henry F. Cary (New York: Crowell, 1897). Subsequent quotations from *The Divine Comedy* are taken from this translation and are given parenthetically in the text. In our copyright obsessed times, this nineteenth-century translation falls safely within the public domain. Readers are encouraged to consult other, more recent translations. For example, a more memorable translation of the phrase in question appears as a title of a recent article by Robert Hollander, "Dante: A Party of One," *First Things* 92 (April 1999): 30–35.

25. Paul Priest, *Dante's Incarnation of the Trinity* (Ravenna, Italy: Longo Editore, 1982).

26. It is striking how small a role Christ himself plays in the poem. The natural explanation for this is that he is present through his representative, Beatrice, except that the chain of authorization behind Beatrice's mission to Dante reaches back not to Christ but to the Virgin Mary, who does indeed appear in pictorial splendor toward the end of the poem. For all of the depictions of Christ in medieval art, he never appears fully pictured in the poem. Another possible reason for this is that so muted a Christ coheres with the apocalyptic thrust of the poem, since, according to St. Paul, at the end of time, Christ subordinates to God to the point of virtually disappearing, so that God "may be everything to everyone" (1 Cor. 15:28, RSV).

27. This is Allen Mandelbaum's translation. For *sospetto*, Cary has "distrust." Dante Alighieri, *The Divine Comedy*, trans. Allen Mandelbaum (New York: Knopf, 1995), 68.

28. Mandelbaum translates this as "the great refusal" (Ibid., 69). Cary captures the same idea through the word "abjured."

29. The contrast is especially troubling if the poem is read apocalyptically. Joachim's third age of Christianity constitutes an apocalypse of sorts for the institutional church of the second age. If the Spirituals strove to realize the church of temporal powerlessness within the confines of their own order, then why is not Celestine, for Dante, a symbolic representation of the same attempt within the confines of the papacy? In time, Celestine was indeed taken to represent an alternative vision of the institutional church. See "Celestine V, Pope," in *The Dante Encyclopedia*, ed. Richard Lansing (New York: Garland, 2000), 152.

30. Though John D. Sinclair calls Plato Dante's "far nearer kinsman." Dante, *The Divine Comedy of Dante Alighieri, III: Paradiso*, trans. and commentary by John D. Sinclair (New York: Oxford University Press, 1939, 1961), 70.

31. See Mowbray Allan, "Two Dantes? Christian versus Humanist?" *MLN* 107:1 (January 1992): 18–35.

32. The Inferno, which dims the intellect, offers no explanation for these fictive bodies. But in Purgatory, which admits the light of reason, and where similarly disembodied souls nonetheless manifest bodily form, we learn from Statius how these "airy bodies" are fashioned from the immaterial soul (Pur. 25:79–108). Still, how seriously can we take the suffering of these bodies?

33. Dante Alighieri, *The Comedy of Dante Alighieri, Cantica II: Purgatory*, trans. Dorothy Sayers (New York: Basic Books, 1963), 287.

34. Sinclair, in Dante, *The Divine Comedy of Dante Alighieri, III: Paradisio*, 381.

35. "The answers are undeniably rigorous, but as the text insinuates, with a measure of irony, they are akin to those of a sophist." See Fortin, *Dissent and Philosophy in the Middle Ages*, 123. Fortin's point is less that Dante the pilgrim is less virtuous than he seems at this juncture than that Dante the poet's own Christianity comes into question here, because his arguments in defense of the faith are so patently unconvincing. Fortin may well be right. Dante's final defense of Christianity is that multitudes accepted it; how persuasive a defense is that coming from a self-admitted "party of one"?

36. If so, then books with such titles as *Praying with Dante*, which mine the *Comedy* for devotional fare, are misguided.

37. Robert Hollander, "Dante Theologus-Poeta," *Dante Studies* 118 (2000): 286. The quote from Singleton is cited here on p. 273.

38. For theological attitudes toward poetry in the Middle Ages, prior to Dante, see Hollander, ibid.; Ernst Robert Curtius, *European Literature and the Latin Middle Ages*, trans. Willard Trask (Princeton, NJ: Princeton University Press, 1948, 1967), 214–27. The attitudes that these scholars cite, especially in Thomas Aquinas, were dismissive at best.

39. Dorothy Sayers, *Further Papers on Dante* (New York: Harper, 1957), 2.

40. Hawkins, *Dante's Testaments*, 269.

41. Dante, *De Vulgari Eloquio*, 2:8:9 in *Opere Minori di Dante Alighieri*, vol. 2, ed. Pietro Fraticelli (Florence, Italy: G. Barbera, 1906). For English see, *Translation of the Latin Works of Dante Alighieri* (New York: Greenwood Press, 1969).

42. Fortin, *Dissent and Philosophy*, 130. Fortin interprets Dante more radically along the lines of dissimulating dissent. His Dante contrives to "masquerade as an accredited defender of the faith" and, in so doing, to support a self-concealing minority "who did not hesitate to disguise themselves as Christians to fight against Christians" (145, 146).

43. If Adam's and Eve's primal act of disobedience also is paradigmatic in human life, then when Milton has Eve bow to the tree of knowledge, after having eaten from it, he suggests that idolatry continues as an ever-present threat to true religion.

44. Irene Samuel, *Dante and Milton: The Commedia and Paradise Lost* (Ithaca, NY: Cornell University Press, 1966), 31–45.

45. "The very fact that eighteenth-century theologians could find *Paradise Lost ex omne parte orthodoxum* shows at least that the unorthodox elements hardly determine or colour the scheme of the poem." See Arthur Sewell, *A Study in Milton's Christian Doctrine* (London: Oxford University Press, 1939), 81.

46. Samuel, *Dante and Milton*, 81.

47. Milton, *Paradise Regained*, 1:415.

48. See especially Neil Forsyth, "Satan: Making a Heaven of Hell, a Hell of Heaven," in *The Devil, Heresy, and Witchcraft in the Middle Ages: Essays in Honor of Jeffrey B. Russell*, ed. Alberto Ferreiro (Boston: Brill, 1998), 241–58.

49. Milton, "From Areopagitica," in *Paradise Lost: An Authoritative Text, Backgrounds and Sources, Criticism*, ed. Scott Elledge (New York: Norton, 1993), 384.

50. John Carey further explores the enigma of Satan's rebellion in "Milton's Satan," in *The Cambridge Companion to Milton*, ed. Dennis Danielson (New York: Cambridge University Press, 1989), 131–145.

51. As he himself attests in his *Apology for Smectymnuus*, where he counts among the highest points of his education "the divine volumes of Plato." Quoted in *The Portable Milton*, ed. Douglas Bush (New York: Viking, 1949), 134.

52. Irene Samuel, *Plato and Milton* (Ithaca, NY: Cornell University Press, 1947), 21.

53. Plato, *Phaedrus*, 248, in *Dialogues of Plato*, trans. B. Jowett.

54. Milton, *Paradise Regained*, 4:518–520.

55. Milton, even at his most un-Trinitarian, and most dismissive of the term *begotten* applied to the Son, still acknowledges a distinction between God as creator of Adam and as Father of the Son. And so we may assume that where Satan misses that distinction Milton means for us to understand that as an error. See John Milton, "Of the Son of God," in *Christian Doctrine*, excerpted in *Paradise Lost*, ed. Elledge, 408.

56. The Platonic reading has the added bonus of forgiving God his stilted, wooden speech. For on this reading, he is really the idea of the Good, which, exalted as it is above speech, can only be subjected to speech at the poet's peril.

57. Samuel, *Dante and Milton*, v. Samuel quotes Eliot but does not reference the quote.

58. See, for example, Carey, "Milton's Satan," 141–142.

59. William Blake, "All Religions are One," in *Blake's Poetry and Designs*, selected and ed. by Mary Lynn Johnson and John E. Grant (New York: Norton, 1979), 13.

60. Blake, *Milton*, 2:25 in *Blake's Poetry and Designs* and many other places in the poem.

61. William Blake, "Prospectus: To the Public," in *Blake's Poetry and Designs*, 395.

62. Blake, *The Marriage of Heaven and Hell*, which appears in *Blake's Poetry and Designs*.

63. Margaret Bottrall, *The Divine Image: A Study of Blake's Interpretation of Christianity* (Rome: Edizioni di Storia e Letteratura, 1950), 112.

64. Mary Lynn Johnson, "*Milton* and Its Contexts," in *The Cambridge Companion to William Blake*, ed. Morris Eaves (New York: Cambridge University Press, 2003), 231.

65. J. G. Davies, *Theology of William Blake* (Hamden, CT: Archon Books, 1966), 8.

66. Blake, *The Everlasting Gospel*, 4:101, in *Blake's Poetry and Designs*, 368.

67. Blake, *Jerusalem*, 77, in *Blake's Poetry and Designs*, 346.

68. Blake, *Jerusalem*, 16, in *Blake's Poetry and Designs*, 319.

69. Blake, *Milton* 32:38, in *Blake's Poetry and Designs*, 290.

70. "There is error, mistake, etc. and if these be evil then there is evil, but these are only negations." Blake, quoted by Henry Crabb Robinson, in *Henry Crabb Robinson on Books and Their Writers*, ed. Edith Morely (London: Dent, 1938), v. 1, p. 329, quoted in Melanie Bandy, *Mind Forg'd Manacles: Evil in the Poetry of Blake and Shelley* (University, AL: University of Alabama Press, 1981), 53.

71. Blake, *Jerusalem*, 98:47, in *Blake's Poetry and Designs*, 358. See especially Bandy, *Mind Forg'd Manacles*, 46–48, for an analysis of this tree.

72. Blake, *Songs of Experience* 47:17, 49:8, in *Blake's Poetry and Designs*, 54, 55.

73. Blake, *The Four Zoas*, 2:2 in *The Complete Writings of William Blake*, ed. Geoffrey Keynes (New York: Oxford University Press, 1966).

74. Blake, *The Book of Urizen*, 10:43 ff., in *Blake's Poetry and Designs*, 148–51. Also *Milton*, 2:10 ff., in *Blake's Poetry and Designs*, 240–41.

75. Blake, *The Book of Urizen*, 23:2–3, in *Blake's Poetry and Designs*, 156.

76. Blake, *The Four Zoas*, 9:225 in *The Complete Writings of William Blake*.

77. Blake, *Marriage of Heaven and Hell*, 6, in *Blake's Poetry and Designs*, 88.

78. Blake, *Marriage of Heaven and Hell*, 10. Color reproduction in William Blake, *The Early Illuminated Books* (Princeton, NJ: Princeton University Press, 1993), 159.

79. Frank Kastor, *Milton and the Literary Satan* (Amsterdam: Rodopi, 1974).

80. Margaret Bottrall, *The Divine Image: A Study of Blake's Interpretation of Christianity* (Rome: Ediozioni de Storia e Letteratura, 1950), 112.

81. G. Ingli James, "The Holy and the Heterodox: William Blake's Transformational Use of Religious Language," *Studia Mystica* 14:1 (1991): 31.

82. Ibid.

83. Robert Ryan, *The Romantic Reformation* (New York: Cambridge University Press, 1997), 46.

84. Blake, *Songs of Experience*, 44:12.

85. A conclusion that bodes ill for Swedenborg, depending on how severely literary criticism judges the poetic quality of his texts.

86. Henry Crabb Robinson, *Reminiscences*, in *Blake's Poetry and Designs*, 497.

87. Robert Ryan, "Blake and Religion," in *The Cambridge Companion to William Blake*, 155.

88. Blake, "The Laocoon," in *Blake's Poetry and Designs*, 427.

89. Patrick J. Keane, *Yeats's Interaction with Tradition* (Columbia: University of Missouri Press, 1987), 139.

90. Yeats, quoted from his *Autobiograhies*, in Cleanth Brooks, *The Hidden God: Studies in Hemingway, Faulkner, Yeats, Eliot, and Warren* (New Haven, CT: Yale University Press, 1963), 46.

91. Yeats, "William Blake and His Illustrations to the Divine Comedy," in *Essays and Introductions* (New York: Macmillan, 1961), 134. Yeats had a high appreciation of Dante, whom he called "the chief imagination of Christendom" [Yeats, *The Collected Poems of W. B. Yeats*, 2d rev. ed., ed. Richard Finneran (New York: Scribner, 1996), 160], and whom he located in *A Vision*, at phase 17, which defines the same personality type as his own [Yeats, *A Vision* (New York: Macmillan, 1956)]. He was less complimentary toward Milton, whom he regarded as a throwback [Ibid., 295]

92. There is the occasional critic for whom it is important to claim Yeats for Christianity. See, for example, Virginia Moore, *The Unicorn: William Bulter Yeats' Search for Reality* (New York: Macmillan, 1954). But the more typical claim either is or implies that Yeats, to the extent that he used Christian symbols at all, adopted, co-opted, and transformed them to his own quite extra-Christian poetic needs. See, for example, Cleanth Brooks, *The Hidden God*, 47, 60; Keane, *Yeats's Interaction with Tradition*, 135, 148; Margaret Rudd, *Divided Image: A Study of William Blake and W. B. Yeats* (London: Routledge and Kegan Paul, 1953), 34, 174, 176; F. A. C. Wilson, *W. B. Yeats and the Tradition* (London: Victor Gollancz, 1961), 15–16.

93. Austin Warren, "William Butler Yeats: The Religion of a Poet," in *Religion and Modern Literature: Essays in Theory and Criticism*, ed. G. B. Tennyson and Edward E. Ericson (Grand Rapids, MI: Eerdmans, 1975), 269.

94. Yeats, *A Vision*, 8.

95. Ibid., 72.

96. Yeats, "William Blake and the Imagination," in *Essays and Introductions*, 111, 114.

97. Yeats, *To the Rose Upon the Rood of Time*, in *The Collected Poems of W. B. Yeats*, 31.

98. Brooks, *The Hidden God*, 47.

99. Wilson, *W. B. Yeats and the Tradition*, 15, 16.

100. Ibid., 199.

101. Yeats, *A Vision*, 68. Here Yeats may have in mind Plato's picture of oppositely rotating circles in Timaeus 36. The symbol can be found in Dante and Blake; see Rachel Billigheimer, *Wheels of Eternity: A Comparative Study of William Blake and William Butler Yeats* (New York: St. Martin's Press, 1990), 26.

102. Yeats, "The Need for Audacity of Thought," in *The Collected Works of W. B. Yeats*, vol. 10, ed. Colton Johnson (New York: Scribner, 2000), 201.

103. Yeats, *Vacillation*, in *The Collected Poems of W. B. Yeats*, 253.

104. Ibid.

105. Yeats, *Ego Dominus Tuus*, in *The Collected Poems of W. B. Yeats*, 161. Note that the title is taken from Dante.

106. Yeats, *A Vision*, 263.

107. Rudd, *Divided Image*, 189.

108. Yeats, *A Vision*, 279.

109. Ibid., 27.

110 Ibid., 280.

111. H. W. Janson, *A History of Art*, rev. and expanded by Anthony F. Janson (New York: Abrams; Englewood Cliffs, NJ: Prentice Hall, 1995), 226.

112. Yeats, *A Vision*, 286. Yeats empowers even liturgical art to dispense with Christianity when he writes: "True art . . . seeks to burn all things until they become 'infinite and holy'"; Yeats, "William Blake and His Illustrations to the Divine Comedy," *Essays and Introductions*, 10.

113. Yeats, *The Circus Animals' Desertion*, in *The Collected Poems of W. B. Yeats*, 347 (vs. 31–32).

114. See Thomas William Heyck, "The Genealogy of Irish Modernism," in *Piety and Power in Ireland, 1760–1960: Essays in Honor of Emmet Larkin*, ed. Stewart J. Brown and David W. Miller (Notre Dame, IN: University of Notre Dame Press, 2000), 240.

115. Rudd, *Divided Image*, 198.

CHAPTER 4: CREATION AND CREATIVITY

1. A coinage of Milton Nahm, *The Artist as Creator: An Essay of Human Freedom* (Baltimore, MD: Johns Hopkins University Press, 1956).

2. Thomas Aquinas, *Summa Theologica*, trans. Fathers of the English Dominican Province (London: Burns Oates and Washbourne, 1937), I, xlv, 5.

3. R. G. Collingwood, *The Principles of Art* (New York: Oxford University Press, 1958), 128.

4. The prayer occurs routinely in Jewish liturgy, as part of the blessings surrounding the Shema. See, for example, *Gates of Prayer: The New Union Prayerbook* (New York: Central Conference of American Rabbis, 1975), 34.

5. Plato, *Timaeus*, 28 in *Dialogues of Plato*, trans. B. Jowett.

6. For Philo, see *On the Eternity of the World*, 13–19 in *Philo*, v. 9, trans. F. H. Colson, Loeb Classical Library (Cambridge, MA: Harvard University Press, 1941); for Justin Martyr, see his *First Apology*, ch. 59.

7. Timaeus (trans. Jowett), 48.

8. Timaeus (trans. Jowett), 52.

9. Translations from the Revised Standard Version. Subsequent biblical quotations throughout this book are from this translation. The citations are given parenthetically in the text.

10. Bereshit Rabbah 1:1.

11. Plotinus, *Plotinus*, trans. A. H. Armstrong (London: George Allen, 1953), V, 2, 1.

12. For example, "Creativity occurs on condition that a new and valuable intelligibility comes into being." See Carl Hausman, "Criteria of Creativity," in *The Concept of Creativity in Science and Art*, ed. Denis Dutton and Michael Krausz (The Hague: Nijhoff, 1981), 77. Kant calls the products of artistic genius "exemplary." See Kant, *Critique of Judgment*, trans. Werner Pluhar (Indianapolis, IN: Hackett, 1987), 175 (sec. 308). The issue of analogy between the goodness of the creators, respectively, of the world and of art objects, is more vexed. Plato, as we have already seen, was inclined to attribute debased moral qualities to poets. To the extent that Platonic and biblical artists lose their personal agency in their artistry, it is a question of whether they are subject to moral judgment at all. We will revisit this question in a different guise in a later chapter, when we consider the relation of ethics to religion and art.

13. See *Torah: A Modern Commentary*, commentaries by Guenther Plaut (New York: Union of American Hebrew Congregations, 1981), 688; Nehama Leibowitz, *Studies in Shemot*, vol. 2 (Jerusalem: World Zionist Organization, 1976), 698.

14. Plato, *Ion* 533, in *Dialogues of Plato*, trans. B. Jowett.

15. *Timaeus* (trans. Jowett), 71.

16. *Timaeus* (trans. Jowett), 73.

17. Stein Haugom Olsen, "Culture, Convention, Creativity," in *The Creation of Art: New Essays in Philosophical Aesthetics* (New York: Cambridge University Press, 2003), 202.

18. For example, "Creativity occurs on condition that a new and valuable intelligibility comes into being," Hausman, *The Concept of Creativity in Science and Art*, 77.

19. Monroe Beardsley, "On the Creation of Art," *Journal of Aesthetics and Art Criticism* (Spring 1965): 302.

20. Carl Hausman, *A Discourse on Novelty and Creation* (The Hague: Nijhoff, 1975), 89.

21. Ibid., 76. See also Berys Gaut, "Creativity and Imagination," in *The Creation of Art*, 148–173.

22. For the history of the concept in early Christianity, see Gerhard May, *Creatio Ex Nihilo: The Doctrine of Creation out of Nothing in Early Christian Thought*, trans. A. S. Worrall (Edinburgh: T and T Clark, 1994).

23. As we have already seen with respect to originality and miraculousness, which, to give only our cited instances, are claimed for human creativity by Kant and Monroe Beardsley, respectively. For a sustained appreciation of the artist's freedom, see Nahm, *The Artist as Creator*.

24. Noel Carroll, "Art, Creativity and Tradition," in *The Creation of Art*, 218.

25. Beardsley, "On the Creation of Art," 297.

26. See T. J. Reed, *Genesis: Some Episodes of Literary Creation* (London: Institute of Germanic Studies, University of London, 1995).

27. *Timaeus* (trans. Jowett), 56.

28. Ibid., 30, 33.

29. Ibid., 30.

30. Ibid., 36–37.

31. Ibid., 31.

32. Berys Gaut, "Creativity and Imagination," in *The Creation of Art*, 163.

33. Berys Gaut and Paisley Livingston, "Creativity and Art: Issues and Perspectives," in *The Creation of Art*, 13.

34. Kant, *Critique of Judgment*, trans. Werner S. Pluhar (Indianpolis, IN: Hackett, 1987), 182 (sec. 314).

35. *Phaedrus* (trans. Jowett), 246.

36. Kant, *Critique of Judgment*, 182 (sec. 314).

37. Ibid., 73 (sec. 226).

38. Ibid., 177 (sec. 309).

39. See, for example, Friedrich Schelling, *The Philosophy of Art*, trans. Douglas Stott (Minneapolis: University of Minnesota Press, 1989).

40. Eliade discusses his dual vocation as literary artist and scholar of religion in "Literary Imagination and Religious Structure," in *Symbolism, the Sacred, and the Arts*, ed. Diane Apostolos-Cappadona (New York: Crossroad, 1985), 171–177.

41. Mircea Eliade, *The Sacred and the Profane: The Nature of Religion*, trans. Willard R. Trask (New York: Harper and Row, 1959), 48.

42. Eliade, "Divinities: Art and the Divine," in *Symbolism, the Sacred, and the Arts*, 58.

43. Eliade, *The Sacred and the Profane*, 22.

44. See, for example, Eliade, *The Sacred and Profane*, 31.

45. Ibid., 82.

46. Eliade, "Reflections on Indian Art," in *Symbolism, the Sacred, and the Arts*. "Before being a work of art, an Indian specimen is a work of creation" (72).

47. Eliade, "Survivals and Camouflages of Myths," in *Symbolism, the Sacred, and the Arts*, 49.

48. Ibid., 176.

49. Northrup Frye, *The Great Code: The Bible and Literature* (New York: Harcourt Brace, 1982).

50. Northrup Frye, *Creation and Recreation* (Toronto: University of Toronto Press, 1980), 12.

51. Frye's claim is actually much stronger than this: "There is no longer any functional place for a divine creation myth at the beginning of things" (ibid., 53). With

Blake, Frye's orientation is more toward the end of things. The "recreation" of this book's title points there.

52. Ibid., 11.

53. R. G. Collingwood, *The Principles of Art* (New York: Oxford University Press, 1958), 129.

54. See Lionel Rubinoff, "Religion and the Rapprochement between Thought and Action," in *Critical Essays on the Philosophy of R. G. Collingwood*, ed. Michael Krausz (New York: Clarendon Press, 1972), especially 88–89.

55. Hegel, *Phenomenology of Spirit*, trans. A. V. Miller (New York: Oxford University Press, 1977), 86.

56. Peter Jones, "A Critical Outline of Collingwood's Philosophy of Art," in *Critical Essays on the Philosophy of R. G. Collingwood*, 42.

57. Collingwood, *The Principles of Art*, 275.

58. Ibid., 294.

59. Plotinus, *Enneads*, trans. Stephen MacKenna(London: Faber and Faber, 1962), V.2.ii.

60. John Fielder, "*Chorismos* and Emanation in the Philosophy of Plotinus," in *The Significance of Neoplatonism*, ed. R. Baine Harris (Norfolk, VA: International Society for Neoplatonic Studies, 1976), 111.

61. Plotinus, *Enneads* (trans. Stephen MacKenna), V.1.vi.

62. Ibid., V.3.xvi.

63. Collingwood, *The Principles of Art*, 117.

64. Plotinus, *Enneads* (trans. Stephen MacKenna), V.4.i.

65. Ibid., V.8.vii.

66. Collingwood, *The Principles of Art*, 22.

67. Ibid., 111, 114, 122.

68. Plotinus, *Enneads* (trans. Stephen MacKenna), V.3.v.

69. Ibid., V.8.i.

70. Rubinoff, "Religion and the Rapprochement," 89.

71. Dorothy L. Sayers, "Towards a Christian Aesthetic," in *Unpopular Opinions: Twenty-One Essays* (New York: Harcourt, Brace, 1947), 30.

72. At least one critic, Leroy Lad Panek, judges Sayers's mystery novels her "best pieces of theology." From *Watteau's Shepherds*, quoted in *Biography Resource Center* (http://www.nypl.org), accessed December 27, 2000.

73. John Hospers, "Artistic Creativity," *Journal of Aesthetics and Art Criticism* (Spring 1985): 243.

74. May, *Creatio Ex Nihilo*, 97.

75. Dorothy Sayers, *The Mind of the Maker* (Westport, CT: Greenwood Press, 1968), 181.

76. The difference between divine and human creativity is that the first is from nothing.

77. Ibid., 40.

78. Ibid., 174. Compare this to Monroe Beardsley's view that the artist's aims change in the course of creating her work.

79. Ibid., 39.

80. Ibid., 111.

CHAPTER 5: BEAUTY

1. Soren Kierkegaard, "On the Difference between a Genius and an Apostle," in *The Present Age*, trans. Alexander Dru (New York: Harper and Row, 1961), 94.

2. Francois Mauriac, *Woman of the Pharisees*, trans. Gerard Hopkins (New York: Holt, 1946), 74.

3. Homer, *Iliad* (trans. Lattimore), 3:149.

4. Ibid., 3:156,158.

5. Ps. 29:2 in the King James version.

6. Lawrence, "Hymns in a Man's Life," in *The Later D. H, Lawrence*, ed. William York Tindall (New York: Knopf, 1952), 384.

7. Iris Murdoch, *The Fire and the Sun* (New York: Viking, 1990), 2.

8. Plato, *Symposium*, 212, in *Dialogues of Plato*, trans. B. Jowett.

9. Ibid., 211.

10. Ibid., 211, 212.

11. Plato, *Republic* (trans. Jowett), 517, 508–509.

12. *Phaedrus* (trans. Jowett), 251.

13. Ibid., 250.

14. Ibid., 249.

15. Origen, *The Song of Songs: Commentary and Homilies*, trans. R. P. Lawson. Ancient Christian Writers, vol. 26 (Westminster, MD: Newman Press, 1957), 29–30.

16. Ibid.

17. From the Enkomia of the Orthos of the Holy and Great Saturday, quoted in John Paul II, *Letter to Artists* (Chicago: Liturgy Training Publications, 1999), 8.

18. Plato, *Republic* (trans. Jowett), 476.

19. *Phaedrus* (trans. Jowett), 278.

20. Ibid., 234.

21. *Republic* (trans. Jowett), 509, 487–88; *Phaedrus*, 257.

22. *Republic* (trans. Jowett), 473.

23. *Phaedrus* (trans. Jowett), 265; *Republic* (trans. Jowett), 377.

24. *Republic* (trans. Jowett), 382.

25. Ibid., 389, 414–16.

26. Ibid., 592.

27. Dorothy Sayers, "Writing and Reading of Allegory," in *Christian Letters to a Post-Christian World* (Grand Rapids, MI: Eerdmans, 1969), 192.

28. Ibid., 180.

29. Robert Lamberton, *Homer the Theologian: Neoplatonist Allegorical Reading and the Growth of the Epic Tradition* (Berkeley: University of California Press, 1986), 186.

30. Jean-Claude Margolin, quoted in Lamberton, *Homer the Theologian*, 186.

31. Northrup Frye, *Anatomy of Criticism* (Princeton, NJ: Princeton University Press, 1957), 82.

32. Ibid., 90.

33. Ibid., 74.

34. Ibid., 89.

35. Aristotle, *Metaphysics* (trans. W. D. Ross), 1078b.

36. Ibid., 1072a.

37. Ibid., 1072b.

38. Ibid., 1072a-b. See also John S. Marshall, "Art and Aesthetic in Aristotle," in *Journal of Aesthetics and Art Criticism* 12:2 (December 1953): 229.

39. Aristotle, *On the Parts of Animals*, 645a, trans. William Ogle, in *The Basic Works of Aristotle*, ed. Richard McKeon (New York: Random House, 1941).

40. Aristotle, *Poetics*, 1451a, trans. Ingram Bywater, in *The Basic Works of Aristotle*.

41. Ibid.,1454a.

42. Aristotle, *Topics*, 102a, trans. John S. Marshall, in *The Basic Works of Aristotle*. See especially John Marshall, "Art and Aesthetic in Aristotle," for a discussion of imitation in art as of the ideal of proportion that nature shows us.

43. Thomas Aquinas, *Summa Theologica*, 1a.xxxix.8, 2a-2ae.clxxx.2–3 in *St. Thomas Aquinas: Philosophical Texts*, trans. Thomas Gilby (New York: Oxford University Press, 1960), 78.

44. Ibid., 2a-2ae.cxlv.2, 2a-2ae.clxxx.2–3.

45. Ibid., 1a.xxxix.8, 2a-2ae.cxlv.2.

46. Thomas Aquinas, *Summa Theologica*, trans. Fathers of the English Dominican Province (Westminster, MD: Christian Classics, 1981), 1a.xxxix.8.

47. Ibid.

48. See Lane Cooper, *The Poetics of Aristotle: Its Meaning and Influence* (Ithaca, NY: Cornell University Press, 1923, 1956), 92–98.

49. Edmund Burke, *A Philosophical Enquiry into the Origin of Our Ideas of the Sublime and Beautiful*, ed. J. T. Boulton (New York: Columbia University Press, 1958), 117 (pt. 3, sec. xviii).

50. Ibid., 1.

51. Ibid., 91 (pt. 3, sec. i).

52. Ibid., 94 (pt. 3, sec. ii).

53. Ibid., 105 (pt. 3, sec. vi).

54. Ibid., 91 (pt. 3, sec. i).

55. Ibid.

56. *Summa Theologica* (trans. Thomas Gilby), 1a-2ae.xvii.1. This thought goes back to Aristotle.

57. Burke, *A Philosophical Enquiry*, 91 (pt. 3, sec. i).

58. Ibid., 174 (pt. 5, sec. vii).

59. Ibid., 170 (pt. 5, sec. v).

60. Ibid., 16 (introduction).

61. Longinus, *On the Sublime*, ch. 1, in *Classical Literary Criticism*, trans. T. S. Dorsch (New York: Penguin, 1965).

62. David Morris, *The Religious Sublime: Christian Poetry and Critical Tradition in Eighteenth-Century England* (Lexington: University Press of Kentucky, 1972), 36. Later, William Blake would cite "the sublime of the Bible," and Kierkegaard would draw particular attention to "the sublime in the pedestrian" life of Abraham (*Fear and Trembling*, trans. Walter Lowrie [Princeton, NJ: Princeton University Press, 1968], 52).

63. Burke, *A Philosophical Enquiry*, 40 (pt. 1, sec. vii).

64. Ibid., 67–68 (pt. 2, sec. v).

65. In so saying, Burke anticipates John Milbank's comment on the sublime, quoted toward the end of this chapter (see note 78).

66. Kant, *Critique of Judgment* (trans. Werner Pluhar), sec. 236.

67. See Rudolf Makkreel, *Imagination and Interpretation: The Hermeneutical Import of the Critique of Judgment* (Chicago: University of Chicago Press, 1996), especially the last section, "Reflective Interpretation and the Human Sciences."

68. Kant, *Religion within the Limits of Reason Alone*, trans. Theodore Greene and Hoyt Hudson (New York: Harper Torchbooks, 1960), 100.

69. Kant, *Critique of Judgment*, sec. 351–354

70. Friedrich Schelling, *The Philosophy of Art*, trans. Douglas Stott (Minneapolis: University of Minnesota Press, 1989), 31.

71. Edward T. Oakes, *Pattern of Redemption: The Theology of Hans Urs von Balthasar* (New York: Crossroad, 1994), 177.

72. Hans Urs von Balthasar, *Glory of the Lord*, vol. 1, *Seeing the Form*, trans. Erasmo Leiva-Merikakis, et al. (San Francisco: Ignatius Press, 1982), 122.

73. Ibid., V:483.

74. Kant, *Critique of Judgment*, sec. 277.

75. Ibid., 264.

76. Kant, cited in Balthasar, *Glory of the Lord*, V:503.

77. Balthasar, *Glory of the Lord*, V:513.

78. John Milbank, Graham Ward, Edith Wyschogrod, *Theological Perspectives on God and Beauty* (Harrisburg, PA: Trinity, 2003), 3. Cf. Francois Lyotard, who says, "Modern aesthetics is an aesthetic of the sublime," in *The Postmodern Condition*, trans. Regis Durand (Minneapolis: University of Minnesota Press, 1984), 81.

79. John Milbank, "The Sublime in Kierkegaard," in *Post Secular Philosophy*, ed. Phillip Blond (London: Routledge, 1998), 131. It was in part the sharp wedge that Kierkegaard drove between religion and beauty that stimulated Balthasar's seekings to recover the value of beauty for Christianity. See Balthasar, *Word and Revelation: Essays in Theology* (New York: Herder and Herder, 1964), 121.

80. See *Fundamentalisms Observed*, ed. Martin Marty and R. Scott Appleby (Chicago: University of Chicago Press, 1991).

81. Nietzsche suggested that Apollo, more than Zeus, was really the father of the Olympian gods. See Nietzsche, *The Birth of Tragedy*, trans. Walter Kaufmann (New York: Vintage, 1967), 41.

82. Longinus, *On the Sublime*, ch. 9.

83. *Iliad* (trans. Lattimore), 5:438–442. Subsequent quotations are from this text.

84. We are seeing a revival of religious and aesthetic discourse on beauty. Some examples include the following: John Milbank, Graham Ward, and Edith Wyschogrod, *Theological Perspectives on God and Beauty* (Harrisburg, PA: Trinity Press, 2003); Denis Donoghue, *Speaking of Beauty* (New Haven, CT: Yale University Press, 2003); Neal David Benezra, *Regarding Beauty: A View of the Late Twentieth Century* (Washington, DC: Hirshhorn Museum and Sculpture Garden, 1999); Elaine Scarry, *On Beauty and Being Just* (Princeton, NJ: Princeton University Press, 1999).

CHAPTER 6: RELIGIOUS AND AESTHETIC EXPERIENCE

1. Immanuel Kant, *Critique of Pure Reason*, trans. Norman Kemp Smith (New York: St. Martin's Press, 1965), B135.

2. Ibid., B307.

3. Ibid., A613–614.

4. Friedrich Schleiermacher, *On Religion: Speeches to its Cultured Despisers*, trans. John Oman (Louisville, KY: Westminster, 1994), [1], 138–39.

5. Rudolf Otto, *The Idea of the Holy*, trans. John Harvey (New York: Oxford University Press, 1958), 5.

6. Ibid., 21, 12–13.

7. Ibid., 26.

8. Ibid., 5.

9. Ibid., 45.

10. Clive Bell, *Art* (New York: Capricorn, 1958), 54.

11. Ibid., 17.

12. H. W. Janson, *History of Art*, 5th ed., revised and expanded by Anthony F. Janson (New York: Abrams, 1995), 729.

13. Bell, *Art*, 44–45.

14. Ibid., 8.

15. Ibid., 45.

16. Ibid., 45, 54.

17. Ibid. 68, 181.

18. Ibid., 110.

19. Ibid., 107.

20. Ibid., 175.

21. Dante Alighieri, *Purgatory*, 17:13 in *The Divine Comedy*, trans. Henry F. Cary (New York: Crowell, 1897). Bell cites this passage, in the original Italian, on p. 47.

22. Oscar Wilde, *The Critic as Artist*, in *Intentions* (New York: Lamb, 1909), 218–19.

23. Ibid., 221.

24. There is an echo of Wilde's countryman, Edmund Burke, in this view.

25. Wilde, *The Critic as Artist*, 191.

26. Bell, *Art*, 68.

27. Otto, *The Idea of the Holy*, 33.

28. Dante, *Purgatory* (trans. H. F. Cary), 17:13–19.

29. Willis Barnstone, *The Poetics of Ecstasy* (New York: Holmes and Meier, 1983), 4.

30. Ibid., 3.

31. Ibid.

32. Plato, *Symposium* (trans. Jowett), 174, 175.

33. See, for example, Philo, *On the Account of the World's Creatio Given by Moses*, 70–71, in *Philo*, vol. 1, trans. F. H. Colson and G. H. Whitaker. Loeb Classical Library (Cambridge, MA: Harvard University Press, 1971).

34. *Phaedrus* (trans. Jowett), 244.

35. R. B. Y. Scott, *The Relevance of the Prophets*, rev. ed. (New York: Macmillan, 1968), 96.

36. Otto, *The Idea of the Holy*, 77.

37. Teresa of Avila, *Life*, trans. E. Allison Peers (Garden City, NY: Image Books, 1960), 274–75.

38. Ibid.

39. Quoted in Robert T. Peterson, *The Art of Ecstasy: Teresa, Bernini, and Crashaw* (New York: Atheneum, 1970), 33.

40. Teresa of Avila, *Life*, vol. 1, *Complete Works of Saint Teresa of Jesus*, trans. E. Allison Peers (New York: Sheed and Ward, 1950), 193.

41. Ibid., 192, emphasis added.

42. Richard Crashaw, *The Complete Poetry of Richard Crashaw*, ed. George Williams (New York: New York University Press, 1972).

43. Teresa of Avila, *Life*, 190, 189, 151.

44. Bell, *Art*, 45, 63, 175, 190, 59.

45. Ibid., 190.

46. Wilde, *The Critic as Artist*, 234: "The artistic critic like the mystic is an antinomian always"; Bell, *Art*, 62: "For the mystic, as for the artist, the physical universe is a means to ecstasy."

47. Bell, *Art*, 55.

48. See, for example, Jerome Stolnitz, *Aesthetics and Philosophy of Art Criticism* (Boston: Houghton Mifflin, 1960).

49. Meister Eckhart, "No Respecter of Persons," in *Meister Eckhart: A Modern Translation*, ed. Raymond Blakney (New York: Harper & Bros., 1957), 175.

50. Eckhart, "About Disinterest," in *Meister Eckhart: A Modern Translation*, 90.

51. Jane Kneller, "Disinterestedness,"in *Encyclopedia of Aesthetics*, ed. Michael Kelly (New York: Oxford University Press, 1998), 2:59–64.

52. Eckhart, "About Disinterest," 83, 88.

53. Ibid., 90.

54. Ibid., 86–87.

CHAPTER 7: ETHICS

1. *Apology* (trans. Jowett), 20.

2. Ibid., 33.

3. J. R. Aitken likens a mosaic portrait of Christ, in S. Maria Maggiore, in Rome, to a "radiant" Apollo. See J. R. Aitken, *The Christ of the Men of Art* (Edinburgh: T & T Clark, 1915), 55–56. Apollo, as sun god, was an iconographic origin of the "Christus-Helios" image. See H. A. Drake, *Constantine and the Bishops: The Politics of Intolerance* (Baltimore, MD: Johns Hopkins University Press, 2000), 132.

4. Plato, *Euthyprho*, 2, in *Dialogues of Plato*, trans. Benjamin Jowett.

5. For example, Plato, *Gorgias*, 469, in *Dialogues of Plato*, trans. Benjamin Jowett.

6. Plato, *Republic* (trans. Jowett), 379.

7. Kant, *Religion within the Limits of Reason Alone*, trans. Theodore M. Greene and Hoyt H. Hudson (New York: Harper Torchbooks, 1960), 3.

8. Karl Barth, *Ethics*, trans. G. Bromiley (New York: Seabury, 1981), 50.

9. Ibid., 83.

10. Ibid., 66.

11. Samuel Johnson, quoted in Robert Grams Hunter, *Shakespeare and the Comedy of Forgiveness* (New York: Columbia University Press, 1965), 38.

12. Kant, *Critique of Judgment*, sec. 351–54.

13. Nietzsche, *Antichrist*, trans. R. J. Hollingdale (New York: Penguin, 1968), s. 62.

14. Nietzsche, *Beyond Good and Evil*, trans. Walter Kaufmann (New York: Vintage, 1966), s. 192.

15. Nietzsche, *The Joyful Vision*, trans. Thomas Common (New York: Russell & Russell, 1964), s. 299. Alexander Nehamas says of Nietzsche, "No one has managed to bring life closer to literature." See his *Nietzsche, Life as Literature* (Cambridge, MA: Harvard University Press, 1985), 198.

16. Nehamas, *Nietzsche*, 193.

17. Ibid., 194.

18. Nietzsche, *Beyond Good and Evil*, s. 192.

19. Oscar Wilde, *Decay of Lying*, in *Intentions* (New York: Lamb, 1909), 59.

20. Oscar Wilde, *The Picture of Dorian Gray*, preface in *The Portable Oscar Wilde*, ed. Richard Aldington and Stanley Weintraub (New York: Penguin, 1981).

21. Wilde, *Decay of Lying*, 27.

22. Ibid.

23. Wilde, *The Picture of Dorian Gray*, ch. 6.

24. Wilde, *Decay of Lying*, 20.

25. Tolstoy, *What Is Art?*, trans. Aylmer Maude (New York: Oxford University Press, 1930), 228.

26. Ibid., 232.

27. Ibid., 235.

28. Wayne Booth, *The Company We Keep: An Ethics of Fiction* (Berkeley: University of California Press, 1988).

29. Tolstoy, *What Is Art?*, 257–58.

30. Ibid., 257.

31. Nietzsche, *Beyond Good and Evil*, s. 52.

32. Ibid., s. 201.

33. Barth, *Evangelical Theology* (New York: Holt, Rinehart and Winston, 1963), vi. Graham Ward generously corrects Barth's negative judgment on homosexuality in his article "The Erotics of Redemption: After Karl Barth," *Theology & Sexuality* 8 (March 1998): 52–72. There he argues that the psychology of difference that Barth takes as normative for eros is as available to homosexual as to heterosexual lovers; in fact, the difference Barth esteems in heterosexual eros conceals a not-so-subtle subjection of women that resolves into the very homosexuality Barth abhors.

CHAPTER 8: LOVE

1. Anders Nygren, *Agape and Eros*, trans. P. Watson (New York: Harper, 1969), 32, 33. Nygren's dichotomy has come under critique. See William Klassen, "Love: New Testament and Early Jewish Literature," in *Anchor Bible Dictionary*, ed. David Noel Freedman, et al. (New York: Doubleday, 1992), vol. 4, 385.

2. *Symposium* (trans. Jowett), 177.

3. Ibid., 196.

4. Ibid., 203.

5. Allan Bloom suggests that the *daimons* personify the strangeness in the world that persists even in face of the clear Greek contrast between gods and humans. See *Plato's Symposium*, trans. Seth Benardete, with commentaries by Allan Bloom and Seth Benardete (Chicago: University of Chicago Press, 1976), 131. Socrates' own inner voice was a *daimon*.

6. *Symposium* (trans. Jowett), 204.

7. Alexander Pope, *Eloisa to Abelard*, in *Selected Poetry and Prose*, ed. William Wimsatt (New York: Holt, Rinehart and Winston, 1972). The Donne and Herbert poems may be found in *The Norton Anthology of Poetry*, 3rd ed., ed. Alexander W. Allison, et al. (New York: Norton, 1983).

8. Clarence Tucker Craig, "The First Epistle to the Corinthians," in *The Interpreter's Bible*, vol. 10, ed. George Arthur Buttrick, et al. (New York: Abingdon, 1953), 172.

9. *Religion and Literature: A Reader*, ed. Robert Detweiler and David Jasper (Louisville, KY: Westminster John Knox, 2000), 75.

10. Simone Petrement, *Simone Weil*, trans. Raymond Rosenthal (New York: Pantheon, 1976), 330.

11. Cicero, *De Amicitia*, trans. W. A. Falconer, Loeb Classical Library (Cambridge, MA: Harvard University Press, 1946), 29. Succeeding references are given, parenthetically, in the text.

12. Montaigne, "Friendship," in his *Essays*, trans. J. Cohen (New York: Penguin, 1958), 97.

13. Gerhart Ladner, "Presentation," to Adele Fiske, *Friends and Friendship in the Monastic Tradition* (Cuernavaca, Mexico: Centro Intercultural de Documentacion, 1970), 0/6.

14. Fiske, 12/2

15. C. Browning, "Friendship, Particular," in *New Catholic Encyclopedia*, ed. Berard L. Marthaler, et al. (Detroit, MI: Thomson Gale, 2003), 6:9.

16. Aelred of Rievaulx, *Spiritual Friendship*, trans. Mark Williams (University of Scranton Press, 1994), para. 1.

17. Ibid.

18. Ibid., para. 20.

19. Ibid., para. 1.

20. Ibid., para. 16–17.

21. Ibid., para. 16.

22. Ibid., para. 18.

23. Ibid., para. 20.

24. Mark Williams, introduction to Aelred of Rivaulx, *Spiritual Friendship*, 21.

25. John Boswell, *Christianity, Homosexuality, and Tolerance* (Chicago: University of Chicago Press, 1980) 222.

CHAPTER 9: DEATH

1. *Iliad* (trans. Lattimore), 21: 463–66.

2. Louis Jacobs, *A Jewish Theology* (New York: Behrman House, 1973), 303–304.

3. *Iliad* (trans. Lattimore), 23:104.

4. *Webster's Third New International Dictionary* (Springfield, MA: Merriam, 1981).

5. Irene Sourvinou-Inwood, *Reading Greek Death* (New York: Oxford University Press, 1995), 13.

6. Anthony C. Thiselton, *The First Epistle to the Corinthians: A Commentary on the Greek Text* (Grand Rapids, MI: Eerdmans, 2000), 1169.

7. Karl Barth, quoted in Thiselton, *The First Epistle*, 1236.

8. Boethius, *The Consolation of Philosophy*, trans. V. E. Watts (New York: Penguin, 1969), 163.

9. See, for example, Thomas Hockersmith, "Into Degreeless Noon: Time, Consciousness and Oblivion in Emily Dickinson," in *American Transcendental Quarterly* 3:3 (September 1989): 277–95.

10. Sometimes Dickinson suggests that the only immortality she trusted was the one her poems could obtain for her.

11. *Phaedo* (trans. Jowett), 67.

12. Jeremy Taylor (1613–1667), *Holy Living and Holy Dying*, trans. P. G. Stanwood (New York: Oxford University Press, 1988–1989), v.2:xvii.

13. See, for example, "Facing Death," in *Gates of Prayer* (New York: CCAR, 1975), 622–23. Consider also Martin Buber: Death "may become a haven, the knowledge of which brings comfort." See Martin Buber, *Good and Evil*, trans. Ronald Gregor Smith (New York: Scribner, 1953), 79.

14. *Death in Literature*, ed. Robert Weir (New York: Columbia University Press, 1980), 385.

15. Tolstoy, *My Confession*, in *Lift Up Your Eyes: The Religious Writings of Tolstoy* (New York: Julian Press, 1960), 50–53.

16. The following quotes are from Dostoevsky, *The Idiot*, trans. Constance Garnett (New York: Bantam, 1958), 60–62.

17. Willa Cather, *Death Comes for the Archbishop* (New York: Knopf, 1927), 293.

18. Joseph Wood Krutch, "The Pathos of Distance," in *Willa Cather and Her Critics*, ed. E. Schroeter (Ithaca, NY: Cornell University Press, 1967), 61.

Chapter 10: Evil

1. *Rites of the Catholic Church*, prepared by the International Commission on English in the Liturgy (New York: Pueblo, 1991), v.1.

2. On stage, the "humorous Iago has been a favorite," comments Marvin Rosenberg, *The Masks of Othello: The Search for the Identity of Othello, Iago, and Desdemona by Three Centuries of Actors and Critics* (Newark: University of Delaware Press, 1961), 156. Iago can be played "with a light touch, a light step, a sprightly wit . . . [who] sometimes charmed the audience." See Edward Pechter, *Othello and Interpretive Traditions* (Iowa City: University of Iowa Press, 1999), 54–55.

3. Bernard Spivak, *Shakespeare and the Allegory of Evil* (New York: Columbia University Press, 1958), 56.

4. When Olivier played Iago, in 1938, opposite Ralph Richardson's Othello, he portrayed him as gay, and in love with Othello. Rosenberg, *The Masks of Othello*, 158–59.

5. The adjectives are Rev. Dr. Roger Ferlo's from a series of lectures on Milton he gave at the Church of St. Luke in the Fields, New York, N.Y., Fall 2002.

6. Frank S. Kastor, *Milton and the Literary Satan* (Amsterdam: Rodopi, 1974), 59.

7. G. Hamilton, *Hero or Fool: A Study of Milton's Satan* (London: Allen and Unwin, 1944), 33.

8. David Tracy, "Iris Murdoch and the Many Faces of Platonism, in *Iris Murdoch and the Search for Human Goodness*, ed. Maria Antonaccio and William Schweiker (Chicago: University of Chicago Press, 1996), 54.

9. Iris Murdoch, *The Unicorn* (New York: Viking, 1963), 106. Subsequent references to *The Unicorn* are given parenthetically in the text.

CHAPTER 11: SUFFERING

1. Catherine Mavrikakis, "To End the Glorification of Suffering," in *History and Memory: Suffering and Art*, ed. Harold Schweizer (Lewisburg, PA: Bucknell University Press, 1998), 124–135.

2. Margaret Sussman, "God the Creator," in *Dimensions of Job* (New York: Schocken, 1969), 87.

3. Andrew Holleran, "Reading and Writing," in *Ground Zero* (New York: Morrow, 1988), 15.

4. Hervé Guibert, *To the Friend Who Did Not Save My Life*, trans. Linda Coverdale (London: Quartet Books), 5, quoted in Mavrikakis, "To End the Glorification of Suffering," 130.

5. John Ciardi, notes to Dante, *Inferno*, trans. John Ciardi (New York: New American Library) 77, 163–64.

6. B Yoma 86a, quoted in *Book of Legends*, ed. Hayim Nahman Bialik and Yehoshua Hana Ravnitzky, trans. William Braude (New York: Schocken, 1992), 559.

7. Hawthorne, *The Scarlet Letter* (Boston: Houghton Mifflin, 1960), 78. Subsequent references are given parenthetically in the text.

8. Aeschylus, *Agamemnon*, 177–178, in *Orestcia*, trans. Richmond Lattimore (Chicago: University of Chicago Press, 1953).

9. Dostoevsky, *The Idiot*, trans. Constance Garnett (New York: Bantam, 1958), 339. Subsequent references are given parenthetically in the text.

10. Robin Feuer Miller, *Dostoevsky and* The Idiot: *Author, Narrator and Reader* (Cambridge, MA: Harvard University Press, 1981), 189.

11. Margaret Susman, "Franz Kafka," *Jewish Frontier* 23:8 (September 1956): 41.

CHAPTER 12: FORGIVENESS

1. John S. Kselman, "Forgiveness," in *Anchor Bible Dictionary*, vol. 2, 831.

2. Seneca, "On Mercy," in *Moral and Political Essays*, trans. John Cooper and J. F. Procope (New York: Cambridge University Press, 1995), 163. In addition, the Greek concept of justice, especially as elaborated for juridical settings, includes elements of Judeo-Christian forgiveness. Plato introduces the idea of *suggnome*, or "judging with" consideration of extenuating circumstances (Hippias Minor 372). Aristotle and Seneca develop the idea. See Martha Nussbaum, "Equity and Mercy," *Philosophy and Public Affairs* 22:2 (Spring 1993): 83–125.

3. It was Mozart, setting a libretto of Pietro Metastasio to music, who gave to posterity the opera *La Clemenza di Tito*, loosely based on the reputation for fair rule that the Roman emperor, Titus, enjoyed. The objects of clemency are in this case already friends of Titus, who rebel against him from complex, cross-purposed motives of ambition and love. That feature of the plot inflects the classical mercy that the opera celebrates toward a case of personal (Judeo-Christian?) forgiveness, which soars on the music that Mozart composed for it, as Judaism and Christianity would have it do.

4. Walter Allen, quoted in Edward T. Jones, *L. P. Hartley* (Boston: Twayne, 1998), 70.

5. L. P. Hartley, *Eustace and Hilda* (New York: Putnam,1958), 733, 735.

6. *Gates of Repentance: The New Union Prayerbook for the Days of Awe* (New York: Central Conference of American Rabbis, 1984), 335.

7. Louis Ginzberg, *Legends of the Jews*, trans. Paul Radin (Philadelphia: Jewish Publication Society, 1968), v. 3:148.

8. "On the whole no Jew feels himself out of sympathy with the [Lord's] Prayer, except with regard to the condition regarding forgiveness apparently imposed in Matthew's form, which has no Jewish liturgical parallel whatever." See Israel Abrahams, *Studies in Pharisaism and the Gospels*, 2nd series (Cambridge: Cambridge University Press, 1924), 97–98. However, the idea of such a condition does appear in the tradition, but only marginally, for example, in the noncanonical Ecclesiasaticus 28:2. On this point, see Alfons Deissler, "The Spirit of the Lord's Prayer in the Faith and Worship of the Old Testament," in *The Lord's Prayer and Jewish Liturgy*, ed. Jakob J. Petuchowski and Michael Brocke (New York: Seabury Press, 1978), 14.

9. Nussbaum, "Equity and Mercy," 105–109.

10. Robert Hunter, *Shakespeare and the Comedy of Forgiveness* (New York: Columbia University Press, 1965).

11. John Garrard, "Casting the First Stone: Vengeance and Forgiveness in *Anna Karenina*," in *Narrative Ironies*, ed. A. Prier (Amsterdam: Rodopi, 1997), 145–46.

12. Tolstoy, *Anna Karenina*, trans. David Magarshack (New York: New American Library, 1961), 400. Subsequent references are given parenthetically in the text.

13. Garrard, "Casting the First Stone," 144.

CHAPTER 13: SAINTLINESS

1. See, for example: Louis Martz, "The Saint as Tragic Hero," in *Tragic Themes in Western Literature*, ed. Cleanth Brooks (New Haven, CT: Yale University Press, 1960), 150; Konstantin Mochulsky, quoted in Robin Miller, *Dostoevsky and the Idiot* (Cambridge, MA: Harvard University Press, 1981), 234; George Bernard Shaw, *Major Barbara* (New York: Penguin Books, 1960), 146.

2. W. H. Auden, "Postscript: Christianity and Art," in *Religion and Modern Literature*, ed. G. B. Tennyson and Edward Ericson (Grand Rapids, MI: Eerdmans, 1975), 115.

3. Gunther Plaut suggests that the Nazirites "may be described as an informal holy order." See *The Torah: A Modern Commentary* (New York: Union of American Hebrew Congregations, 1981), 1060.

4. Kenneth Woodward, *Making Saints* (New York: Simon and Schuster, 1990), 67.

5. Simone Weil, *Gravity and Grace*, trans. Arthur Wills (New York: Octagon, 1983), 120.

6. Dostoevsky, *The Idiot*, trans. Constance Garnett (New York: Bantam, 1958), 289. Subsequent references are cited parenthetically in the text.

7. Leslie Johnson, "The Face of the Other in *The Idiot*," *Slavic Review* 50:4 (Winter 1991): 868.

8. Ibid., 871.

9. George Eliot, *Middlemarch* (New York: Signet, 1964), 381. Subsequent references are cited parenthetically in the text.

10. Emphases on reason and self-sufficiency in Platonism make it an unlikely context for saints.

11. Sherry Mitchell, "St. Teresa and Dorothea Brooke," *Victorian Newsletter* (Fall 1975): 35.

12. *Gates of Prayer: The New Union Prayerbook* (New York: Central Conference of American Rabbis, 1975), 623.

13. Theodore Dreiser, *The Bulwark* (New York: Doubleday, 1946), 327. Subsequent references are cited parenthetically in the text.

14. Gerhard Friedrich, "Theodore Dreiser's Debt to Woolman's Journal, *American Quarterly* 7:4 (Winter 1955): 385.

15. Ibid., 391.

General Index

Aaron, 90, 114
Abelard, Peter, 173
Abraham (Biblical character), 157, 199, 236n62
Abrahams, Israel, 245n8
Adam and Eve, 26, 100, 117, 182, 188, 189, 190, 226n43. *See also* Index of Fictional Characters
Adultery, 8, 198, 209–210, 220n13
Aelred of Rievaulx, 176–178
Aeneid (Virgil), 30
Aeschylus, 3, 31, 199
Afterlife, 204. *See also* Immortality; Resurrection
Agape and Eros (Nygren), 171, 175
Aggadah, 98
AIDS, 195
Aitken, J. R., 240n3
Akedah, 160, 199
Allan, Mowbray, 225n31
Allegory, 28, 32, 33, 35–36, 55, 119–121, 156, 182
Allen, Walter, 245n4
Alter, Robert, 42–43, 224n15
Amalekites, 160–161, 162, 168
Ambiguity: in allegory, 119–121; and the arts, 2; in beauty, 112, 126; in Blake, 70, 71; in Dante, 42, 45–46, 52; in evil, 192; in freedom, 131–132; in Hawthorne, 6–9; as ideal, 10; and literature, 6–9, 42, 45–46, 52, 70, 71, 77, 202; in love, 172–173; and

monotheism, 3; in myth, 40, 71; as principled, 70; and sensuality, 42; in Yeats, 77
Among Schoolchildren (Yeats), 75
Amos (Biblical book), 148–149
Analogy, 83–84, 111–112, 123, 137
Angels, 47, 53, 67, 70, 150–151
Anger, 33, 35, 177, 203, 208
Anglicanism, 6, 14–15, 71–72, 204
Animals, 123, 125
Anna Karenina (Tolstoy), 5, 17–19, 167, 208–210
Annunciation, The, 33
Anthropomorphism, 114
Antichrist, 182
Apocalypticism, 75, 225nn26,29
Apollo, 1, 33, 43, 135–136, 158–159, 237n81
Apologetics, 30
Apology (Plato), 15
Apophasis, 122
Archetypes, 99, 100
Architecture, 98
"Areopagitica" (Milton), 59
Aristotle, 28, 50, 51, 115, 121–124, 127, 128, 130, 160, 172, 190, 245n2
Ark of the Covenant, 88–89, 206
Ars Moriendi, 179, 184–186
L'Art pour l'art, 130
Artist(s), 83, 85, 90, 91, 93, 104, 105–106, 111, 164, 165, 166, 190–191, 193, 231n12

247

Burckert, Walter, 222n18
Burke, Edmund, 115, 124–127, 129, 133, 238n24
Byzantium, 77–78

Calvin, John, and Calvinism, 7, 8, 28–30, 31, 32, 57, 220n12
Capitalism, 8
Carey, John, 227nn50,58
Carroll, Noel, 231n24
Cary, Henry F., 225nn24,27,28
Cathedrals, 14–15
Cather, Willa, 185–186
Catholic Church, 6, 8, 13, 28, 29, 33, 39, 44, 57, 58, 187
Cause and Effect, 128–130, 131, 141, 154
Celestine V, 49–50, 225n29
Cervantes, 4–5, 9, 28–29
Cezanne, 143–144
Chaos, 59, 64–65, 68, 75, 86, 87, 97–98, 100–101, 193
Chase, Richard, 223n3
Cherubim, 89, 90
Christ, Jesus: in allegory, 32, 117; Apollo as, 159; as artist, 73–74; as beautiful, 111–112, 117, 124; Blake on, 69, 72–74, 77; Dante on, 32, 225n26; and detachment, 154; as dual, 46–47; and ethics, 159–160, 162; opposed to evil, 188, 190; in literature, 200–201, 214–215; and love, 172, 174, 177–178; Milton on, 64, 72; as resurrected, 181, 182; as Son of God, 64, 72, 117, 124; as tempted, 188, 199; Yeats on, 77. See also Trinity
Christianity and Judaism (paired): and allegory, 120; and beauty, 117–118; and covenant, 162; and creation, 84, 93; and forgiveness, 203, 205–207, 210, 245n3; and history, 45; and nature, 44; opposed to literature, 1–3, 6–7, 33, 35; as mythic, xii, 40; in relation to Platonism, xii, 1–3, 36, 84, 85, 87, 92, 120, 125, 148, 199, 203; and

revelation, 84; and the Suffering Servant, 199–200; and the textile arts, 114. See also Judaism
Church of England. See Anglicanism
Church of S. Apollinare Nuovo (Ravenna, Italy), 78
Church of S. Maria Maggiore (Rome), 240n3
Ciardi, John, 244n5
Cicero, 28, 32, 175–177
Circus Animals' Desertion (Yeats), 79
Cistercians, 178
City of God (Augustine), 30
Clemenza di Tito, La (Mozart), 245n3
Coleridge, Samuel Taylor, 191
Collingwood, R. G., 84, 101 109, 166
Color, 124
Comedy, 5, 207
Commandment(s), 159, 162, 189. See also Law
Confession (Tolstoy), 17, 18, 184
Congregationalism, 6, 7, 10, 14
Contrapasso, 44, 48, 59, 64
Cooper, Lane, 236n48
Corinthians (Biblical book), 171, 172, 174, 181, 182
Covenant, 162, 196, 202, 205
Craig, Clarence Tucker, 241n8
Crashaw, Richard, 151
Creatio Ex Nihilo, 85, 86, 87, 91–93, 100, 234n76
Creation: in analogy with religion and literature, 4, 12, 83–109, 137; as Fall, 68; according to Genesis, 40, 85–88, 91, 92, 97–98, 100–101, 204, 232n51; as God's, 31, 37, 202; according to Plato, 62, 85–88, 92, 93–94, 96; according to Plotinus, 104–106; and Satan, 64, 191; and the Trinity, 106–109. See also Genesis; Timaeus
Creativity: as analogous to creation, 83–109; as cosmogonic, 98–99; as devilish, 69, 70; as a product of contraries, 72; as dialogic, 93; as divine, 12, 73, 80, 84–85; as emotional, 103–104; as

Picture of Dorian Gray (Wilde), 165, 168
Plato: on beauty, 115–123, 127, 129, 130,
    132; and Blake, 73; and Calvin, 28; on
    creation, 84–87, 92, 93–94; and Dante,
    225n30; on death, 179, 183, 184; on
    ecstasy, 148; on ethics, 157–159, 161,
    166, 167; on evil, 188–189; and for-
    giveness, 203; on ideas, 95–97,
    227n56; on literature and art, 32–37,
    90–91, 96, 106, 108, 146, 162, 231n12;
    on love, 171, 173; as mythic, xii, 2–3,
    40; as poet, 41–42; and religious sensi-
    bility, 3–4, 36–37, 83; and saintliness,
    246n10; on suffering, 196–197, 199;
    and Yeats, 75–77. *See also* Good(ness)
    in Plato
Platonism: and Aelred of Rievaulx, 178;
    and the arts, 83, 106; and Hans Urs
    Von Balthasar, 133; and Blake, 67–68,
    and Burke, 125; and Cicero, 175; and
    Dante, 54; and George Eliot, 215; and
    D. H. Lawrence, 11, 12; and Milton,
    61–66; and Iris Murdoch, 192–194;
    and Dorothy Sayers, 108; and Oscar
    Wilde, 165; and Yeats, 75–76. *See also*
    Neoplatonism
Plaut, Guenther, 231n13, 246n3
Plot, 123
Plotinus, 87, 101, 104–106, 107
Plymouth Brethren, 25
Poetics, The (Aristotle), 123
Poets and/or poetry: as angry, 35, 231n12;
    as creators, 87, 92; as devilish, 69; as
    divine, 73; as false, 33–37; as love-
    medium, 171–175; as musicians, 146;
    as myth-makers, 40–44, 74, 224n15; as
    numinous, 145, 147; and pathos, 197;
    as anti-Platonic, 76–77; as possessed,
    90–91, 119–120, 231n12; as priests,
    79–80; as prophets, 66, 73; as protago-
    nist, 67; as religion-challengers, 41–80,
    133, 140; as religion-makers, 56; as
    rhetoricians, 118; as sacred, 55; as sub-
    lime, 127; as truthful, 31
Polytheism, 33, 39, 40
Pope, Alexander, 172–174, 180

Poseidon, 126, 135
Postmodernity, 134
Predestination, 8
Pride, 33, 54, 58, 191
Priest(s), 79–80
Priest, Paul, 225n25
Process Philosophy, 108
Prophets: Biblical, 148–150, 152,
    160–161, 182, 189, 196–198, 206;
    Greek, 41, 148; as poets, 73; poets as,
    55, 66, 74; versus priests, 80; and pun-
    ishment, 44, 196–198, 206
Proportion, 123, 124, 125, 235n42
Proverbs (Biblical book), 56, 86–87
Psalms (Biblical book), 42, 97, 114, 180
Punishment, 48, 60–61, 66, 67, 69, 165,
    179, 180, 182, 187, 196, 197–200, 202,
    203, 207–209
Puritan(ism), 7–9, 10, 17, 57–58, 61, 62,
    165, 191, 220n13
Purpose, 86, 96, 105, 123, 128–132
Pushkin, Alexander, 16, 201

Quakerism, 12, 13–14, 57, 217–218

Rabbinical Judaism. *See* Judaism
Rachel (Biblical character), 114
Rahab (Biblical character), 97–98
Ranters, 71
Reason, 7, 34–35, 61–62, 64, 73, 86, 91,
    92, 94–95, 131, 134, 135, 144, 158,
    175, 183, 202
Rebecca (Biblical character), 114
Redemption, 88, 97, 198, 202
Reed, T. J., 231n26
Reformation, 28, 44, 57, 62
Religion (the word), 2, 56
Religion of art, 74, 77, 79, 145
Religion within the Limits of Reason Alone
    (Kant), 236n68, 240n7
Repentance, 198–199, 204–210
Republic, The (Plato), 3, 32, 36–37, 91,
    96, 118, 119, 159, 234nn11,18,
    235nn21–26
Resurrection, 155, 179, 181, 182, 183,
    184

Index of Fictional Characters